GW00692281

James Valentine has been a part of ABC Local Radio for over a decade. He presents Afternoons on 702 ABC Sydney. He is also the presenter of the *Showtime Movie News* and regular All Star on Channel Seven's *Sunrise* program.

James has been a rock musician playing saxophone with The Models, Jo Camilleri, and Wendy Matthews, among others. His career in media began on ABC Television when he was the host of *The Afternoon Show*.

He is also the author of the JumpMan series, a humorous time travelling trilogy for younger readers.

The Form Guide

The Customs of the Contemporary World

Not what you should do,
but what you do do

JAMES VALENTINE

ABC
Books

To Mum and Dad.
Thank you for all the early instruction, but you should know:
'I no longer have a butter knife.

Published by ABC Books for the
AUSTRALIAN BROADCASTING CORPORATION
GPO Box 9994 Sydney NSW 2001

Copyright © Valentine Media 2007

First published March 2007

National Library of Australia
Cataloguing-in-Publication entry
Valentine, James.
  The form guide : not what you should do, but what you do do :
  the customs of the contemporary world.
  ISBN 978 0 7333 1958 7
  1. Manners and customs - Humor. 2. Etiquette - Humor.
  3. Social norms - Humor. I. Australian Broadcasting Corporation.
  II. Title.

395

Designed by saso.com.au
Typeset by saso.com.au
Cover design by saso.com.au
Set in Devin 9/13pt
Printed and bound in Australia by Griffin Press, Adelaide

5 4 3 2 1

CONTENTS

ACKNOWLEDGEMENTS

Thank you to my producers at 702 ABC Sydney, Jennifer Fleming and Marion Frith. Because of them I only have to talk to great callers: they get the nutters. Thank you to my 702 colleagues, especially Stephen Amery, Richard Glover, Roger Summerill and Michael Mason. Thank you to Susan Morris-Yates at ABC Books and Megan Johnston for excellent editing and laughter. Thank you to Pam Every, Sarah Hopkins and Lulu Serious for reading. To John Bartlett, Beth Gunnell and Lynne McDonald for taping and transcription. Thank you to Joanne, Ruby and Roy for letting me mine their lives and for all the love.

Thank you to the 702 listeners and callers. We are now old friends.

INTRODUCTION

A Brief Guide to the Views of the Author

I don't like Manners. I'm suspicious of Courtesy. I detest Etiquette—the very word *looks* annoying—it's in the same group as potpourri and doily. It's twee—and I hate the word twee. Politeness! Be polite! What does it mean when someone suggests you should be polite? To me, it always means start using all the behaviours I use around people I can't stand or anyone who looks like they might tip suddenly into psychopathy.

But, like anyone else, I have no desire to upset my friends, my colleagues, my family, my neighbours, passers-by or complete strangers. I don't want to do anything that annoys anyone. In whatever situation I find myself, I'd like to get it right every time. But I don't think you achieve that by referring to a body of rules known as 'Manners' or 'Etiquette'.

Manners and etiquette always suggest to me public forms of behaviour designed to mask real emotions and allow us all to get along without killing one another. I have seen the British use manners to cut each other to the quick and to establish immediately their class status. I have seen the Americans use a formidable combination of puppy-dog-like enthusiasm and formal conversation rules to ward off any actual personal contact. I have watched my own tribe, the Australians, pretend to have no manners at all. Yet, they are, of course, deeply offended by tiny imagined slights.

I hate the phrase 'impeccable manners'. I don't like people who think of themselves as 'well brought up'. That's always about class. We of the middle/upper upper/middle class use our forks this way and if you want to be one of us then you had better learn how to do it (see 'The Fork Wars' on page 8 in Chapter One).

Many also seem to be of the belief that we live in rude and uncivil times: simple daily courtesy has been replaced by road rage, coarse language and Paris Hilton. I don't buy that either. Courtesy was demanded of servants, shop assistants and underlings who, if they failed to deliver it, would be punished or dismissed. People who believed themselves to be genteel and of significant family had no qualms about being rude and uncivil to anyone they regarded as beneath them. We doffed our hats and opened doors and left calling cards lest we be cast out of the society we were desperate to be in.

Lynne Truss—author of *Eats, Shoots & Leaves*—in her recent book *Talk to the Hand* suggests that we live in a time of great rudeness. Dismissive expressions like 'Whatever', common use of four letter words, people yelling into mobile phones and giving each other the finger whenever they can, all say to her that civil society has ended. The young people who are rude to her in shops are Visigoths, Philistines, Yahoos, Delinquents, Punks and Slackers all rolled into one ill-mannered and ungracious mob. I think she's completely wrong.

Manners, like all aspects of human behaviour, are in a constant state of development. They are no more fixed than our language, our laws, our beliefs, our child-rearing habits, our diet. They are always changing. They change if you move towns. They definitely change if you move countries. What is simple courtesy in one nation will get you killed in another. What indicates respect in one city will be a gross insult in the next.

The great *Oxford English Dictionary* (*OED*) developed a system of tracking our words. In the face of an overwhelming belief that our language is flat and fixed for all time, the *OED* charts the wild evolution of our words, showing with millions of citations how the meaning attributed to any one collection of letters and sounds in our language is constantly changing and is determined only by common usage. Not by one class, or a governing body, or by a reference to some better days, but by how the word is used right now by most people.

Manners are the same. There is no absolute right way to use a fork. The right way to use a fork is in a manner that allows you to get food into your mouth without looking like a pig. (You really must check out 'The Fork Wars' on page 8.)

I don't find it necessary any more to bow. My wife is unable to curtsey and finds most days there is no call for her to do so. I rarely find it necessary to write a letter, but if I did I wouldn't begin it with 'My Dear Sir', or sign it, 'Obediently Yours', 'Your Humble Servant Etc, Etc'.

Pick up a book on manners and etiquette from only fifty years ago and you'll find long chapters on calling cards. Calling cards have disappeared so entirely that it's almost not worth explaining. By the time I get to the end of a description of a strange ritual of leaving calling cards on each other's tables in the hallway and which card you should leave when, and what it meant to have your name on the left-hand side and your husband's name on the right, you'll be so bored that you'll put the book down and go and buy something else. But they're a fine example of how one generation can have a practice that is meaningless to the next.

Hats are another. At some point, and I don't know if there was an international covenant passed, or some kind of mass telepathic thought went around the globe, but around about the time men walked on the moon, they also hung up their hats. Take a look at a cityscape in any western city in the world pre-Beatles: every man is wearing a hat—a hat with a brim if they were on their way to the office; a flat hat or variation of if they were going down pit. Same street post-Woodstock and the hats have disappeared. There's longer hair, there're bigger sideburns and there're a couple of old codgers with hats on, but the hat has largely gone.

It's the same with women. Hats and gloves and dressing up to go to town were once the norm for women of a certain class. Now the same ladies can wander into the cosmetics floor of any department store wearing a fluoro pink leisure suit and no one would bat a botoxed eyelid.

There was a lot of etiquette around hats and it was considered bad form to wear them inside. Older Citizens (OCs) will often ask now, 'Why don't young people take their hats off indoors?'. Inquire of the OC what the issue is and they reply, 'It's a question of respect. It's disrespectful to wear a hat inside. It's just plain bad manners'. Now this is a classic example of an etiquette where you need to know the rule in order to be well mannered. The action itself has no meaning either way.

A hat on a head is not in any way an insult to anyone observing the hat except that they take it so. In 1956 it was common knowledge that it was disrespectful to wear a hat inside. But that was then and that was a hat—not a baseball cap or a beanie. The twenty-year-old doesn't think of his headgear as being in some way separated from his overall attire. You may as well ask him to remove his T-shirt. So it's changed, hasn't it? The hat is different, the way it is worn is different, and there is no disrespect being implied by continuing to wear it inside because the wearer has no idea that it might imply disrespect.

This is what I've tried to do with *The Form Guide.*

The Form Guide operates along the strict principles of the *Oxford English Dictionary.* It's all about common usage. It's an attempt to gauge what we're actually doing: not to refer to the Queen and ask her what we should be doing; not to look at what we used to do back in some mythical age of good manners, but to ask people about actual situations they've found confusing or confronting and see how we actually handle them.

My research has been conducted via the extraordinary medium of talkback radio. Talkback radio is largely regarded as a major contributor to the end of civil discourse. This is true for all other programs except my own and those of my colleagues at the Australian Broadcasting Corporation. The usual talkback radio style is blunt. Announcer makes outrageous pronouncement on current event and invites callers to debate him (rarely her). Caller takes bait and announcer can swing into prolonged rave, be rude to caller, talk over them and do anything they like so long as it produces radio ratings. This is Stone Age talkback.

Those of us operating in the twenty-first century have discovered many other ways of encouraging the listener to become a caller and thereby provide free content to the program and entertainment and infor-mation to the other listeners. 'The Form Guide' is a fine example of New Millennium talkback. I invite people to tell me about a recent moment where they've been unsure what the current standard of etiquette or behaviour should be. They ring in and tell me their story. A classic would be 'The Wine at the Dinner Party'. 'James,' says caller. 'I went to a dinner party the other night, and took a very nice bottle of wine I'd been saving for a special event. The host took the wine and put it away. They then served a very cheap and nasty wine throughout the dinner. Should I have asked for my bottle to be opened? Would it be okay to take it back at the end of the night?'

Now, crasser forms of talkback would then involve me, the announcer, pronouncing what I believe to be the rules. Not here! What I do is invite other listeners to call in and tell us what they would do; what they believe is the appropriate behaviour and response for this situation.

Here's how the callers respond:

'He should keep the special wines for his own dinner parties.'

'Yeah, that's just rude. He should have gone and got it out of the cupboard and opened it himself.'

'Maybe the host doesn't know much about wine. He could have chosen a moment and just said quietly without embarrassing the host, "Hey, that bottle of red I brought would be perfect with this main course. It's a fantastic wine, let's have a glass now".'

'When you take a bottle of wine to a dinner party it's not necessarily to be drunk there. It's a gift to the hosts. The hosts can do what they like with it.'

Sometimes the callers stay like that—a range of responses, some helpful suggestions for easing a tense situation, but nothing very definite. Sometimes they find consensus. And in fact 'The Wine' issue is one where they usually do.

The consensus is that you are taking the wine as a gift. You could choose flowers or chocolates or a much-loved book for your host, but the general convention is at dinner parties you take wine. Often it's drunk on the night, sometimes it's not. But the wine-giver should realise that he's taking it as a gift and it's up to the host to determine what happens with it. The only regular exception to that rule is French Champagne, which should be guzzled immediately. If the wine-giver is bringing something special from his cellar, then he should say something like, 'This is twenty years old. I've been saving it for a special occasion. Let's drink it tonight'.

'The Wine at the Dinner Party' also shows us that nothing has changed. Here is a particular class considering an issue peculiar to their class. They want to do the right thing and a lot of it is how you wish to be perceived. The wine-giver is peeved in two ways: his gift wasn't recognised and displayed for the rest of the party, and he didn't get to drink some decent wine. Class comes into this because if you're not on this particular social strata then the problem seems ridiculous. Non-wine-drinking class: bunch of wankers—what on earth does this kind of crap matter? Wine-drinkers-with-own-cellar: the problem never occurs.

And, of course, it's changed with time. Dinner parties are a more common form of entertainment and it's common to bring a bottle of wine. A generation or two back, bringing wine would have been considered peculiar and probably insulting: are you implying that the host can't afford wine?

Everything we consider on 'The Form Guide' is like that. It's all peculiar to a particular moment, to a particular set of circumstances, but, regardless of the particulars, callers ring because they've all reached the same impasse.

1. There's behaviour we don't like.

2. We want to express our view about the behaviour, but we don't want that to be a cause for offence.

3. We would like the behaviour to change.

'The Form Guide' is always about exploring that territory. Am I right in feeling this is wrong? If I'm right can I get them to stop doing it? Is there a way I can communicate my dissatisfaction, my discomfort, my displeasure at what's happening here?

These are the constant themes of 'The Form Guide'.

Children's birthday parties, RSVPs, emails, car parks, workplaces, schools and supermarkets; wherever homo sapiens gather and communicate, form guide dilemmas follow. And in all of them we are being asked to consider: how do we want to live right now? How can we get on so we can all enjoy the life we're living? If someone's rubbing me up the wrong way, how can I get them to rub me up the right way?

And although we often reach a conclusion, and we often form an opinion about what this particular caller should do in this particular circumstance, we never create an absolute rule; an etiquette or protocol that will show that we are well behaved and those who don't do it the way we do it are animals.

'Look,' you say, 'this is all too trivial. War, poverty, cancer, environmental degradation on a catastrophic scale are all around us and you are concerning yourself with Shiraz.' Excellent point! But as Edmund Burke noted two hundred years ago, manners are what barbarise or refine us. I believe a society that places importance on manners is a society that places great faith in human beings. Societies that attempt to proscribe all human behaviour are societies without faith in human beings. They put their faith elsewhere or they treat their people like domesticated animals to be herded and controlled. Societies with fluid notions of etiquette and behaviour are truly civilised.

Each chapter of *The Form Guide* works like this: there'll be a brief and possibly humorous summation of our previous attitudes to this particular area, then you get the caller who poses the initial problem, some interjections from me, and then other callers who are wanting to comment on the problem along with further interjections from me. I then sum up. Some of the callers' names have been changed as they don't want to be identified and many people choose a pseudonym—a radionomic?—when they call talkback lines.

So, wander around the streets, the schools, the workplaces, the parks, the restaurants, the dinner and birthday parties, the weddings and funerals visited in this book. Reading these dilemmas is as good as poking your nose over the back fence and having a good gawk at what other people are up to. You'll be amazed at how similar they are to you.

CHAPTER ONE

DINING OUT AND DINING IN

A Brief History of Dining Out and Dining In

The idea of eating out and the dinner party are relatively new inventions. Eating out used to be frowned upon: it was extravagant and only indulged in by flappers, bachelors and the idle rich who had more money than sense. Perhaps on a significant wedding anniversary Father might take Mother to dinner in the dining room of the first-class waiting room at the railway station. She would wear her second-best dress and chide him throughout the meal for the unnecessary fuss and attention; however, if he didn't do it, she would become sullen for several years and overboil his potatoes.

There were no restaurants. Hotels had dining rooms frequented by travelling salesmen and ladies who had come to town to visit their gynae-cologist. The menu consisted of soup, a choice of roasts—lamb, pork or beef—and possibly Peach Melba for dessert if you were in a capital city. Fish was compulsory on Friday. Smoked cod was the only fish available and a working knowledge of fish knives was the mark of a well-bred man or woman. Men would tuck the table napkin into the collar of their shirt; women were expected to eat very carefully.

The only meal regularly taken out was afternoon tea. This was a major recreation that came about with the rise of the motor car. Motor cars were considered to be like horses: they needed some regular exercise. Father might putter into work in the car each day, but on Sunday the valves needed a bit of a stretch. It was also considered a wonderful thing to be able to reach some local bushland, mountains and nearby hamlets in only two hours and there stop for scones and a cup of tea—coffee was unavailable and viewed with suspicion. After partaking of refreshments and looking at the view, the family would get back in the car and drive home again, stopping only to let the children out of the back seat to vomit by the roadside.

If going into town and unnecessarily delayed, ladies were permitted to dine in one of the new department store cafeterias. They would eat a ham sandwich and sip a cup of tea and keep their hat on at all times.

The serving of alcohol was not a feature of any of these meals. If dining in a hotel dining room, a glass of sherry might be taken before dinner, but not if dining alone. Wine was unknown and drunk only from flagons by First World War veterans suffering from the effects of trench foot, mustard gas and shellshock. Beer was never served with a meal except to men in pubs who had to drink their quota before the pub closed at six o'clock in the evening. After six, they would vomit and then move on to the sly grog shop. An SP bookie was usually nearby to relieve them of the rest of their pay packet.

And while Cousin Anne and her brood might stay for tea and eat sausages and mash, dinner parties at home for guests were only indulged in by the wealthy. They were an elaborate ritual involving weeks of negotiation about who would take whom into dinner, whether there would be a toast to the Queen, and if all the guests really understood how to use the fish knives.

After the Second World War, refugees and workers on the Snowy Mountains Scheme arrived in great numbers. They were used to sitting in cafés for long periods of time. Jimmy Chu's Chinese and the Gundagai Roadhouse didn't work for them. So they imported espresso machines and olive oil and open cafés for one another. After several decades some longer term residents wandered into these hitherto exclusively ethnic eateries and discovered gnocchi and multiculturalism.

This began a rapid rise in eating out and takeaway food. Takeaway food began as an informal arrangement with the local Chinese café which sometimes allowed you to bring in your own saucepans and take the chow mein home. Then someone who'd been to America discovered that if you built a place and put a car park around it, people would pay a lot of money for fried chicken covered in vast quantities of salt or a hamburger made largely of sugar. Soon we had lost the art of cooking. We now watch fascinated as appealing people on television make meals and occasionally, when we want to impress our friends, we make the same things at home.

Then: it was all meat and potatoes and you could be jailed for using a fork incorrectly. Now: you can stick it up your nose with a chopstick if you wish, and the food's never been better.

AND HOW WILL SIR BE PAYING?

Olivia: We were invited to a dinner party and my boyfriend took a bottle of Veuve Clicquot. The hosts took the bottle and put it away. At the end of the night they asked all the guests for fifty dollars to pay for the dinner. I've never been so astonished in all my life. We paid up.

BEN: Should have asked them if they take VISA. Ask them back and charge them sixty dollars.

STEVEN: I'd be offended if nothing was said beforehand. They could at least take a swipe of my card when I arrived.

LYNN: I have been at something like that where they were doing it as a fundraiser. We knew beforehand what was happening so we went into it ready to pay. But if it ever happens again, perhaps you could say, 'Oh, I'm sorry. Are you trying to buy a goat in India or support your foster child?' or something like that.

GARY: I think they were doing a cull. It was a way of getting rid of friends. 'How can we most offend them? Get them over for dinner and then charge them money. We'll never see them again.' Sounds like it's working.

LYNDALL: I would have deducted the price of the Veuve from the meal: meal, fifty dollars, Veuve seventy-three dollars. Actually, you owe me twenty-three dollars.

JV Times are tight, but if it's got to the stage where you're charging for dinner parties, cancel the dinner party. At least mention it when you invite people and claim it's to cover the cost of importing the truffles. The wine question here comes up all the time. Is wine taken to a dinner party to be drunk there? General consensus is that when you are students, you are taking alcohol for the party and everything is to be drunk immediately. At adult dinner parties, the wine is a gift for the hosts and they can determine what happens to it. The clear exception is French Champagne and expensive local sparkling whites—they are to be guzzled immediately by all present.

AL FRESCO

Ian: I've been wondering, with all the restaurants and pubs that put tables out on the footpath, what's the best thing to do? Are you allowed to stop and have a look at the people eating and what they're eating or should I avert my eyes? Am I just a pedestrian passing through, or can I be part of the social experience? Maybe taste someone's food?

JV: I would say, straight off, that's going a little too far—helping yourself to a chip like you're some sort of errant seagull.

IAN: I went past a pizza restaurant the other day that had tables all over the footpath and I couldn't help but look at everyone's pizza.

JV: And did you get a feeling that people found this a little off-putting?

IAN: Absolutely.

CHRIS: James, there's a particular Asian food court that we spend time at, probably two or three times a month, and my wife actually looks at people's tables to get her meal idea. She looks and says 'That looks okay' or 'I might try that one' and 'I wonder if it has any chilli in it?'. She'll stop and ask people or pinch me to ask for her.

JV: And do people mind?

CHRIS: Generally they haven't seemed to, but they could be just sort of keeping that to themselves.

PETER: I think it's okay to sample the food on another person's plate, provided they've finished and possibly left. I was down in Cooma last weekend, as a matter of fact, at one of these Italian pizza-type places. I was standing there, 'cause they were quite busy, and a couple left, leaving a third of a pizza and about a third of a bottle of red wine. So I thought, oh, I'll just tuck into their leftover pizza while I was waiting. It was quite nice. It was what I would have ordered and so, to cut a long story short, I had some pizza and a third of a bottle of wine—didn't cost me anything. I just rounded it off with a bit of garlic bread on the table next to me, 'cause the people were just leaving and I said, 'Would you mind if...?'. 'No, no, that's fine.'

JV: You drank the red wine?

PETER: The third of a bottle of red wine from one table and the third of their remaining pizza, and lifted the garlic bread off the table next to me.

JV: What was your problem—couldn't find a salad?

PETER: No. I'm not into the salads—but I think they were quite happy that it wasn't wasted.

JV Peter has a delightfully laidback approach to restaurant etiquette usually only found among people who wander the streets muttering and barking—or perhaps in Cooma things are pretty casual. Whenever you see a dish you like, I think it's okay to stop and say, 'Hey, that look's great, what is it?'. However, timing might be important here—it is intrusive, people are eating and they don't like to be interrupted. Fork in mouth, don't ask; masticating, same; dabbing at mouth with napkin, go right ahead.

OH, I'M SORRY, WOULD YOU RATHER COOK?

Charlie: I love to cook so I'll be making dinner for people I've invited over and they come in while I'm crushing the garlic and say, 'Oh, I don't like garlic, don't put too much in', or it might be the cream or the butter or salt. Why do people think it's okay to comment while I'm cooking and what should I say to them?

PETER: I try to find out what people like or dislike beforehand, but when I'm the chef, get out of here. You can't go into someone else's kitchen and tell them how to prepare a meal.

DOUG: When you cook, you need to focus to get it right. It's like with anchovies: if people aren't familiar with them, then they always look at them and say, 'No way, don't put any of them in'; but if that's the dish then they're going in. And once it's served, they'll be fine. Halfway through preparing something, you can't accommodate them.

MARGARET: Some people are allergic to things. I can't stand coriander, for example, and really if it's got coriander in it, I can't eat it. But I'd say that beforehand. The cook should check what you can eat, but if there's something you can't eat then you should tell the cook beforehand. Peanut allergy, for example—you have to tell people about that.

I cook all the time, and the salt agents, the cream police, the garlic Nazis, the butter patrol drive me insane. It is with certain knowledge that the garlic Nazis, the cream police, the salt agents will declare your meal delicious if they are ignorant of the amount of garlic, cream or salt that has gone into it. Anyone who comments on such matters during cooking is not welcome in my home and I want them to stay on the commune and eat brown rice and never come to my table again.

THE FORK WARS

Peter: The other night I was sitting down with my European-bred, seven months pregnant partner and, doing the guy thing, I cooked myself some chilli con carne because she's not much of a meat-eater. All of a sudden she shot me this glance, and said, 'Of course, when our child's born, we will be teaching it how to eat correctly'. To which I thought, well, what am I doing wrong? And I looked at myself and I was only armed with a fork. Now, according to her, this is just not on. But being a simple bloke, I thought I'd got the correct tool for the job, wasn't making a mess, and...well, how am I supposed to eat it? She suggested you would do it with a knife and fork, which I thought was almost impossible. Is there a right way to eat?

STEPHANIE: I'm Italian and I have a couple of things to say to Peter and his German wife: first of all, using the fork to smash the food is a major crime, because you are actually squashing the food. It's not polite.

JV: So, what, with a dish that really only needs one utensil, you shouldn't use the fork?

STEPHANIE: You can scoop it but don't squash it.

JV: So, if you're using a fork in a scooping motion, then that's okay?

STEPHANIE: But squashing it, really, it's insulting for the cook.

JV: I tend to eat a bowl of pasta with only a fork...

STEPHANIE: Never use a spoon—never!

JV: Why not use a spoon? A lot of people will scoop a bit into the spoon and then twirl the fork around it.

STEPHANIE: No, because there is a technique to actually scoop the pasta out of the plate. You catch a few strands with the side of the fork, then you make room on the plate, and then you twist with the fork touching the bottom of the plate. So you don't need anything else.

GLENDA: I was always taught that if you've got the fork in the left hand you only ever use it with the tines down so that they suit the roof of your mouth. If you've got it turned round the other way, you're using it as a shovel, as my mother would say. You were sent from the table in our house if you used your fork as a shovel.

JV: Well that may have been then. What do you think now?

GLENDA: In fact, it offends me when I see people using their fork as a shovel.

JV: How do you eat a green chicken curry?

GLENDA: I put the fork in my right hand and then I can use it turned round the other way. But that's the only time you can turn the fork around.

JV: Yes, but using the shovelling motion.

GLENDA: Yes, but it's in your right hand. So with the chilli con carne, I would feel Peter was using that the right way—if he had the fork in his right hand and he was using it that way. That, to me, would make sense.

JV: So, left-hand shovel, offensive; right-hand shovel, perfectly okay. What if you're left-handed?

GLENDA: Then you've got a problem.

JV: Why is the left-hand shovel in any way offensive?

GLENDA: Because you have the fork in your left hand and the knife in the right. It's like if you're left-handed, you'd have the fork in your right and the knife in your left—that would be appropriate. But if you're using it as a right-handed person and you've got the fork in your left hand and you're using it as a shovel—No, no, no!

JV I'm fascinated by this one. It's one of those beauties where there are schools of thought that are deeply at odds with one another and will never countenance the other's view.

I have found people who say the shovel-fork motion is fine in the right hand and abhorrent in the left, and others who say the exact opposite. Both believe they are well-bred and describe parents who were obsessive and adamant about such things. So is there a correct way to eat? I'm always suspicious of any code that starts with, 'Well, I was always taught...', that will inevitably be a class rule. In order to be recognised as a paid-up member of the middle-class British order, make the little concoction on your fork, tines down, so you never have to transfer the fork to the right hand and commit the sin of shovelling. Europeans will differ and Americans have a relationship with the fork that others find obscene. In actual fact, we now have to be extremely adaptable and be able to eat finger food with our fingers while not spilling our drink; wind up long strings of mozzarella cheese while catching a drooping slice of pizza before it hits the floor; and handle sloppy curries and rice with chopsticks. The panic comes for many with their children. How do I teach them to eat correctly in this age of chicken nuggets? I don't want them to ever be embarrassed by their eating habits. Of course, you have to teach your children how to use a knife and fork and how to sit at a table and eat a meal, but, remember, you are eating food from the twenty-first century not the nineteenth, so don't panic too much about what hand the fork is in.

IF I'D KNOWN I'D HAVE BROUGHT MY FERRET

Patsy: Every time I go to my brother's place for dinner, he insists on feeding his cat at the dinner table with the humans. I hate it, and I need to know how to approach him and persuade him to stop doing it.

JV: Have you tried, 'Get that stinking cat off the table?'.

PATSY: Oh, he just loves it so I can't.

GRAHAM: Look I agree with you, I think it's just 'Get the stinking cat off the table. Now!'.

JV: Is that the form of words you would use? Pretty much?

GRAHAM: And just add 'I'm never coming over here again until you stop eating with that stinking cat'.

JOY: I think she should try and get hold of a baby and just casually go over for dinner. Be very happy and friendly and all the rest of it, and then just casually change the baby's nappy on the table. I think that could be equally disturbing for the brother.

JV: Yes, you could well be onto something there. I was thinking perhaps download a little bit of information about the parasites cats carry, hookworms or something.

JOY: Drop it casually into the course of the conversation.

JV: Well you could just email some of those sorts of things to your brother. Say, 'If I get there and that cat is on the table, this will help you understand why I'm not going to stay'.

SEAN: I'd be reminding the brother that cats don't actually use toilet paper—that overall thought should get through.

JV: Yes, I can see another excellent point there. I think we come back to Graham's solution, 'Get the stinking cat off the table', don't we?

SHIRLEY: Well actually my solution is to suggest that perhaps she sits on the floor and eats her food on the floor.

JV: She should turn up and say, 'Oh no, I'm sorry, could you put mine in a bowl and I'll just eat it on the floor'.

SHIRLEY: Yes, just a little bowl of milk will be fine.

JV 'Oh no, don't bother cooking something for me, just some Snappy Tom like the cat.' I mean, look, if it was a very sophisticated cat—good on the knife-and-fork work and a terrific conversationalist—then we'd all be happy to share the table with it, but otherwise, try developing a cat allergy. Really, it's time to say something. No matter how much affection your brother might have for his cat, you don't have to eat with it.

AND WOULD SIR LIKE A TODDLER WITH THAT?

John: My wife and I go out for dinner quite regularly and I find it very annoying to have other people's children running around the place. Can I tell them to be quiet? Can I go and have a word to the parents? I mean, it really does destroy the relaxed dining experience.

JOCELYN: Can I get a list of restaurants he's likely to frequent so I make sure I never run into him? Look, how are children going to learn how to behave unless we take them out? I'm raising restaurant-goers of the future, but if they're being that bad, sure, come and talk to me and I'll deal with them.

MIRO: I was at a restaurant with some pretty annoying kids. In my bag I had one of those pens with a bubble blower on the top of it. I pulled it out and started blowing bubbles for them: stopped them in their tracks! I gave it to them and we didn't hear a thing from them for the rest of the night. Maybe he should get some bubble blowers and hand them out when he goes in.

MICHAEL: We only take our kids to a Chinese restaurant that has a television. We try to time our outings with 'The Simpsons'. We can usually get a glass of wine, some crispy skin duck, a little conversation and get the kids to eat some noodles in the half hour. I'm with that caller. I don't even like my own kids in restaurants.

STEVE: If you're at a restaurant at about 9–9.30 pm, then I think you've got every right to go and tell the parents to discipline their children. But if you're there early, like about six or seven, well, that's when parents go to restaurants with their kids. If you don't like it, don't go there till later.

JV If it takes a village to raise a child, at what point is the village allowed to send that child to the naughty corner? While John does sound like Mr Grumpy, he does have a point. He was going out to dinner not to a crèche. I think parents have to find child-friendly restaurants, they should be there early and if any diner has any kind of problem in a restaurant, get the owner, the maître d, or anybody in charge over and tell them. Get them to deal with it, rather than approach other customers directly.

WE MUST HAVE YOU OVER...

Max: We often go to friends' houses for dinner, but we don't reciprocate—we're too disorganised, we just can't get it together. How far can we push this thing? And when we do reciprocate, do we have to invite all the other people who were at the dinner parties as well? Do we have to provide multiple dinner parties or can we just do the whole thing at once?

HELEN: Call the local Country Women's Association (CWA), hire the local hall, invite everyone. The CWA will do simple catering that won't cost you a fortune. The ladies will have a great time, the blokes will get around the barbecue and have a beer and everyone will think it's very original and a very special day—better than yet another dinner party. The CWA will get some money out of it, and so everybody's happy.

JV Brilliant! The formal response is: of course you should invite your friends back to dinner, but that doesn't work for everyone. You might live in a tiny flat, you might be a lousy cook, you might have a dog that stinks. This solution has the makings of an annual event where he repays all of his hospitality at once. Saved from the brink of social extinction, transformed into social legend!

A LITTLE MORE OF THE LOBSTER
I FLEW IN FROM BROOME?

Sam: We have friends whom we have over for dinner a lot but they never reciprocate. I think people who don't throw dinner parties don't realise the effort and the cost. Driving all over Sydney to get Portuguese tarts, parking at the fish market and checking out the scallops. Are they being selfish or am I?

MARYANNE: Oh, he's worrying far too much. It's obvious his friends can't cook. He's setting a standard that's way too high for most. Next time just give them bangers and mash—don't bung it on all the time. But if he's that unhappy, I'm free, I'll come for dinner.

PETER: He obviously sees dinner parties as a kind of legal tender. He's expecting his friends to trade in return. Genuine hospitality means you wouldn't care about being asked back. It would never occur to you. If he likes dinner parties and likes the people, what's his problem?

JV I once spoke to a woman about dinner parties in the seventies. She said it was like being a show dog: your beef wellington had to be better than anyone else's; your cheeses stinkier; your red wine bigger and red winier—it was horrendous. I believe she was describing a simpler time. Today, the dinner party is at once an expression of hospitality to our friends and also for many a blunt display of status: this fish came off the trawler this morning, my seafood supplier saved it for me, I have garnished it with fresh greens from my vegetable provedore and the spices—which were growing in Sri Lanka yesterday—I ground them myself all afternoon. The wines, of course, are the latest—no Chardonnay—it's all Pinot Gris now. And so on. Yes, many people go to a lot of trouble with food and wine for a dinner party. I'm one of them, I'm as big a food wanker as anyone, but, please, come and eat anytime. I love cooking, I love having my friends over, I love drinking with them. They don't have to ask me back: some of them don't cook; some of them have little kids; some of them can't be bothered. I'm not keeping score, I believe that's hospitality.

SALT? COLD WATER? BI CARB AND VINEGAR?

Anna: We were invited over for dinner and the hostess used the 250-year-old hand-crocheted tablecloth that's a family heirloom. They served copious amounts of red wine, we all got a little tipsy and my husband spilled a glass. The hostess went mad. She shrieked and was terribly upset for the rest of the evening, which I thought was very rude of her.

JV: So you don't mean, should you get it cleaned? You think the hostess was over the top.

ANNA: Yes. Of course we offered to have it cleaned, but why use these things at a boisterous dinner party and then be so astonished that it got wine spilt on it? Am I wrong?

JANET: I wouldn't bother going there again. If you're going to use the best stuff, you have to expect it to be broken and dirtied. When the grand-children come to dinner I don't put on my best clean linen. And if you're serving wine and it's a good party some of it's going to get spilt, isn't it?

MARTIN: Well the concept of a tablecloth is you put it down on the table to protect the table. So if you've spilled the red wine on the tablecloth and she's going off, you say, 'Well, thank God I spilled [wine] on the tablecloth and didn't ruin your table as well!'.

CLARE: I think she has definitely gone too far. If she was any kind of hostess she would have picked up the bottle of wine, poured it on the table herself, and that would have been the end of that. She should make that man feel comfortable.

JV: If they'd been the fifty-dollar wineglasses, would it be the same thing? So you've broken the fifty-dollar wineglass, it's the same thing, isn't it? Don't use them. They're going to break.

CLARE: That's right. And you don't want the other person to feel uncomfortable.

MELANIE: I had something similar happen. I was helping wash up and a wineglass broke in the sink. I said, 'I'm terribly sorry, I'll replace it'. And the hostess said fine and proceeded to tell me how much, what shape and size to get and where I should get it. It's just part of the dinner party. It wasn't my fault, I was just washing up. She took eighty dollars for the glass and we've never been invited back.

JV While guests will take all care to ensure that they don't destroy hosts' home, hosts will bear all costs for any damage done. Use paper plates and plastic beakers if you're worried about the best china.

STOP THIEF!

Greg: I run a restaurant and I want to tell you: big groups don't tip! What happens is everyone throws in fifty dollars, say, and one gallant man collects all the money, but only pays the bill and pockets the tip. Happens all the time!

GARY: I go out with this group all the time and one guy was notorious for doing it. I got sick of it and I said to him, 'If you're not going to leave a tip can I have my change, please?' Stopped him!

PHILIPPA: When I was a waitress, we had a policy of taking the bill to the table. If the person brings the money up then we just say we're too busy and we'll bring the bill over in a minute—much harder to pocket the tip at the table in front of everyone.

TOM: Tip theft is rife in society today. Running a restaurant, I make sure that everyone is watching their table and do that next bit of service, deliver the bill to the table. We allow people to pay separately too, which always increases the tip.

BRAD: I thought everyone knew this. I never trust the guy who gets up to collect the money. They do it all the time. I always say to the guy loudly, 'Make sure you pay them the tip'. And I check with the table that we're all tipping and ask them, 'So you think the tip should be like fifty dollars?' That sorts them out.

And you thought it was tough dividing the bill up at the end of the night. Now you can't trust the person who volunteers to do that. Isn't this one that just destroys your faith in everyone? You can't trust teachers, priests, policeman, politicians or the self-appointed treasurer at a group dinner.

CHAPTER TWO

IN PUBLIC

A Brief History of Being in Public

Going out in public was a rare treat. To leave the factory or the farm, the schoolhouse or the kitchen and go about with no purpose other than for entertainment was considered frivolous. If there wasn't a war on, there was probably a Depression and all hands were needed to make tanks or build dams. The only exception was church.

Church was compulsory. There were some Jews who had to go to synagogue on Saturday and they were excused, but otherwise everyone had to go to church on Sunday. There were only two types of church: ours and theirs. Our church was full of everyone we knew; their church was full of skinny children with ringworm and nits and an evil priest who was drunk. Our church had just the right amount of piety and some charming ritual; their church was excessive and wrong. Our church had a lovely Sunday School, where you could colour in pictures of Jesus; their church sat the children in rows on hard pews and lectured them on Hell. Our church barely mentioned guilt at all; they drank it in with their mother's milk. But it didn't matter to which one you went: faces were to be scrubbed, hair plastered down and best clothes donned. Children had to behave or they would be beaten with belts and wooden spoons when they got home.

Afterwards there might be a cup of tea in the hall or simply some standing around exchanging pleasantries out the front.

To church and at any other time outside the home, a woman had to wear a hat and gloves. If a woman had to go to the letterbox she would put on her hat and gloves. If she went to the grocer, on went the hat and the gloves. A woman without a hat and gloves was considered 'fallen' and would find herself taking in boarders and the subject of much gossip in the street. Men also wore hats, but if a man wore gloves he would find his hat being tipped off by ruffians who would tease him in the street and question his masculinity. Other than church, going out meant the annual agricultural show or perhaps a wedding or funeral.

The introduction of moving pictures did see a rise in going out, but only among fast city folk who would stop to see a newsreel on their way to the train. Occasionally on a Saturday night they might go to the pictures to enjoy a Dad and Dave film or anything with Chips Rafferty in it. Wealthier types might take in a musical. But in general people stayed at home. Women could go for days without leaving the house, speaking only to the rabbitoh and the greengrocer's boy on their rounds. Once a week they would go to the grocer for flour and tea and if they met anyone they knew they were permitted to converse about the weather.

As we have observed in Chapter One, 'Dining Out and Dining In', no one ever ate out, so there was little reason for anyone to be out and about in public. Men might attend the races or the football on a Saturday, but there they would be drinking and betting until their pay packet was gone and then they would stagger home to beat the wife for an hour or two before bed.

Then: to be out was to be an object of suspicion—you must be a woman of the night or a footpad. Now: many live their entire life in public and feel a sense of failure if found at home.

CROTCH OR CRACK?

David: In the cinema or theatre, if making my way to a seat in the middle of a row, which way should I face—towards the person, thus presenting my crotch area to their face, or away from them, thus presenting them with my rear end?

BRIAN: If you think about it spatially, it's easy. If you go down the row facing the audience, then you bend a little forward at the waist to make your way through and your bum hits the heads in the row behind you. Plus you're always just about to fall forward into the laps of the row you're moving along. If you turn and face the stage, when you bend a little forward, your bum occupies the space above people's laps and you bend over the tops of the heads of the row in front of you.

JV: It's like stacking chairs.

BRIAN: Exactly. This way you minimise the number of people you annoy in trying to get to your seat.

JV: Why are people so annoyed when I have to get to my seat? What did they think: those middle seats might go unoccupied? I'm not coming in late, I'm just after them and it so happens my seat is on the other side of them, but people always act like there's some problem.

BELINDA: I can't answer that, James, but there is something annoying about people pushing past you. I've noticed at concerts or at the cricket, women face the stage, men face the exit—gender is at issue here as well. But that guy's right, you should face the stage. We're anatomically designed to spoon our way to our seat.

JV: It's evolution.

BELINDA: Very true. You also don't miss any of the show if you face the screen and you're running late.

JV And can someone tell me why no one stands up when you're moving past them to get to your seat? I do. No, really, I do. I don't need you crunching on my toes and shoving my choc top into my shirtfront. I'll stand up and through you go. On planes, I prefer an aisle seat. If someone has to get to the window seat, I get up. Could you start to do it as well, please? Then the whole crotch and crack issue disappears, you can skip down the row to your seat.

CINEMA STAND-OFF

Scott: I went to the cinema earlier in the year to see a big blockbuster, and it was quite full. There was a couple that was sitting towards the back, right in the centre of a row, and I squished my way along and said to them, 'Excuse me, would you mind moving along one?', because they had a seat spare on either side of them, and then my girlfriend and I could have sat down together. And they said 'No'. So I stood there for a bit and felt a bit stupid and said, 'You won't move along one to let us sit down?'. And they said 'No, we chose these seats'. And I stood there feeling silly and thinking—was I right to ask? Should I have asked, and should they have moved along one, or was I being thoughtless because they'd chosen the seats first?

JASON: Well, yes, of course they should have moved, but if people aren't going to move, I would never try and force the issue. Just simply ask once and then move away.

JV: You don't reserve those seats. If things change, the crowd changes, you've got to move to accommodate that.

ANDRIANA: I hate anyone sitting next to me in the movies. I always try to block them off with my bag or something.

JV: In a crowded cinema?

ANDRIANA: Yeah, well, then I suppose you have to let them in, but possession is nine-tenths of the law, isn't it? If they had a problem, ask the ushers to make them move.

JV: But then you don't want to sit next to them once you've done that, do you?

ANDRIANA: Well, too bad. They should have got there earlier.

JV Cinemas have lost any sense of formality. It's fast food entertainment—we're there to consume a very familiar product. The audience for a popular blockbuster will consist of large groups of kids and teenagers out for the night, twenty-somethings straight from work and a drink, and, for many, the movie is something they're going to see here and then consume again on DVD, so there's not much sense of occasion about it. That doesn't excuse anyone being rude and not moving—or talking or taking a phone call—but it explains why you won't get much satisfaction if you complain. The audience no longer sees it as a place where you have to behave. And good luck if you want to complain.

There's no projectionist, the manager is eighteen, the ticket-ripper fifteen, and no one working at the popcorn bar is interested in crowd control.

MIND IF I FLOSS?

Sally: I want to know: is it okay to floss in public? You've got that piece of food stuck between your molars and you can't concentrate on the conversation...do you get out the floss or don't you?

JV: Well, I don't. I don't carry floss. Do you carry floss with you?

SALLY: Always, in my handbag.

JV: Do you floss often?

SALLY: Yep, all the time.

JV: Do you floss in public?

SALLY: Well...very, very discreetly.

JV: Gee, it's hard to floss discreetly.

SALLY: Well, you can. It's hard, you need to practise. I'm not so sure if it's the right thing to do or not.

JV: What kind of reaction have you had when you've flossed in public?

SALLY: People sort of look the other way.

JV: Would that be answering your question then?

SALLY: So I should go to the ladies?

JV: Let's find out.

ANDREW: As a dentist, I can only recommend as much flossing as possible. Go for it! The other thing, of course, as a pick-up line, you know you're not looking at dentures. So flossing in public is quite acceptable.

JV: I see, it's a way of boasting about the vitality of your teeth.

ANDREW: If you've got them, floss them. You only need to stop flossing the teeth you don't want to keep.

JV: In terms of a public health drive, do we need to get rid of the taboo around flossing?

ANDREW: For sure.

JV: If we floss in public—let's say we're at a restaurant and we've just had the steak and I'm flossing now. Then I have a piece of string with some half-chewed bits of meat on it.

ANDREW: You don't, actually, because if your dentistry's up to scratch, James, basically nothing's going to come out on that floss. If you're flossing regularly, that string's going to be spotless when it comes out.

JV: Let's say that my floss does come out beautifully pristine, as you say—where do I deposit my floss?

ANDREW: What I do with mine is I roll it round my finger, tie it in a figure eight, do a little loop around it just because I'm anally retentive, then just put it in the ashtray, because that's the only thing ashtrays are for.

JV: They're now flosstrays. I like your little figure eight, tie the loop around it.

ANDREW: Oh yes. It shows your dexterity as well.

JV: Andrew, we weren't able to show your face because you are a dentist...

ANDREW: I'm actually standing here half-naked at the moment.

IRENE: I can actually floss with one hand. You wind it round the pointer finger, then around the next one, and it depends where it is, if it's right up the back molars it is a little...

JV: So you make a V, wind it round the top, and then...

IRENE: Yes, and your other hand can then be used to discreetly cover your mouth.

JV: Why stay at the table? Surely you'd just go to the bathroom.

IRENE: But you might miss out on something very intelligent that's being spoken about.

JV: Yes, but you don't sit there and endure bladder pain...I'm just saying, when you go to the toilet, why wouldn't you have a quick floss then?

JOAN: I'm opposed to public flossing, and as for that dentist who says he does it in public and isn't it wonderful and then puts all his floss in the ashtray—I think he ought to go back to infection-control classes and find out how filthy the mouth is. I think that's the same as leaving needles all over the city.

JV: But we've only got to go back a few years and we would have left our cigarette butts which had been in our mouths sitting in the ashtray.

JOAN: Just because we have learned not to do something filthy, doesn't mean to say we can do another thing that's filthy now. He can take a little plastic bag with him and pop it in that, if he insists on doing it in public so that he can show everybody how great he is.

ROSEMARY: I'm a great believer in flossing. I probably floss my teeth two or three times a day. But I just don't think—you know, you've got to get it twisted around each finger, you're getting it in there, and then it flicks over the table to someone...Not a good look.

BEN: I think public flossing is really revolting, and it's on a par with picking your nose. I wouldn't even do it in front of somebody that I know really well.

JV: So if you had a partner, for example, you wouldn't do it; if you were sharing the bathroom, you wouldn't do it?

BEN: No. I'd do it in the bathroom when they're not there.

ADAM: Maybe it's a matter of public awareness, too, because for a long time the cigarette industry rode on the fact that it was portrayed on the television and in movies as the cool thing to do. So, maybe we just need a few movies where, after a meal, Nicole Kidman or someone just leans back and flosses almost erotically, and suddenly the kids are doing it; it's great for dental hygiene, it's out there in the community, and it's the new black.

JV Yes, I can see many a famous movie scene being reworked without the cigarette but with the dental floss. I am yet to encounter a public flosser: an occasional toothpicker, sure, but I haven't seen anyone floss. Despite the claims to flossing prowess by several of our callers, I was left wondering why you wouldn't do it in the bathroom? No matter how dexterous you think you are, you're still going to be sitting next to me with your fingers in your mouth probing bits of old food out of the cracks in your teeth. Do I want you to join in the conversation when you're doing that? If you need to do that, don't you need a little privacy as well? We may as well be discussing cleaning your teeth at the table: you pull out a little toothbrush, scrub away discreetly and then spit quietly into a wine glass. Sounds as stupid to me, but stranger evolutions have occurred in our social practices and I for one will be excited to wake up and find in decades to come that public flossing is all the rage.

THE SNIFFER

Julia: I have a problem with men who either don't have a handkerchief or perhaps haven't learned to use a handkerchief. Recently I was at a function and the fellow beside me decided to sniff his way through it. Do people not use handkerchiefs these days? Is it not fashionable? What's the story?

JV: Yes, well, what *has* happened to the handkerchief? Look I haven't carried a handkerchief for years, but I tend to have a tissue handy.

JULIA: I did suggest to him that there were tissues available in the toilets if he would like to use them, but he didn't even take any notice. So I thought okay, well, what else can I do? I can't really pull out one from my handbag and offer it to him. So I just shut up and put up by that stage.

ANNE: You've got to hand them the tissue, absolutely.

JV: Have you ever done it?

ANNE: Yes, I have. My most notable one was when I was watching the American Dance Theatre in England—I was living there for a few years—and I handed some tissues to some guy behind us who was sniffing at regular seven-second intervals; it was driving me bananas. My English boyfriend was mortified.

JV: And what was the recipient's response?

ANNE: 'Thank you very much.'

NEIL: There was a time at uni many years ago during the exams and this guy behind me was sniffing away, and it just got too much and I turned around and said, 'Listen pal, you can blow it or let it drip' and it was quiet after that. So I presume he let it drip.

Hankies! What happened to them? Time was when you had a neatly folded handkerchief in the top pocket of a suit; when a child would have had one pinned to her tunic; when a set of three hankies was a perfectly good Christmas present from a great-aunt. The tissue dominates and I wonder if that has led some to conclude that it's okay to sniff back up one's nasal excess. It's not! It never is, and I think offering a tissue to anyone sniffing in close proximity is perfectly fine. It should probably be mandatory. It opens up the line of conversation, 'Do you have a cold or the flu?' and when they say they do, you can tell them to go home and get away from you.

PUBLIC TOENAIL FILING

Ian: Beautifully presented coach, going around Sydney transporting American tourists. A couple got on, sat opposite me in the front row, and the man was wearing sandals—JCs type of thing—and he pulled out a nail file and started to file his toenails.

JV: Filing toenails on the bus...

IAN: Well it was a coach, not just a bus. Beautifully vacuumed and presented, an immaculate thing. I thought, now is that just the height of rudeness or in America is it considered normal?

JV: If the woman had been filing her fingernails, would that have been okay?

IAN: That would be different, I think.

JV: Did he clip as well?

IAN: Just filing, noisily.

JV: Did anyone else seem worried about it?

IAN: No, it was his wife sitting next to him and then me. Did he think: you're just the coach driver and I'm gonna do my toenails in front of you on your beautiful coach? Because I know over there Greyhound bus drivers are considered a dime a dozen.

JV: Did you remonstrate with him in any way?

IAN: No. When he got off, I said, 'That's all right, sir, I'll clean that up later'.

JV: Perfect response.

DAVID: Oh, look, public grooming in general I find a little nauseating, especially when it's in a coach, a place where somebody is then going to have to go to the effort of cleaning up and removing it. I would regard that as being a bit antisocial.

DIANA: I'm actually a podiatrist, so I see a lot of feet, a lot of nails. And I find it quite repulsive that people would actually do this in public. I'm really against it. I don't particularly like girls doing their nails in public either. If somebody breaks their nail and you see them filing it, well, that's not so bad; but to actually get out a file and file all their finger-nails, I think those types of things should be done behind closed doors.

LIZ: Oh, James, I can't believe all these stitched up people, honestly! Where did they learn all this stuff? I was very well brought up and my mother did try to instil these things in me. But let me tell you a story: I lived in Brazil for a couple of years about twenty years ago, and I went to my first beauty parlour. The Brazilians are very body-conscious, as you know; they go to the beauty parlour all the time, and I wanted to go and get my underarms waxed. I was used to English beauty parlours—which are the same here—where you go into little cubicles with little discreet curtains drawn and nobody sees what the other person's having done. It's all very genteel and hush hush. But you go into the Brazilian beauty parlour and it's just one big, glorious room, and everybody's there and they're all unashamedly having everything done out in the open. They're talking and laughing and gossiping and they're having hair removed from all sorts of places and all sorts of intimate things are being done. And it's just a lot of fun. And it showed me how stitched up we are—we sort of UK-based races. No, I can't see anything wrong with public nail filing, myself.

JV Liz's South American sojourn has put her in a different state of mind and she'd obviously be quite happy with any amount of public tweezing, exfoliating and dousing. The rest of us might tolerate a little emery board on the fingernails, but I think we draw the line at the toes. So flossing, sniffing and filing of toenails have all occurred in public and in places we share, but do most of us think that it should continue and become standard? No!

OUT OF MY WAY, I'M ON A PB

Roz: *Swimming in lanes, in the swimming pool, doing laps. When is it acceptable to overtake?*

JV: Is the swim lane etiquette hard to figure out?

ROZ: Well, basically I just stay behind, and when I get to the end, if there's someone that's a bit faster than me, I normally say, 'Oh, do you want to go in front?'. But if I'm going continually and not stopping—

like I may do twelve laps at a go—normally that's the way, but there was this fellow obviously took umbrage at me overtaking him.

JV: It sounds like you've been swimming for a while, if you're doing twelve laps at a shot and you can overtake people and that sort of thing. So what do you think of the usual? If someone's faster than you, it's beholden on the slow person to hang back?

ROZ: Normally you pick your lane: there's slow, medium and fast. I go in the medium. And if there's someone going a bit slow, if there's no one coming the other way I would overtake and then just keep going. But I often wonder whether you should just wait till you get to the end and let them get a long way ahead, or is it correct to overtake at any point mid lap?

SHANE: Roz has described one of the biggest problems you ever have. I think the etiquette is pretty simple, because if there's no one coming the other way you should be able to overtake. But the most important part of the etiquette is that the swimmer being overtaken should not accelerate and should not move into the middle of the lane to try and stop you, which happens all the time.

JV: Slower swimmers get out of the way and allow faster swimmers to pass?

SHANE: I think that's right. Everyone's got their own speed and everyone accepts that. But a lot of people will just get in the lane, they get in the fast lane and do breast stroke—and I think the only people who should be doing that are Olympians—but they don't look and they don't care, so one is entitled to overtake as long as the other lane's clear. And if people accelerate, you should give them a very stern talking to at the end of the lane.

JV: And usually you can pause at one end to let somebody pass—it's like golf, isn't it?—you let them play through, sort of thing. Off you go, I'll give you a third of the pool and then I'll come up behind you.

SHANE: That's right. And if you're paying attention to the people swimming around you, you'll know when they're coming up, and you'll know that right at the end of this lap, you'll probably need to just pull over and let this person through.

TONY: I'm glad you're taking on this issue. It's a major one that's been fraught with danger for some time.

JV: Well, I think there're more and more people swimming.

TONY: It's been an issue that I've struggled with for many years, and my easy solution was to stand up in the pool, before I touched the end of the pool and turned around and went the other way. You're immediately in front of the person that you're trying to overtake.

JV: But there's no real instruction is there? You turn up at the pool thinking 'I'm going to start doing some laps', and no one at any point says, 'Look, this is the way it should be done', do they?

TONY: No. It's a bit of commonsense.

JV When we go to exercise we head out with a very personal focus: this is my time, this is about me, and I'm doing the right thing, I'm getting fit. We only have a limited time in which to do it, we have personal goals to achieve, it's an odd combination of doing something we enjoy and something which is often relaxing, but in a kind of intense and disciplined way. It's not a

38

moment where there's a lot of tolerance. Observe the jogger on a crowded path, the lycraed cyclist in the park, the swimmer in their lane, someone working out in a gym. I'm in a routine here, I'm in the zone, I need to do this, all must give way to me. I think all of these situations are awkward when you first go into them. There are a lot of unwritten rules in the pool and the gym and it can be a bit hard to talk about them with strangers when you're nude in the shower afterwards. Wait until you're all dressed and walking back towards the car park.

OVERTAKING PART TWO

Nicky: I'm a mum with an eight-month-old baby, and my main form of exercise is walking with a stroller. And sometimes I need to overtake people who are walking slowly—elderly people, for example. As I'm walking at a fair pace, I tend to give them a bit of a fright when I walk past. I don't mean to, and I'm seeking guidance as to how to negotiate this.

JV: Are you suggesting you need a bell?

NICKY: Yeah...

JV: But then you'll wake up your sleeping baby.

NICKY: That's right, or do I need to say, 'Just coming past...' What's the right way to do it?

MICHAEL: Perhaps you need a quiet kind of noise that creeps up on you. A squeaky wheel—if you let the axles rust a little bit, you'll get this 'eee, eee, eee'. Something very subtle, quiet, seems to be effective.

JV: Or one of those little clickers we used to have on the bike.

MICHAEL: Well, possibly. The other idea, of course, is to have the baby trained to—they've got those little steering wheels nowadays on the front of prams, you must have seen them in the shopping centres—and...

JV: She has a little horn.

MICHAEL: But the other thing is, these days prams are so modern, you could almost go bush with the thing. Throw the accelerator into the 4WD mode and go round on the bit of grass.

JV: That's right. She should be able to fang it off onto the nature strip, dodge the acacias and get back onto the tar.

MICHAEL: Absolutely. You'd hear the rustling coming...

JV: But you'd also hear her dropping down a couple of gears, wouldn't you? Maybe she could just learn to whistle.

MICHAEL: I always thought it was quite appropriate to make a very gentle but non-threatening kind of approaching sound. It seems that people don't seem to know which side is left. We used to pass each other on the left side of the sidewalk, and these days we don't any more.

ANDY: I remember when I was a young bloke and I wanted to get through a crowd or something, I'd just sing out, 'Lady with a pram' and everyone would turn around and this avenue would appear. And here we really have a lady with a pram, why can't she do that? Then people would just turn around, they have respect for you because you're a lady with a pram. They feel that it's not a good thing to be angry with a lady with a pram. You've got a kid, you know, that's your ticket to everywhere.

CATHY: My advice to Nicky is enjoy the fast walk while you can with your eight-month-old, because within four or five months they'll be wanting to walk, be hopping out of the pram, and the oldies will be overtaking Nicky.

JV: So just relish it, zip up the inside there. She shouldn't feel embarrassed about just singing out, 'I'm coming...on your left there' or 'Excuse me...'.

CATHY: Not at all, but for the next four or five years she'll be walking so slowly that this is a joy, to be fast-walking.

JV The cyclist on the shared pedestrian path reports the same problem: if you ring the bell or call out, you often frighten the pedestrian; if you zip up the inside of them, you frighten the pedestrian. And now, when every pedestrian has their ears filled with headphones, neither works. The cyclist or the pram person has to call out, however, and it's perfectly okay—people strolling don't want you hard on their heels—a cheery 'coming through' or 'Good morning, can I just get past?' should work.

GET OFF MY CHAKRA

Angela: I have a gym dilemma. I'm a regular gym-goer. I have my normal days I attend, but occasionally—due to changes in my work roster—I go on a different day. This happened to me recently. I set up my steps for the step class, and I was obviously in someone else's regular spot. They set up so close to me I had to move. I'm wondering, does this woman own the spot, or can I just use it sometimes? After this happened to me, I remember a friend telling me that she went to a spin class, you know, the stationary bicycle class, and she was warming up and getting ready for the class to start and another woman came in and said, 'You're on my bike. That's my bike'.

JV: But these are public gyms, where your membership fee entitles you to the use of any equipment, and you don't book specific bits of equipment.

ANGELA: No. So my question is: does regular attendance to a particular class give you ownership of the spot and/or the bike?

JV: So, if you always do the Wednesday at five o'clock, are you always on the furthest bike on the left?

ANGELA: I do another class and there's one guy who attends on a Wednesday morning at 6 am, and he stands in one spot. But when he attends the Saturday 8.15 class, he uses a different spot. So he has his two different spots.

TERRY: I think the pecking order established in the gym seems to be based on some people's idea of how good they think they may be. So,

Angela's particular problem may be that the person thinks they own that piece of equipment based on superior athletic performance on a step machine or a treadmill.

JV: Yes. I can bench-press this weight or I can do this in the spin class, you seem like a fat amateur to me.

TERRY: That's right. I own the bench press, this is mine. You can go and have the squat rack.

JV: Is that what you've seen?

TERRY: Certainly have, yes.

JV: And do people tend to ask nicely, or do they just sort of assume?

TERRY: I've never seen anyone ask nicely. I've seen them assume, usually accompanied by a lot of very transparent body language.

JV: So there's an essential sort of strutting posture that says 'This is mine, get off it'.

TERRY: It's much more complex for the women, though, because part of the thing with the women is it also depends on exactly how you're looking at the present moment and how you've managed to dress. And that goes in two levels. The really serious ones tend to dress down, whereas there are the ones who still think somehow that dressing up is the requirement—so you get a bit of a clash there as well...

DENIS: Oh, that's real simple, 'cause I get the same problem when I go to the gym. I even got into trouble for going to a yoga class, everyone thought I was trying to pick the women up when I was in yoga class. I pay membership as well, thank you.

JV: So have you said this to people? Have you said, 'Look, just back off, wait your turn?'.

DENIS: Yes, I have. I said, 'I've paid membership. You can wait until I'm finished. I'll be finished in twenty minutes' or 'I'll be finished in five sets'...If it's a piece of machinery and they can't share, just tell 'em the timeframe that you'll be finished—or if it's a piece of machinery most people actually can join in together, 'cause you do need to rest when you're doing weights.

JV: So there's a lot of this goes on where people are sort of, 'Look, I'm on my routine and you need to move now'.

DENIS: Occasionally, but very rarely. Then you generally find that they're pretty selfish people. They're probably people that cut you off when they're on the road anyway.

SONG: I'm a regular gym-goer, and I do have my little spot that I like to stay in, my little comfort place. But I think nobody owns that spot. To me, if you come first, that's yours.

JV: But have you noticed this kind of thing where people do seem— you know, it's like—you're in my spot? I wanna be there, can't you be somewhere else?

SONG: Very rarely. I think people just sort of move aside and let someone else have it.

JV We do have our little corners of paradise, don't we? A little spot in the sun where we like to eat our lunch, a part of the beach we think of as ours, a corner of the bar, a spot at the cinema, a desk in a library; all public spaces, but if we're a regular user we think of it as ours. So, if someone has taken our corner can we ask for it back? Well, probably only if there's a suitable alternative on offer. Otherwise, go somewhere else and think of it as an opportunity to break out of your rusty ways.

FUR-TIVE

Joanne: I have a difficult question. I'm going to a black-tie dinner soon. I have a lovely dress but it's sleeveless, and I anticipate feeling rather cold. I have a couple of wraps, but I don't think they'll be warm enough. I asked my mother recently whether she ever comes across fake fur. And she said, 'Funny you should ask, I have three in the cupboard upstairs'. It turns out my parents have three real furs which must be at least eighty years old, and are probably quite valuable. They'd inherited them from distant, wealthy relatives. I've had a mixed response on canvassing family and friends. So far, the dominant opinion is that it will be okay to wear the furs, and if asked, I could pretend they were fake. Let me just say that I would never buy a real fur because I think it's wasteful to kill an animal for clothing when there are plenty of good alternatives. However, these furs were made well before I was born and, as my husband said, you had nothing to do with the death of those animals. Should I refuse to wear them on principle and go out and buy a fake instead?

JV: Well, what do you think? If you're opposed to wearing fur, but there's a fur in front of you that is old and antique and dates from the days when no one cared a rat's about a mink—well, why not? Can you stick it on, can you wrap the stole around you, its little claws down there in your derriere, in your cleavage? Can you put on the lovely big coat because it's fifty years old, it's one hundred years old? Beautiful bit of sable, lovely piece of Russian fox or something? And you don't care that it was killed in some extraordinarily nasty circumstance back in 1927, because it happened back in 1927—and there's the coat, it's sitting there. What do you do, set fire to it? Get rid of it?

REBECCA: I think the reason that furs were worn in the first place is because they are so beautiful and so warm, and despite the tragic circumstances in which the poor animals have died to produce them, if they're not worn and they're old furs—and so a historical thing—if you don't wear them, the animals died in vain. You're not appreciating the fact that it died to produce this gorgeous garment.

JV: You're looking for any excuse...

REBECCA: No, I'm not, actually, because I don't promote the wearing of currently killed furs.

JV: But doesn't it promote the wearing of currently killed furs, if it shows us how beautiful it is?

REBECCA: But as a tribute to the animal.

JV: It's a tribute to the animal that died.

REBECCA: Yes. Otherwise, if it died and it's made into a coat and the coat just gets thrown out or burned or whatever, the animal has completely died in vain, and there's no appreciation of what it died for at all.

SANDRA: I suppose my views are not dissimilar to Rebecca's, really. I'm in a similar situation to the woman who rang in initially to raise this, because I inherited a woollen coat with a very large fur collar on it, from my mother.

JV: What's the fur?

SANDRA: I think it's only fox, it's not mink.

JV: I always like it if the little paws are in the front. It doesn't have that, it doesn't have the little paws?

SANDRA: No, I'm not sure I could quite come at that, actually, or a flattened head. It just goes round, no attachments.

JV: Have you worn it out, has anyone ever commented?

SANDRA: Yes. And they have, and I just turned around and said, 'Too bad, you live with it. This fur died before I was even born'.

JV: How did they react, did they go, 'Oh yeah, fair enough'?

SANDRA: They didn't say much, I can be fairly obstreperous.

JV: This sounds like a very blokey comparison, doesn't it? Is it like getting around in a '68 Mustang and not giving a fig about the environment? This car's always been here, it's still there, it uses petrol and pumps out poisonous carbon and lead, but I don't care.

SANDRA: No, I do see it a bit differently from that, because the coat's not doing any more damage. The coat's been there since...

JV: But doesn't it promote the wearing of fur? You look beautiful, you make other women jealous and want one...

SANDRA: I don't see it like that. You're not likely to go out, I don't think, and buy a coat like this just on the basis of having seen somebody wear one. You're either going to go and buy one, which I would not encourage, or you really like it and you get lucky like I did and you get it handed down from your mother.

JV: There needs to be a label on it that says 'Old Fur', doesn't there?

SANDRA: That might be a good idea.

MARY: Old fur is like old coral or old ivory. You can wear it, but if it's new, depending on your disposition, no, you don't wear it.

JV Look, one man's elephant foot umbrella stand is another's crime against the animal kingdom. It's a fascinating one. If Great-great-grandfather shot a tiger while staying with the Maharajah, is it okay to display the skin on your study floor in an ironic juxtaposition to your own obvious ecowarrior credentials, like your hybrid car and paid up Greenpeace membership? As well as the '68 Mustang already mentioned, I also covet an aged Steinway and I'm pretty sure the eighty-eight keys will have been ripped out of some Kenyan tusker. So is it okay to maintain an antique that represents a set of values perhaps at odds with even your own current thinking? The anti-fur lobby says don't wear it. By wearing old fur you are maintaining the links and the presentation and encouraging others to wear it. All the 'animal died in vain' arguments just make you feel okay about wearing that particular garment. To encourage real change in the world, you have to change what you do. 'I abhor slavery, darling, but Mtubu has been with us for years and is part of the family.' Same thing!

I'M WALKING HERE, BUDDY!

Paul: What are the rules about walking on the footpath? Who gives way to whom?

ROBBIE: I have the same irritation as your caller and my solution is you stand right where you've been walking. You stop and they have to walk around you.

JV: You stand your ground. Do you do it every time?

ROBBIE: It's quite simple, all I do is give a big cough or a sneeze, and you get plenty of room on the footpath.

ANNE-MARIE: I have a solution for the footpath. What you do is you just keep your head down and guaranteed, people will just clear the way for you. It works!

MAL: During World War Two, when we had blackouts, in Pitt Street and George Street they painted a yellow line down the middle of the footpath with an arrow either left or right, and in the night you could walk along. It's easy. And I wrote to the council about this, but of course I didn't even get a reply.

SIMON: Keep head down, footpath clears in front of you. The head-down rule could end in tragedy if everyone does it. If everyone's got their head down, no one's giving way—clunk. It's going to be painful heading down the footpath, isn't it? It could be very bloody in our streets if that sort of thing takes place.

SARAH: Since I was a kid, my mum said 'You always stay to the left like you're on the road'. And I went to school and it was very strict, all the girls had to stay on the left-hand side and go single file, and it's always surprised me when I'm walking along footpaths that people don't stick to that rule, 'cause I just thought everybody knew that.

JV: I think it should be enforced.

SARAH: I agree.

JV: I'd like to see footpaths policed. Police on little scooters with the flashing blue light.

SARAH: Yes. If everybody stayed to the left like they did on the roads, I think we'd be a much happier place.

The keep-to-the-left rule seems pretty straightforward and should be encouraged. I don't seriously want to see police on little scooters except they'd look funny. But actually there is an emerging problem on the footpaths: phones, people walk along talking—now that's fine, but they miss all the cues they would get if they weren't otherwise engaged—so they walk into you or they stop in just the place they shouldn't stop, so you bang into them, or their head is down as they text and they stand in the middle of the escalator, oblivious to you trying to pass. Ditto iPods: ears crammed with headphones, no sense of anyone else around. Beware of the person with the phone and the iPod, texting a friend on a rainy day carrying a large umbrella—you may lose an eye. Solution? It will come with time. Just as we learned not to shout on the phone when in public, so we will learn how to walk and talk at the same time. Our adaptability as a species is amazing. It's been happening ever since we came down from the trees.

UMBRELLA WARS

Nick: I noticed walking around the centre of town yesterday that when it started raining, everyone seemed to be actively attempting to take my eye out—with their umbrella. Everyone had the brolly up, but they forget that it's a metre out from their head. People should be more aware of others.

DONNA: The point here is that umbrellas have got bigger. Every health insurance company and bank and car dealership is handing out these huge golf-style umbrellas and people put them up and walk down the street and they take up half the footpath. That's the problem right there.

BEN: Yeah, that's it, spot on. Umbrellas used to be little folding things that you shook out and were no bigger than your shoulders really. Now, like she says, everyone's unfolding these giant things like they're on the back nine and the heavens have opened.

JV: It's a Sydney thing. People have to have a bigger one: bigger car, bigger child stroller, now big inflated umbrellas. It's a real estate claim, really.

DAVID: No one shorter than me should be allowed to have umbrellas. Everyone thinks they're tall and everyone forgets that other people's eyes are right at the level of the outside spokes of the umbrella. It's a dry climate thing. People in Sydney don't get enough practice. Go to New Zealand, live in Wellington—get to practise every day—and over there if you used one of those big ones, the wind'd pick you up and blow you over here.

SUSAN: Far too many umbrellas, don't need all of them. Any one of the big ones can accommodate two, even three. I think a roster system to decide who is going to bring the umbrellas to town: like odd-numbered houses on Monday, Wednesday, Friday; even-numbered on Tuesday, Thursday, Saturday. And then we just share. I don't get the umbrella thing. How wet can you get walking from your office to the car park or from one shop to another? Much easier just to get a few drops on you than to worry about the whole umbrella thing.

JV This is a Sydney issue, or at least a dry city issue. In London people know how to use an umbrella and how to behave around umbrellas. In Sydney, where it doesn't rain for weeks on end and then you have a couple of days of it, no one knows what to do. It is also true that like houses, cars and barbecues, umbrellas have got bigger. Perhaps the corporate-style golf umbrella should be banned and the only umbrella issued be the one that is no wider than the shoulders. Otherwise, see pedestrian rules in 'I'm Walking Here, Buddy' on page 49 and walk carefully in Sydney when it's raining.

BUTT OUT

Stuart: What should you say to people who drop their cigarette butt on the footpath? It's litter, it's wrong, but smokers today are pretty defensive and it's hard to say something that's not going to agitate them. I tried it once and nearly got punched out.

AMANDA: I suggest you just quietly pick it up in front of them. I think that adequately shames them, and you solve the litter problem.

JV: That's good because you're not verbalising. As soon as you say something, it can become sarcastic or it gets people's backs up.

ANN: Actions are much more constructive.

JEAN: I'd do that and with a dainty tissue. You can act out how disgusting it is to pick up someone else's cigarette butt.

JV: I like that with the tissue. Would tweezers be going too far?

JEAN: With a specimen jar.

JV: Would you actually do something like that?

JEAN: I'm the sort of person who does that sort of thing. In fact, I've done it for other bits of litter. I pick it up and say to the person, 'Can I get that for you?' and they kind of look at you, and I say, 'No, really, it's my pleasure'.

DANNI: He could carry around a few spare film canisters and hand them out. A film canister is the perfect thing to put your own butts in.

The smoker just throws it out at the end of the day. You're just being helpful; you're not having a go at them.

GORDON: I'm a smoker and look, this is all very well, but picking them up and being all smug and smart, it's still taking a dig at the smoker and we need to have respect for people's individual choices, even when they're wrong. We smokers need not inflict our habit on other people but others need to respect us as well. We know how bad it is and we don't need to be victimised any more. Because of the intolerance of smoking there is no provision for it any more, so there is nowhere to put your butts and no ashtray and no place to smoke and so on. I'm a friend to all creation but at the same time I've got this butt to get rid of. People yell at me about smoking when they're driving past in their cars. Which one of us is doing the most harm to the planet? I like the idea about the film canisters, though—I'm going to do that and hand them out: 'Here's your little present from the fairy penguins who don't want to choke on your butt'.

Gordon, you're an extraordinarily balanced individual and if only we could all approach our own foibles and responses with this level of self-awareness, this would be a very short book. I think Gordon's analysis of his own smoking, people's reaction to it and what he should be doing is an example of completely civilised behaviour. Even though he believes on balance he's not doing anything much in terms of environmental damage, he's going to adopt the film canister idea. What else should any of us be doing in response to any problem we have or perceive?

EXCUSE ME WHILE I KEEP MYSELF ALIVE

Robyn: I've recently been diagnosed as a type-one diabetic, and so I have to inject insulin four times a day. It's only been a couple of weeks and I'm having a problem knowing where and when to inject. I have a friend who has the same condition, and he doesn't have any problem at all injecting in front of people at the dinner table. I personally don't really like to do that, but I also don't really like doing it in the toilets, either, in the stall of the toilet. I'd rather be outside at the sinks rather than sitting on a toilet seat. So I need to know how other diabetics handle this. I mean I have to do it all the time, but I understand that for some people it might be quite unusual. Other people don't like the sight of needles at all. So I don't want to upset them either.

CAROL: I have a friend who's diabetic and she has to inject herself as well—and she does it basically under cover of the table. She just lifts her shirt up a bit and just jabs away. The first time you see it you wonder 'Oh, what's she doing?' but after that it's fine.

RICHARD: I've been a diabetic for forty-one of my forty-six years. In my youth, I'd have one needle a day, which was a big, pre-boiled glass syringe clunker and it really hurt. I hate needles. But at this stage in my life I have about six or seven needles a day, and what I do is, I shoot up. It's my life and it isn't the case for everybody else. If they don't like it, that's their problem, not mine. I'm going to live my life and I'm not going to be ashamed of having diabetes. I'm not holding myself out to be sickly or anything of that nature. I have diabetes, it's well controlled, I'm a very fit person—and I'm shooting up. And if they say, 'What are you doing?', I'm shooting up. And I don't look for discreet ways of doing it, I do it.

POSS: I had a woman turn up at a party I was giving and she walked in the door and said 'Hello' and then pulled out all her paraphernalia and shot up. And we all sort of went, ugh! She had a half-hour drive to get here—why can't she sit in the car and do it? I'm sympathetic, but I don't feel that it has to be in your face. I found it really quite offensive.

SHARON: My daughter's twelve and has had diabetes since she was seven, and she's been injecting in public quite happily since then. And I think the more people do that, the more others will understand about type-one diabetes and what it means to be a diabetic.

JV: Now what's the situation at school?

SHARON: Yes, she does it in public at school—she has no problem. A few of her friends when she was younger were completely grossed out. But then she explained that she had to do this to keep herself alive, and it became just part of her deal.

JV: So she sits on the bench in the playground and does it?

SHARON: Yep!

At the risk of sounding like a cheap self-publicising media outlet, Robyn called back a few months later. She had rung us, had a discussion, gone on to a Diabetes Clinic where she'd met several people who'd heard the discussion. Everyone offered further advice and she wanted to let us know that calling us and talking about it had helped her enormously to get over the first few weeks of dealing with her condition. She now shoots up whenever she needs to, wherever she is.

LISTEN, LOVE, WE'RE AT
THE $#%@&* FOOTY!

Simon: *I have season tickets to the Swans with the same seats every week. And last week a lady who has a seat brought her young son with her. And I tend to get very passionate and might use the odd expletive so I was getting extremely dirty looks. Now, I think football is the type of place where people do get a little bit passionate. I'm not vulgar, but I'm wondering whether I just politely say to the lady, 'Well, look, if you're going to bring your young son to the football, I think you've got to expect this type of thing'—or whether I need to shut my gob.*

JV: Let's cut through the euphemisms, without using the language—would you say that most of your calling out to players or umpires uses four-letter words?

SIMON: Fifty per cent.

JV: And do you call out a lot?

SIMON: Yes.

JV: And it's 'You effing idiot...'

SIMON: Yes. 'Get on with it, you're playing like a member of the opposite sex', or something like that, you know.

JV: But you would argue that this is part of the footy...

SIMON: Very much so. I don't think in myself it's vulgar. In the party there're four of us, and two of them are female and they don't seem to get distressed. You bring your eight-year-old to the footy, it's sort of what you're gonna get.

JV: That's it, isn't it, if you're not prepared to, then go to some other...

SIMON: Go to The Wiggles.

BILL: Simon's moved me to ring a radio station for the first time because I've taken my kids to the football many, many times over the years. They're adults now, but if I took my daughter who's eighteen and I sat beside Simon and every second word was a four-letter one, we'd be having a little chat. And I think his barracking might get a lot quieter and certainly more muffled.

JV: So you would happily comment on it? Look, I'm not a footy-goer. I don't go to the footy often, but isn't that sort of full-blooded barracking pretty common?

BILL: No. You can go, you can cheer, you can yell, you can scream, you can laugh, you can cry, you can do anything you want, it's fantastic, the atmosphere, when it's going. I'm no shrinking violet, mate, I'm a truckie; I've coached and managed and played rugby league all my life. But if he sat beside me, he'd be in strife. You've got to be able to behave like a human being, for God's sake.

DAVID: I'm a Mexican by birth. I've lived in WA and I've been to a lot of AFL. I was down in Canberra on Sunday, for example, took my son to see West Coast and North Melbourne. Simon is definitely out of order. What he ought to do is learn a bit of repartee. He can say things like 'white maggot', 'bludger' and all that sort of stuff for the umpire. I think you've got a duty to entertain the crowd a little bit, and you've got to come up with something funny. I have a lot of fun doing that, but as for swearing, if it's not really accepted in the street, it can't be accepted at the football.

JV: So there's not a lot of swearing in the barracking at the footy?

DAVID: No. There're things like 'bloody' and stuff like that, but there're no 'effs', no 'cees'. And I'm with the previous caller; you don't need to carry on like that to express yourself.

HELEN: I agree with the previous two callers: Simon's definitely out of line. My husband and I went to the A League and we had a spectator sitting next to us who was most foul-mouthed, and my husband asked him to stop and he was told that he had to expect this at the footy. But one day the young man brought his girlfriend along and there was not one bad word during the whole match!

JV: So we need to get Simon partnered up.

HELEN: I think so. He should behave himself as he would if his mother was sitting next to him.

JV Well, according to our callers, a football crowd watching the Sydney Swans in Sydney behaves as if they have their mothers, their precious daughters and several nuns sitting beside them. And even though this was the evidence of the callers, I still find it hard to believe. A sporting crowd? A few beers in them? An idiot of an umpire? Your team is losing? And in a world where fruity language is considered not so fruity any more, no one in the crowd tells the team to pull their F$%#@*ing finger out? Bad language is interesting. Older men believe it's deeply offensive to use it in front of women. Younger people understand that it's offensive to older people. On stage, screen and radio, language that would have had the program banned and the announcer fired is now commonplace. On my radio program broadcast I wouldn't use four-letter words, but if a caller does or if it pops up in a music track, we don't censor it. Complaints? At most one or two, compared to a dozen for a factual error and three dozen for grammatical slips. But according to regular match-goers, screaming obscenities from the grandstand is not on, and if Simon wishes to continue, he should think about getting a tent at the top of Mount Panorama for the Bathurst car races where strong language is not only tolerated, it's fully encouraged.

CHAPTER THREE

MODERN COMMUNICATIONS

A Brief History of Modern Communications

Communications used to mean letters. Letters were very important. People were in a constant state of writing letters. They wrote letters to everyone they knew; it was nothing to write a dozen a day. They wrote letters to their sister in Brisbane, a monthly chatty letter full of accounts of the interesting doings of the family. Letters began with, 'Hope this finds you well...' and finished with, '...Must go if this is to catch the post, TTFN', and then three Xs if you were an effusive kind of person. You could be funny on envelopes in times of war. SWALK was very popular, an acronym meaning Sealed With A Loving Kiss. This was considered very racy and a prelude to an offer of marriage. There were raunchier versions still involving Knees Up and Knickers, but these were only to be used between married couples if the husband had been posted to battle-grounds overseas.

Letters had to be set out properly. The address and date in the right order on the left-hand side, the person you were addressing and their address on the right-hand side, a proper margin, a 'Dear Sir or Madam' and then you had to begin, 'I refer to your letter of the 22 Inst.'. Handwritten letters were much more personal than typed ones, but occasionally unmarried young women living in the city and smoking cigarettes would own a portable Corona and type racy accounts of their doings for their younger sisters still back home on the station.

Most people spent most of their time writing thank you letters, or bread and butter notes as they were known. There was no more important form of communication. After any social event, it was imperative that you write and express your gratitude. The thank you note must arrive by the second post on the day after the event, but it should suggest that some time and thought had been spent on its composition. Dashing off, 'That was great, see you soon, love Elsie' on the back of an Eskimo Pie wrapper in a taxi cab on the way home could end the friendship. The thank you note should imply that Elsie has arrived home, removed her make-up, put on a Chinese wrap, sat at her night desk and, on a piece of creamy thick notepaper—perhaps embossed with her address—spent twenty minutes composing a sincere note of thanks. Some mention should be made of the menu or the decor to prove that you were paying attention: 'How do you get your trifles to stay moist?', 'Your lampshades are exquisite. One rarely sees such taste nowadays, does one?'.

The telephone arrived, but nothing much changed. The telephone was not a device for chatting on except by loose women who drank in the afternoon and would hang on the party line for hours sniffing for gossip. You answered the telephone by saying your number and then your name, '649, hello, Mrs Peter McCafferty speaking. Who's calling?'. Information would be relayed and the handpiece returned to its cradle. There was only one phone in the house. It never occurred to anyone that the children could use it. No one rang overseas or interstate unless someone had died. Only immediate family could call after sunset and only if a close relative had died. Some sophisticated—read lazy—women in the city phoned in their butcher's order.

There were telegrams as well. These cost around fifteen pounds a word and you had to put 'Stop' in them all the time: 'Dad dead STOP Stopped tractor with head STOP Order new tractor STOP' and so on. You could also send witty ones to weddings you weren't invited to. These were read out by the best man and a certain risqué tone was acceptable: 'Good Luck Joan STOP Lie back and think of England STOP Or at least of Leslie Howard STOP'.

Then: we treasured each letter, bound them in ribbon and placed them in a camphorwood chest. Now: we are bombarded with messages from people we barely know and we do little else but communicate.

FRIENDS, ROMANS, COUNTRYMEN, GIVE ME YOUR EMAIL

Patrick: I'm still unsure about how to address an email. 'Dear Sir' seems formal, 'Hi' too casual, and I have no idea what to do with a group one. Should that be 'Hey everybody', 'Dear all'? I just haven't got any of it figured out.

COLIN: I've been experimenting a lot lately with the email. I start generally with 'Hi', but my sign offs are getting elaborate. All that 'Regards' and 'Yours sincerely', seemed ridiculous. I've been trying 'Ciao Miao' and 'Party on' and 'You rock' with good results.

CLARE: You have to have a good understanding of the relationship you have with the person you're emailing. A formal business email should have the same formality as a business letter.

DAVID: I like the group email. It gives me a chance to start with things like 'My people, hearken unto me, o yea' and 'Now I will set forth for you all'. I don't think you need to be boring in an email and 'Dear all' just doesn't make any sense. How can you be 'Dear all'?

JV The email has been with us for a while now and I still find it hard to put tone into it. It's hard to indicate whether I'm being funny or formal. Some of the traditional letter forms work, but not always. And then addressing a group 'Dear all', has got to be wrong. I think it's very specific. To strangers in a business context, err on the side of old-fashioned letter formality. To groups, reflect on your relationship to the group and the content of the message. 'Hey fun lovers, drinks this

Friday?' is fine; 'Hey fun lovers, apply for redundancy now!' probably doesn't work.

IS THIS TOO LATE FOR YOU?

Sarah: I want to know what time you stop calling people at night? The other night I got a call at 9.30 from someone who wanted to know if I was going to follow up on an inquiry I'd made about a holiday three months before. She's ringing at 9.30! I've got little kids and to me 8 pm is the cut-off. Anything after that you're waking my kids up and I'm not wanting to talk to you.

ELIZABETH: The rule we have is nine and nine. Not before nine in the morning, and nothing after nine at night. The exception is really close friends who know what we're like. I'm often up till midnight, so I don't mind hearing from a girlfriend at eleven. But I'd be astonished if a business or someone I didn't know broke the nine and nine rule.

DIANA: I was brought up never to ring anybody after 9 pm and not before 9 am on a Sunday. Monday to Saturday you can ring at 7.30 am, but on Sunday never before 9 am, and at night never after 9 pm. And I brought up my children to be the same, and it's fair to everybody then.

BRIAN: Listen, mate, those people who don't want the phone calls during dinner—any time, eight o'clock—take your phone off the hook.

PETER: I run a home delivery service and we specialise in catching people when they're at home. We can't talk to them at work so we have to call them at home. And the latest you can call is definitely eight o'clock. You can call them between eight and nine in the morning. Pointless after that, they're not home; and the other stipulation is I don't call people between six and seven, or just after seven, because they're eating their dinner and if you interrupt their dinner they're very angry with you.

JV: When you're in that sort of work, Peter, as you say, you suddenly realise that everybody's got pretty much the same habits.

PETER: Oh yes, I think everyone watches the ABC seven o'clock news: if you ring anyone at that time, they don't want to talk to you. By twenty past seven, it's okay again.

The nine and nine rule is good, isn't it? I have kids at school and parents ring one another about things for school tomorrow at nine-thirty at night, or at seven-thirty in the morning. It's acceptable because it's got to be dealt with, but let's also notice here how this reflects old-style use of landline phones: a home phone. People who build their communication network around their mobile phone will have a completely different attitude. In that world, you can ring when you like. If they want to talk to you, it's on; if they don't, it's off and you leave a message, you text them and so on. Very different from how we used the phone when there was only one of them sitting in the front hallway. If you're still a landline person, get a voice message service and don't answer the phone after your own cut-off time.

CALL WAITING, OR 'I'M SORRY, SOMEONE MORE IMPORTANT THAN YOU IS ON THE LINE'

Jo: Is there any right way to use the call-waiting function on the phone or is it always just rude? I'm talking to someone and another call comes in, they put me on hold and then leave me there—or you can be the second caller and they do the same thing. I just don't think it works. Why not just have a busy signal or a message service and then there's no problem.

LINDEN: With call waiting, I just hang up. Someone puts me on hold like that, I find it very rude. This is at home, they're not a business, so I just hang up, then they get back to me. I just say we were cut off or something, but I'm not going to sit there on the phone waiting for them.

HELEN: I don't think I've ever called anyone who knows how to use call waiting. They don't know how to jump from call to call. And if you do, then why not just immediately tell the second caller you'll call them back. Unless you're a business, why in your personal life do you really need that function?

RICHARD: I hate call waiting. It implies that even though I'm speaking to you, I want to speak to someone else. And even if I don't take the call, there's this incessant beeping and it says you've got more friends than me, your life is busy and interesting and I'm a lonely loser you want to get off the line so you can talk to your more interesting friends.

MELISSA: I hate it, but I have teenage children who never get off the phone, and if there's another person trying to contact me or my husband, they can't get near us. So I tell the children if it beeps, to answer the other line and if it's for me, they have to give up their call and let me speak.

JV Again, we have to consider the difference between a one-phone family and a household where everyone is connected to mobiles. This problem and the one preceding it date from a year or two back and they're a good illustration of how rapidly things have changed. Take mobile phones, for example. When I first began doing 'The Form Guide' we got lots of calls about people talking loudly in restaurants on mobiles. People with mobiles were still regarded as wankers. Now people know how to go outside and talk on the phone, they know to redirect the call to a message bank rather than answer it. It's been possible to watch the etiquette develop in only five or six years as phones have gone from an affectation to an essential.

YOU TRYING TO KILL ME?

Mark: What do you do when you see someone driving their car and talking on their phone—not with a hands-free set but with the actual phone? I always feel like catching up to them and grabbing the phone and throwing it away. It's illegal, it's dangerous, I get quite incensed about it.

JV: Is there a gesture? We need a gesture.

TONY: You know when you park somewhere you're not meant to and they put a sticker across your windscreen? I want one of those that reads 'Idiot' to stick it across the front of anyone's car who's talking on the phone. The stupid thing is, the cost of a kit, fitted, which I have, is less than the fine, let alone three demerit points.

JOHN: I reckon the police should have clippers on their belt and whenever they catch anyone they clip a bit off their thumb. Each time, lose a bit more, and then move on to the fingers. There is nothing more annoying when you're driving down the highway and you've got someone next to you using the phone or texting and not concentrating on what they're doing.

JV: So you find it absolutely infuriating.

JOHN: It's very dangerous. There should be a sign that we can use or whatever where we can get the message through, because it's dangerous, and obviously people have been killed by this in the past.

JV: I've got the sign. You know when you do the phone with your thumb and your little finger, you put it up to your ear, and then you move it away from your face and you jerk it up. You are taking your hand off the steering wheel, but you're driving along, you do the phone sign, catch their eye, and then just jerk it up.

DOMINIC: You've got to embarrass them. I travel all week on the roads in the metropolitan area and whenever I see these people on their phones, I yell through their car window at them. I yell 'Get off the phone and come back to bed!'. They have no idea what's going on, and I love the thought of the person they're calling hearing that. It's fantastic.

JULIE: There was a woman in front of me driving up the Pacific Highway last week and she was all over the lanes. And I was getting so angry. I inadvertently ended up next to her, and she was still on the phone. I put my phone up to my ear and yelled 'Get off the phone!' at her. Then I took her registration number and when I got home I rang the police. They said they have to catch her in the act but they have her number and they're going to ring her up. I thought, 'Great, I can start a vigilante group'.

HELEN: I think the sign is the thumb across the throat. The one that they use to say to people, 'Wind up the conversation'. I think that's a very good sign.

JV: So it's frown, dark look and then run the finger across the throat.

HELEN: Otherwise, if you're near enough to the car, you bang loudly on the window and say, 'Get off the bloody phone!'.

There are two groups on the road: one who recognises that any distraction from driving is dangerous and the other who believes that their driving skills make them perfectly capable of this kind of multitasking. The second group are cretins. Ellen DeGeneres has a joke: 'Anything that requires both hands probably means that the brain should be involved as well'.

I MIGHT HAVE TO CALL YOU BACK

Prue: I have noticed recently that many people seem to think it's okay to be on the phone when they're on the toilet. Obviously, with mobile phones today it's possible, but is it really okay to call someone or keep talking while you're otherwise occupied?

KATE: Placing and receiving calls—no problem. Flushing or straining away, choose your audience. You don't know women. We talk about all sorts of stuff. Women are physically very graphic. Most of my women friends happily call me and one another. But it's a very special friendship that can accept the flush.

LISA: When I come through the door, the first thing I do is go to the loo because I can only comfortably go on my own in my own place. If my phone rings, I answer it. And sometimes I have my mail in my hand as well and I'm sorting it, I have a kind of mini office going.

JV: So what's the status here? Is it very special friends who get called from the toilet or does it indicate that you're so low down the list that it doesn't matter that someone's calling you from the toilet?

VANESSA: The real question is to wee or not to wee? If you're in the middle of a long chat, it's perfectly acceptable to pop off. We're girls, we have to, but you shouldn't make it too loud or splashy and you certainly shouldn't flush. I think this happens only with very dear friends. You should say where you're going because there can be a bit of a toilet echo which might sound strange. It's a badge of honour with closest girlfriends. If you can say to someone 'I'll put you down for a minute, I just have to unzip my jeans', I think that's lovely.

JV Life has really sped up, hasn't it? If we have to multitask to the extent of communicating while evacuating or micturating, then I think we all have to stop for a moment to consider what happened to stopping for a moment. I think of this moment (and I don't share this kind of information lightly) as the one true break in the day. I plan for it. I schedule it. I take uplifting reading material. I don't want to talk to anyone—but I'm out of step. It seems women, in particular, are perfectly comfortable with this.

HAPPY BIRTHDAY LOL :-)

Elizabeth: I think it's rude to text message birthday greetings. I put it in the same basket as ringing someone hoping you'll get the voice mail so you don't have to actually speak to them. A close friend of mine texted birthday greetings and I thought as a friend she should have done something a lot more personal.

LISA: I think it's a bit cheap. Text messages don't cost much and it's like she's sent a cheap little message and she hopes that the birthday girl will be all excited and ring her back. It's like you get to say Happy Birthday and have a chat for no real cost.

MARIE: Oh, look, just be glad you got a Happy Birthday. Maybe the friend was trying to be a little hip and she thinks it was a fun thing to do. Better than getting some rotten card you just throw out. I mean what's that? Two seconds in the supermarket, buy something with a stupid poem on it, stick it in an envelope. Does that really mean anything more than the text?

JULIA: I love the text. It's such a quick way of keeping in touch. My son is travelling and I can contact him every day. You could never do that before. People were off the radar for weeks.

SUE: I've got teenage boys and it's much easier for them to text me and it means they stay in contact. It was my sister's birthday yesterday and I texted her and she rang to say she was really happy I'd thought of her.

JANE: It depends on who it is. I got a text from my cousin on my birthday and I thought, how lovely. But then I got one from my brother and I thought, hang on where's my phone call?

JV: There's an emotional radius. Draw a set of circles out from yourself and those closest to you, family and the like. It's landline, then mobile, then maybe email, then text—or is it the other way round?

JANE: Text and email equal. I texted my brother back and said, 'Thanks, but where's my phone call?'. He rang.

JV As well as the emotional radius, there's a kind of timeline: the newer the technology, the more people think it's impersonal; as it becomes more common, the more people accept it. Back when mobile phones were new—for younger readers: this was around the end of the last century—people felt it was a business tool, it wasn't personal, and there were lots of issues about how rude it was to call someone on their mobile. It was the same with email when it was fresh and new. But it changes and it changes rapidly. I doubt there's a fourteen-year-old anywhere who thinks any kind of text is ever offensive.

I'LL JUST PUT YOU ON SPEAKER

Jan: Whenever I ring my brother he always puts me on speakerphone. I find it really off-putting and it seems kind of harder to talk in a real way. Maybe I'm too sensitive about it but I always have an image of him staring out the window and not really listening to me—and there could be someone else in the room. I feel really awkward about saying something about it, but I really don't like it. It's less intimate.

NATALIE: I'd put him on speakerphone too so he can hear how rude it sounds.

SHEILA: First of all he's being a jerk, so she has to address that. She could call him on his mobile only, and tell him she'll only call him on his mobile till he stops using the speakerphone.

SUSIE: I think what she should do with her brother is tell him that the echoing annoys her, because I know I have friends with a speakerphone and I can't hear them very well. So she should just say that she can't hear him, so could he pick up the phone?

LEO: It's interesting. I have a colleague in Melbourne and every time I ring up he asks me if I'm on speakerphone. If I say 'Yes', he lets out a very loud four-letter word, and I quickly take him off speakerphone. He does it every time, and it works every time.

JV: And it traps you every time.

LEO: Every time.

JV: Have you ever had anyone else in the office?

Leo: Oh yes, both in the car and the office.

JV: You'd think you might have learned by now.

LEO: Nope, gets me every time.

 I'm not sure why Jan can't just say to her brother, 'Don't put me on speakerphone'. It's fascinating how little changes in technology change the style of communication. Speakerphone is less intimate and you always have an image that the person is doing something else and not really concentrating on you. Only for use in conference situations!

HEY! BRING IT DOWN WILL YOU, PEOPLE ARE TRYING TO WORK

Louise: I've got a colleague at work who constantly emails me in a very large font and it sort of comes across like he's shouting at me. And when he wants to emphasise something he puts it in red. I've actually emailed back and said stop font-shouting and could you use a smaller case.

JV: Font-shouting—that's a new expression on me...

LOUISE: Well I've created it because it's the only way I can describe it. But you see the name come up on the screen and you go to open it and you almost have to push your chair back a bit, like it's just CAN YOU PLEASE DO THIS FOR ME. So I don't know what to do about that.

JV: So it always seems a little bit hysterical, it has the air of being imperative, it must be done now.

LOUISE: It's sort of angry and 'I'm the boss, you have to listen to me' — which, I mean, it works.

JV: Does he do it to everyone?

LOUISE: Yes.

JV: Do others have a problem?

LOUISE: Yes. We have had roundtable discussions about it. That's where the word 'font-shouting' came from.

JV: Is he in about twenty-four point?

LOUISE: More than that. Sometimes it could be a couple of screens' worth. I'd like him to go back to a ten or a twelve.

JV: How to get someone to speak in a normal tone of voice at about twelve point.

LOUISE: And just a nice calm blue.

BILL: I received some advice recently by email, and this **works**: if you hold the Control key down and you twiddle the little wheel in the middle of your mouse, it reduces and enlarges the size of the font. So if you know that this person always sends you a loud one, you could twiddle it as you were opening it to reduce the size, so it would come out in a much smaller font.

JV: Okay, so it's kind of the equivalent of being around a loud talker and covering your own ears.

BILL: Yeah, it's a bit like a muffler.

JV: He seems to be doing it to everyone. I'm not quite sure why the entire office can't go round and say, 'Hey, buddy, it's kind of annoying'.

BILL: He might be the boss.

DAVID: I think this solution addresses a technical point more than the psychological point that this guy's obviously got a problem. But what you can do is disable HTML in your email client and just change it to 'plain text only'. That way it's gonna not be red, as well. It'll just be pure plain text.

JV: And does it bring it down to twelve point or something?

DAVID: Yes, and you can even make it smaller if you want to.

JOE: I had a colleague who was a font-shouter.

JV: How did you deal with the font-shouter?

JOE: Well, this particular fellow not only was a font-shouter, but he also used catch-phrases. And the 'in' phrase that drove us all mad was 'project'. So we all ganged together and sent him a message in five point, headed 'Project compromise'.

JV: And five point would be very small...

JOE: It was so small you had to enlarge it to be able to read it.

JV: Project compromise—and that was?

JOE: The message was, 'You probably can't read this, because it's too small. Your fonts are too big. How about we compromise and all send each other messages in eleven point?' And it worked.

JV: Isn't that good? How large was he sending things?

JOE: Oh probably eighteen to twenty point, but it was a very heavy font as well, so, as Louise was saying, you had to really roll your chair back to be able to get it into focus. But our message was done in a light-hearted manner and it worked one hundred per cent.

JV: I think one of the interesting things about email is that it's actually very hard to get tone into it, do you know what I mean? It can be a bit toneless. It's hard to indicate that you're being funny or sarcastic or...

JOE: I agree with what you're saying, but that comes back to compromise, doesn't it?

JV: Yes, but what we're dealing with here is a very definite tone. If you use a large font, it has this kind of shouting sense. It's kind of a bit annoying.

JOE: Absolutely, and there's no need for that.

JV I find tone in email and text very interesting. Emails often seem flat to me and nuances of humour and irony absent. It may be as a creaking old 45-year-old I'm simply unable to detect it. Little symbols and acronyms tacked on the end don't do it for me, but is that just lack of familiarity with the form? Is tone something that you can get happening when you're in regular communication with someone? But I still make a joking reply and get a puzzled response back from people I know well. I thought one of the best things about this response was the fact that this group of people was able to get together and deal with the FONT-SHOUTER. It was a clever idea and even if he was THE BOSS there was nothing they did that could cause any grief for any of them. Hard to do in the workplace where you can live with the consequences of a mistimed comment or complaint for years.

WHAT DO YOU MEAN CTRL ALT DEL???

Lyn: This is to do with computers and having computer-literate people in the house and computer semi-literate people in the house. I'm the latter, and often I just need a bit of help. What does this error sign mean, or which button is it again to find that file? I always ask my son, but I notice a little bit more tetchiness in his voice as he's had to explain these things to me twenty times or more.

JV: How old's your son?

LYN: He's twenty-six.

JV: And does he live in the house?

LYN: We've got the sort of revolving-door house, so, yes, they come and go, they study, they travel, they work and then—he's actually a freelancer, so he's very busy.

JV: Do you ring him up and say, 'Look, I've just got the program open here, what do I click on'?

LYN: Something like that. 'And I know you can do it and I know you can do it fast.' 'Well, look, I'm really busy at the moment'—that's the sort of response.

JV: I'm assuming that you gave him a fine education which allowed him to get to the point where he's adept with the computer. So why can't he repay that without begrudging it?

LYN: Well, I guess that's my point.

JV: So I suppose you want to know, is it time for you to stop asking him, or is there a way of saying...

LYN: He would sort of think, yes, there's plenty of courses and people out there to help, and now it's time, Mum.

JV: Or is there a way of saying to him, 'Look, darling, I'm going to continue asking you to do this, and I'd like you to get over your attitude'.

LYN: Oh, look, he's very sweet most of the time.

JV: I'm sure, but that's the dilemma, isn't it? You'd like to say something to him so that he continues to help you, but doesn't continue to get increasingly tetchy.

LYN: Maybe it *is* time for me to go and actually become more independent.

JV: Oh, I don't know. What's the point? If he was a motor mechanic, what, you're not allowed to ring him up and say there's something wrong with the car? What does he ring you up to ask for advice on?

LYN: Oh, he's pretty self-sufficient. We mostly get along really, really well, and we have lots of really wonderful times together. He cooks, he does all sorts of wonderful things. I just think it's the ineptitude of the older generation with computers while the younger ones have just lived with them and really know them inside out.

DON: I think she could convey the same point in a couple of different ways. One would be to take the son into the laundry and to point to the washing machine and say 'Just imagine that's a computer; I'd be glad to give you advice on how it works at any time you'd like to seek it'. Or you could say to him that you're thinking of using the time that you'd normally spend in that laundry, or on any other domestic chore associated with his needs, and going and doing a course instead of doing those things. I think there's a lot of ground to be made up when you're still twenty-six.

JV: That's right. The balance is still with the parents.

ADAM: I think it goes back further than that. I think any person that's twenty-six years old has got a question debt that goes back a long way, and for every time he asked 'Why, Mum?' there's a corresponding question that she's allowed to ask.

JV: I've looked under Edit and I can't see what I should do.

ADAM: That's it. And so from that period of five years old to fifteen years old where he said 'why' or 'where'—I think there are questions that can come back the other way.

JV: Could you also then calculate from age fifteen to twenty every night she was up until four in the morning waiting for him to come home?

ADAM: How would you ration those—one hour, one question, or one hour, five questions?

JV: Oh, I think one hour, five questions there, easily. What about for every thousand dollars lent?

ADAM: And every driving lesson—there's a whole bunch of them.

JV: Every car borrowed. And I think as Don was pointing out, if he's twenty-six, every load of washing equals a question.

ADAM: I think she should use her new-found skills on the computer to write an Excel spreadsheet and do a whole list for him and she can present it to him and not only get corrections to the mistakes in it but also he can see the value of what he's already racked up.

JV I think there's a new frontier opening up here: parenting your adult children. I get this call all the time, 'My twenty-plus is still at home. Do I pay his medical bills/parking fines/buy his bed linen/accept board from him/wipe his bottom?' Well, not the last one, but it's kind of the same. Twenty, twenty-three, twenty-six years of age, working and earning a wage and living with the parents like the flatmate from hell. Does a bit of cooking and takes own washing to laundry. Wow, isn't he a clever little man? What's happened is that it's just evolved. The parents often didn't expect it and weren't really prepared. Nothing was laid down and it all remains a little indefinite. Is the kid moving out at the end of the year? When he comes back from overseas? When he breaks up with this girlfriend is he coming back again? And so someone you have raised for twenty-six years who is still draining your mortgage has the gall to be a little petulant when you ask for help with the computer? I'd change the locks.

CHAPTER FOUR

TRAVEL

A Brief History of Travel

Despite the reality of planes crammed with Krispy Kreme-toting fellow passengers and seats only wide enough for the anorexic, trains that lurch from one crisis point to another and buses that reek of a toxic combination of LPG and BO, we seem to retain a strong memory of travel experiences from other days.

The word Travel seems to contain in it a hint of a large wardrobe trunk opened in a first-class cabin to reveal a range of outfits to be worn at the Captain's table over the next few weeks. It suggests deck quoits, reading Somerset Maugham in a deck chair, and perhaps enjoying a gin sling with Somerset Maugham as the sun sets over the first-class deck as you steam out of Colombo en route to Singapore.

Travel implies a hop over the Atlantic in BOAC, seated in a stuffed lounge chair, smoking and playing cribbage while dressed in a suit and tie. It suggests coming down a flight of stairs onto the tarmac and waving to the paparazzi. It's a dining car on a train with Cary Grant and Grace Kelly and a kindly conductor who brings hot milk to your sleeping compartment.

Unfortunately travel was only ever like this for about two decades during the middle part of the twentieth century and only while war or Depression wasn't happening.

Before that, if the potatoes failed or the satanic mill became too satanic, a member of the family would be nominated to travel in steerage to the New World. Steerage offered a coffin space in which to lie down in an area under decks shared by about three or four hundred others. The journey would take weeks to the Americas, months to Australia, and travellers would occupy their time by dying in painful ways. Those who survived would do so by eating rats and some of the few potatoes spared the blight and presented to them by the village priest on the eve of their departure. Childbirth and the subsequent death of the mother was also a common on-board recreation.

Upon arrival in the colony, after a night drinking fermented pig scraps with a local employment agent, new chums would find themselves strapped onto a stage coach with the luggage and embark on a six-day journey to the goldfields. Passengers would alight to push the carriage uphill and rests were taken to water the horses. Bushrangers (Australia) or Varmints (America) would stop the coach twice daily to rob the passengers of their grandfather's watches.

When the train came through a new era of travel arrived. Now travellers could reach the goldfields in only two days, arriving covered in soot and ash to have grandfather's watch stolen by pickpockets. Trains were strictly divided into classes: First Class—a seat to yourself and the company of the Archbishop and a Titled Widow; Second Class—a compartment shared with twelve others, some of whom might well be grocers; Third Class—a carriage shared with goats and lambing ewes.

So, today, although travel is swift, each journey is a slice of eternal torment. Being on a plane is like being packed in a vegetable crisper; a long train or bus journey is like being packed as a vegetable in a box, and all forms of public transport require the individual to maintain a Zen-like calm in the face of daily indignities. Then: we could love travel as every journey was an adventure. Now: if we could say we love travelling, we really mean we love arriving.

I GET ENOUGH OF THIS AT HOME

Vicki: I get an early train and there's a snorer in the carriage— always there, always snoring away. He hasn't actually sat next to me, but he ruins the dynamic of the carriage. Early morning trains are often quite peaceful and calming but here's this one snorting away. If he was next to me, I'd give him a little nudge, but is there anything I can do if he's not?

LYNNE: One of the kids will get one of those little water pistols on Christmas Day. Swipe it, and in the train just give him a little squirt. It'll only be a drop but just enough to wake him up.

BEN: Lean over and grab him on the nose. It's very offensive and he should be told.

JV: I have a certain sympathy—he is getting some sleep.

BEN: Oh well, buy him one of those nose things or something, but he needs to be told. It's like sitting next to someone burping or who has flatulence on the train. It's horrible.

The early-morning commute is a bad confluence of personal ritual and public demands. Coffee must be sourced, the paper, book and MP3 player all working and ready. If you like to sit facing forward in the upper deck in a window seat on the eastern side, then you'll need to make that happen. Once there, hopefully you can rock your way happily into work, but it doesn't take much to upset that. A snorer, a too-loud set of headphones, a mobile phone going off and, worse, answered, and the sense of calm Vicki describes is ruptured. If you told the snorer he was snoring, I doubt he would ever sleep on the train again. But, of course, early morning commutes also involve running into the same people every day, so do you want to have a long-running feud with this person? Get yourself some of those noise-blocking headphones, or in these days of the iPod and MP3 player, grab one of those and load it up with your favourite radio podcast or music from around the world and you'll never hear the snorer again.

I WANT TO BE ALONE

Sylvia: I travel a lot and often, when I've been working, I'm exhausted, so on the plane I just want to kick back, watch a movie, eat and go to sleep—but the person next to me wants to chat. And when I tell them I work in film, it's even worse. They want to know about famous people and talk about movies, but I'm exhausted, I don't want to have that conversation.

JV: Headphones and a book won't do it?

SYLVIA: I had a guy once who talked for fourteen hours and in the middle of the movie he nudged me and wanted to know what I thought of it. I told someone once I worked for the CSIRO and we were trying to develop odourless pigs. He turned out to be a venture capitalist and became very interested in the project. When I finally had to admit I was lying he got very surly.

PAUL: Oh, this is easy. I tell people I work for the Tax Department and I've just been promoted to Random Audits. It shuts them up real fast.

Psychiatrist often works as well. They feel like you're analysing them.

JOHN: I munch a clove of garlic in the queue as we're boarding. Anyone wants to chat I give them the full blast. They don't want to engage after that.

JV I was thinking, when Sylvia called, I haven't encountered a chatterer on a plane for years. I'm not flying around the country every week, but maybe once a month, and it seems to me as though people are very reserved and keep themselves to themselves. They burrow into the in-flight entertainment, they pull out devices as soon as possible, they have thick books and on international flights the masks and the blankets are out as soon as possible and people make camp. What do you do, though, when it happens? Be brief but courteous and hope the sleeping pills start to work.

MARKING OUT TERRITORY

Brian: On planes and in the cinema, what do you do with armrest thieves?

JIM: In a row of fifteen cinema seats, there're sixteen arms. That's one for everyone. Everyone should have one arm on one armrest.

JV: But what if someone's hogging two? And what if you've got an armchair hog on both sides?

JIM: That's tough. Maybe suggest a time-sharing arrangement.

JILLIAN: Mainly planes men take over the armrest. I put my elbow behind where their arm is and just gradually push it forward. I read my book, I don't look to the right or left, I just gradually move it forward and they eventually move. Stuck in the middle of economy you can lose both and you have to do something.

PETER: Start coughing uncontrollably. 'So sorry, it's that damn tuberculosis.' They pull right back and you might get them to move and get a whole extra seat.

GERALDINE: On a trip from Sydney to Los Angeles, my eldest son sold his armrest to his little brother. He had to pay ten bucks to use it.

JV: Could you do that with adults? With strangers on a plane?

GERALDINE: I don't see why not. Two vodka tonics, some duty free Chanel No 5—it would depend on how badly they want it.

JV It's a land grab. I think in former colonies like Australia or the US, we're used to this. Possibly in Europe and the UK, they ask permission, they book the armrest ahead of time, but here we take. Having taken we must retain. At the slightest opportunity, the armrest can be seized by another. You must remain alert to the possibilities or subtly move them on as Jillian has so effectively described.

NEVER MIND THE GAP,
LOOK OUT FOR THE PASSENGERS

Richard: In trying to get off a train, it's very difficult when people push their way on before you can actually step off. I had a lady with a pram who actually jumped the queue, came belting up and hit me in the ankle with her pram as she was getting on. I just wondered if you should call the guard. Twice I've had a very bad experience, and ended up bruised.

MALCOLM: I've just managed to get back from England safely using the underground. They make announcements all the time about waiting for people to get off the train before you get on.

JV: It's like lifts, isn't it? Isn't it obvious you have to let people off before you get on?

KEVIN: People are incredibly rude trying to get on trains. You've just got to fight fire with fire, I think, and be equally rude back. I used to have a briefcase with reasonably square corners; I'd leave half a pace between me and the person in front who was getting off, then I'd make sure I was on the upswing as I was stepping off. If people trying to get on are crowding in front of you, it just catches them under the knees. They learn fast.

ADAM: You're going back to the deadly art of every person for themselves. State Rail does actually have a voice saying, 'Please stand back and wait for all passengers to get off the train'. But with the standard of State Rail and the way that they run to such a fantastic timetable, you've just got tempers flaring. You want to literally rip the person out who's getting off and you want to get in.

ANDREW: I've had a broken arm and people have shoved me out of the way to get on. It doesn't matter who you are, if you've got a baby, you're pregnant or you're an invalid—people are vicious.

JV And we wonder why public transport isn't more popular? It's worth remembering that these calls emanate from Sydney. Sydney's rail system has been in slow decline since the war. What was once a swift and pleasant trip in from an outer suburb or across the harbour has now become a crap shoot: the train may or may not arrive; it may reach your destination or it may continue on without stopping. Adam is right, Sydneysiders arrive at the station already defensive and prepared to do battle with a system that lets them down day after day. If a train is there in front of them, they're getting on it, as there is no guarantee there'll be another one along any time soon. In other more civilised parts of Australia and the world, of course, we let people off before we get on. Although I'm astonished how often I get out of a lift and am confronted by people standing right in the way who look put out that I'm trying to exit. I can only assume they're down from the country and it's the first time they've seen such a contraption.

I BAGSED IT

Malcolm: I was getting on a bus last night to go home. A guy sat there and saved a seat—through several stops. The bus was full, people kept trying to sit in this seat or ask him to move and he kept saying, 'No, I'm saving this seat'. Can you reserve a seat on a public bus?

LUKE: The bus etiquette, as far as I understand, is that you can only save seats on school specials. So, on a school special bus when you're going to the zoo, you can say, 'No, this one's for my best friend. You can't sit here'. It has a lot to do with superiority. The older you get at school, the more power you have to reserve seating on the school bus.

BRAD: I think the school special cuts out at about Year 6. By Year 7, you're going to have to fight for your own seat, let alone anyone else's. On public transport, it's not yours. And if someone else has paid their fare, then they should be able to use the seats.

JV Here's the dilemma that faced our seat saver: I must stare down strangers who want my seat or face the wrath of my beloved who has demanded I save a seat for her. Of such dilemmas is great drama made. The inner turmoil he would have faced; the choices he would have to make and, if life had a great director, it would have sent to seek the seat, in poignant succession, a hugely pregnant woman, an ancient limping crone and a badly twisted cripple. However, life lacks a director—and usually even a half-decent scriptwriter—so, unfortunately, public transport remains just that: public; available to anyone who has a ticket. You want to save seats for someone? Get a car!

THE REAL PETROL CRISIS

Jennifer: Petrol-bowser etiquette! My problem is that people fill up, and then they lock their car at the bowser, they don't move it over to a parking area so you can move in and fill up your car.

JV: I moved the car once and got told off by the attendant.

JENNIFER: Well I don't think that's right. I think you're allowed to move the car.

RITA: Oh, please, move your car! There's a particular petrol station I go to and there's at least five people deep across seven pumps. And people to in to pay and they buy candy and they buy Coke and then they come back out. Drives me nuts! I move my car every single time and there's never been a problem.

MARY: No, James, don't move the car. I did that out of consideration, I used to do the same thing, until one day I got caught out and I paid somebody else's bill. I don't know how the confusion happened. I moved the car, went in, and I said, 'No, that's not mine,' and they said, 'Well, that's been paid.' It was about thirty dollars difference and the attendant said to me 'In the future don't move the car'. It often makes things confusing.

STEVE: Mate, you should definitely move your car. It's the height of rudeness to sit there. Servos these days are mostly supermarkets as well, so you've got to wait for someone to find what chips they want and biscuits and whatever else they've forgotten—maybe a pie as well...

JV: Leaf through a few magazines...

STEVE: And it's not bad manners to get stuck into anyone who doesn't move their car.

JV: Oh, you think it's okay to say, 'Hey, mate! Move it!'.

STEVE: Definitely.

JV The official view of the Service Station Association of NSW is that it is up to the owners of the individual stations to determine the rules. So you'll never really know what to do any time at any service station. Sorry.

HANG ON, I'LL JUST GET ON MY MASK AND CAPE

John: I'm wondering what the correct behaviour is when you're confronted with road rage, but you're a disinterested bystander? I was at an intersection and a man got out of a car with a baseball bat and threatened to bash another car. I wanted to intervene, but he could have attacked me with the bat. Not intervening is the safest thing to do but it doesn't leave you with any great feeling of civic responsibility.

MICHAEL: A friend of mine was involved in something like that. A guy was coming at him with a crowbar and he got out his phone, which had a camera on it, and yelled, 'I'm taking your photo, I've got your picture!'. The guy got back into his car and drove off.

ROB: I'm a policeman and I have intervened when off duty. I basically stood back and described what I saw of the incident and it calmed them down and on they went. But if someone's armed, you shouldn't get involved. The risk to yourself isn't worth it. But you should make some show that you are witnessing it and that you're contacting the police and passing the details on.

JV: Will the police do anything?

ROB: Absolutely. If you can pass on the car registration, they'll notify police and they can be picked up. I'd be quite demonstrative with the camera phone, which is great in this kind of thing, and it might well circumvent the assault or whatever.

ROD: A person parked across our driveway and I had a go at him. He came at me with a baseball bat. I cooled things down, got his number plate and it turned out he was wanted for armed robbery and rape. He's in Long Bay, cooling his heels.

Being of the stature of a slim girl, and an ageing one at that, it never occurs to me to interfere in moments of public violence. With the preponderance of phones with cameras attached, though, it's remarkable what a concerned citizen can achieve from a safe distance.

I SAY, YOU FELLOWS, TONE IT DOWN!

Bill: I travel on public buses a lot, and I'm often overhearing children in school uniform swearing amongst themselves, whilst in the company of adults. Do I invade their privacy by admonishing their behaviour or do I just ignore it?

JV: Yes, this is an interesting one, isn't it, because the kind of behaviour has changed so markedly from one generation to the next. I'm sure when you were a boy swearing was an extreme behaviour.

BILL: Well, it's commonplace now because our standards have dropped. The morals of society have dropped to the stage where we just ignore it, but we need to kind of, you know, get back to some sort of standard of decency.

JV: What stops you saying to a group of kids on a bus, 'Excuse me, that language is unacceptable'?

BILL: I'm afraid that they may gang up. I don't want any sort of confrontation. Sometimes it's a big group and they can be big young men, really.

MICHAEL: I went through that situation when there were quite a few elderly people on the bus with kids, girls actually, swearing their heads off. I just worked out which school they were from, phoned the principal up and told him, and apparently at assembly everyone got a warning.

JV Bad language again but, unlike our football fan (see page 57), here one could still say it's uncalled for. The difficulty is that most adults don't want to confront a group of young people about anything at all. Young people can seem threatening. Getting a third party to intervene is a good move, but at another time we had a similar call about bad behaviour in family restaurants and the caller said he approached the kids, told them to calm down and they did. The young people are often not as threatening as they appear and they are, underneath, young. They're used to being told what to do. It may be that you have to recognise that you're the grown-up and it's time for you to stand up for the way you want your community to be.

LEFT-HAND DOWN, DARLS

Gwen: Why is it that whenever I reverse park, men appear out of nowhere and insist on directing me? Women know what I mean. They would never do it to another man, but they do it to women and then they want you to be very grateful and gracious. I find it totally patronising and in today's cars with power steering and so on, I'm just fine.

MALCOLM: If she parked the car right the first time, she wouldn't have this problem. I do this, I'm a good Samaritan in the car park. If they're having trouble I try to help out. No one's abused me or seemed annoyed, they're always grateful. I do it in a way that doesn't annoy.

ALAN: She's not quite as good a driver as she thinks she is. You see these people everywhere and you wonder how they ever got a licence.

JOHN: Wind down the window and say, 'Out of the way, dopey, I'm trying to park the car!'.

JUDY: She's right. Men don't do it to men but it happens all the time to women. Listen to those first two blokes, they've got no idea that they're being insulting. They're patting themselves on the back for what good fellows they are. I have been known to stop in the middle of reverse parking and say, 'Goodness, I don't know how I've managed to do this for the last forty years without you'. It's so common, my mum and I observe it all the time. We say, 'Oh, here we go, there's another one of them'. Just because you don't slide in first time, doesn't mean you don't know how to park a car.

JV I like the confirmation from both sides that this does happen. I like the irreconcilable divide here. Helpful bloke will never notice that the woman wants to run him over. Tell him to stop if it annoys you that much, but don't actually run him over.

CHAPTER FIVE

ACQUAINTANCES

A Brief History of Acquaintances

All was once clear in all relationships at every stage of life and between every person. Father was Father until the day he was laid out in the front parlour with coins in his eyes. Two men would stand at their clerk's desk in the shipping office for thirty-seven years and address one another as 'Mr Fogdyke' and 'Mr Thinwhipple' (it was common in such times for a person's surname to be quite Dickensian). Anyone in service or in shops was addressed by their trade: 'I say, Blacksmith, my horse is lame in the right hindquarter'; 'Shipwright, where's my frigate?'. Occasionally a man might learn the name of his tailor if his father and grandfather had been going to the same firm before him, or a woman might learn to know the name of her butcher if she'd been buying suet from him for several decades. Otherwise it was Mr and Mrs, ma'am and sir all round.

There were very strict rules for getting to know one another. Two men could meet at a formal dinner but choose to ignore one another if crossing a bridle path with a person of a lower rank. A woman should never greet a man unless introduced to him by her father or a member of Parliament. Women would call on one another and leave a calling card. This card would indicate when they were going to call again. They would call and pick up a card left by the mistress of the house. That card would indicate a time at which they might call in order to pay their respects. If intimate, they might be offered tea. A gentleman arriving at an 'At home' should bow first to his hostess and then to each lady in turn in descending rank. After fifteen minutes conversing about the weather, he should leave, bowing in ascending rank before exiting without turning his back on his hostess.

These were the rules of good society—and many of these manners are still observed in European courts and in three houses in Toorak and Vaucluse. Of course, most quaint was the way the lower classes aped their betters. This began once Queen Victoria ascended the throne in England. She settled in for most of the nineteenth century and during this time the middle class of England found a rule for every behaviour. Tea was to be drunk with the little finger poked out, the further out the finger poked the more genteel the drinker. Some ladies had their little fingers broken and re-set at the right angle. The correct reply to 'How d'y'do' was 'How d'y'do', to which the correct reply was, 'I do believe it looks like rain' to which the correct reply was, 'How dare you sir? My second will call on you'.

The word 'leg' was never to be mentioned. Legs were banned and the most refined ladies had theirs removed. The peak of society was to be a gentleman. No one could define what a gentleman was but they all knew one another so it didn't matter. A gentleman's manners were always impeccable, especially when getting the second chambermaid pregnant, thrashing his valet and refusing to pay his tailor.

The working classes barely had time between being born and dying of consumption, industrial accidents and overdoses of gin to develop any social customs of any interest apart from bawdy humour and rhyming slang.

The manners of the Victorian era and the rules of Acquaintanceship stayed firmly in place until Elvis Presley and The Beatles showed a new generation, the Baby Boomers—or, as we now know them, self-funded retirees—that it was cool to be rude. Rock music, the Pill, Germaine Greer, marijuana, getting rid of the strap from schools, the end of National Service, television (replacing comic books and radio as the great scourges of youth), all played their part in erasing manners as we knew them and left us where we are now; making it up as we go along and hoping no one gets hurt.

LOST FOR WORDS

Bill: How are you—what's the response?

AMELIA: I work in sales and I say 'How are you?' a hundred times a day and I love it when people say, 'I'm having a crap time' or 'the kid just vomited in the car' or something. When I say 'How are you?' I'm inviting conversation.

PHILIPPA: The response varies. With a close friend, I respond personally—it's a genuine inquiry. If it's an acquaintance on the street and I get a list of problems back, well, I don't think that's what I was looking for. I agree sometimes it is hard to know quite what is intended when someone asks 'How are you?'.

CHARLOTTE: I work on the supermarket checkout and I say 'How are you?' and I expect you to answer based on how many groceries you have. The amount of swiping I've got to do will determine how much detail you go into. And you've got to make it entertaining. If you had your back molars taken out, well, then I want the full gory details. If it's just a bit of a sore knee, don't bore me with it. The important thing is when someone asks you 'How are you?', don't be boring. Use it as a chance to open up some conversation.

Is there anything simpler? 'How are you?' is the starter for all interaction whether with stranger or spouse. How I felt for Bill, a middle-aged man who'd spent a lifetime unsure of what to say at the very beginning off all conversations. Charlotte's right: use it as a chance to open up some conversation. That means when asked, you have to be prepared to give a little. In the supermarket queue that might mean, 'I'm well, which must mean the flu shots are working!' (offered in a sympathetic manner of, course). With an intimate, you should be able to judge if it's a casual inquiry or if they're keen to know what's really going on.

CAN A SKIP SAY WOG?

Kerry: We've recently had the driveway stencil-creted—you concrete it and then use stencils to create an effect over the top—and everyone says it looks woggy. I've been very unsure about this; is woggy an acceptable term these days?

KATE: Wog *is* an acceptable term these days and by the way what she did to her concrete driveway is in no way woggy. No self-respecting wog would cover good concrete with stencils. I got into a lot of trouble with my in-laws for jacking up good concrete.

BRIAN: I think it's still a very offensive word. It's not that long ago when wog and dago were very insulting words...I don't like Irish jokes for the same kind of reason. If you are a wog, you can use it, but otherwise I don't think so.

JOHNNY: The correct term for the architecture she's describing is the Art Dago school. I would hope that we would soon see a heritage order on a fine example of an Art Dago house.

JV: Or entire suburbs?

JOHNNY: Punchbowl, Luddenham, around Liverpool—whole streets of Art Dago—some magnificent Art Dago mansions.

JV: How about Italianate? Could we use that?

JOHNNY: Well, Italianate describes a tribute architecture of the nineteenth century. It's a particular style and there's plenty of that still around. Art Dago is far more proletarian than Italianate.

DAVE: I'm a real wog and it's all in the tone. She's using woggy in a good way. It's like bastard or mate, you can say these things so that they're really cutting or really friendly. And that other woman's right. Stencil-creting is hardly woggy. Woggification means columns, lions, the works. Stencil-crete is like decaf wog.

ANNA: Italianate is a completely different style. I wouldn't find wog offensive, but my father's generation still does.

If, instead of woggy, you said something like 'I've seen this effect practised on some of the homes owned by our more recent arrivals', is that any less offensive? Although wog and woggy have been dewogged to a certain extent by comedians and by general overuse, it can still be an insult if used insultingly. Many derogatory terms get adopted by the groups at which they're aimed and are recycled as terms of pride. However, the terms can usually only be used by the group itself. Skips need to be careful if using wog and woggy and realise that people who don't know you well or are of an older generation mightn't appreciate it. Art Dago is brilliant.

MY NAME TOO HARD FOR YOU?

Susan: *I like to be called Susan. Eighty-five per cent of people call me Sue. If I say to them, 'Please, my name is Susan', they get annoyed and defensive. I have a neighbour who's been calling me Sue for fifteen years, and I hate it. I don't mind Suzy or Susanna, I just hate Sue.*

LAURENCE: This really gets up my nostrils, this shortening of my name. I was Laurie during my school years, but after that I always said 'I'm Laurence' and people do get stroppy when you correct them. They think I'm putting it on. What's wrong with Laurence?

JV: I'm a James. I'm never a Jim and was Jamie only when I was five. People try it, but with me the Jims don't stick.

DAVID: I've been David for sixty-four years. My boyfriend and I have been together for twenty-two years and about six months ago he suddenly started calling me Dave. What was I to do, call it quits? I know some people think I'm a bit on the formal side, but I don't worry too much about the Daves, and the occasional Davo. What am I going to do, dump everyone who doesn't call me David?

SUSAN: I get the same thing, obviously. I don't worry about it, unless it seems as though there's a friendship there, an ongoing relationship, and then I might say, 'Really, I prefer Susan'.

JV: People shorten your name as a gesture of friendship. When you correct it it's like you're rejecting their gesture. Perhaps you're right, you have to choose your time to do it.

EDWARD: It gets up my jersey, people calling me Ed, like I'm Mr Ed the talking horse. In my book, Ed is reserved for those who want to be ignored.

VALMAE: You have to respect someone's choice of name. I get called Val, and I just repeat it, 'No, it's Valmae'. No one gets upset and they get the message. I work with a Jennifer and a Rebecca who get Jenny and Becky all the time and they hate it. The way they use the names between themselves, though, is very funny.

JV Why is it so hard? This is my name; this is what I prefer to be called. But the problem is Williams become Bill and Katherines, Katie because we are trying to be friendly. It's one of those instances where both sides have to understand the other. The Susans of this world have to ask for their name of choice in a way that doesn't reject the friendly overture. And then we have to respect a Susan who wants to be Susan.

THE MISSING MISTER

Peter: I have three young children. I introduce myself as Peter, but other parents often insist on using my surname. I don't really feel like 'Mr Smith'; I'm Peter. In this day and age, unless it's a schoolteacher or an authority figure, the 'Mr' and 'Mrs' thing creates a separation. Have 'Mr' and 'Mrs' pretty much gone? We don't do it between adults much any more, do we?

JV: You know where I noticed it recently? I flew with an airline that's meant to be really young and fun. And at check-in they all call me

'James', whereas on the older more formal airlines they still say, 'Here's your boarding pass, Mr Valentine'.

ALAN: I've got a teenage daughter and most of her friends call me by my first name. I prefer it, it makes me feel younger. I notice in the course of my work that if I'm not happy with people, I call them 'Mr' and if I think they're going okay, I call them by their first name.

AARON: I think with kids, you should introduce the person as 'Mr' or 'Mrs' and then if they wish they can say to the child, call me 'Jack' or 'Ruth' or whatever. I think that's still the correct courtesy. Between adults, I don't use it much. I do property maintenance work and I find a lot of the tenants expect to be called 'Mr' or 'Mrs'. I think to myself you weren't baptised 'Mr Jones' were you? I use their first name. I think I'm old enough to do it and it's an egalitarian society we live in.

MARIA: I might have Mrs Robinson Syndrome, but I insist on my son's friends calling me 'Mrs'. I see it as a rite of passage. When they turn eighteen, I will invite them to call me by my first name.

JV: They'll never be able to do that.

MARIA: I know, when you've called me 'Mrs Smith' all your life, you can't suddenly call me 'Maria'. But I insist on it and try to make them aware of what I want to be called because my son said to me once, 'I never know what to call people, "Mr" or "Mrs", and so I call them nothing'. I think you have to let kids know what you want.

EDDIE: Out there in the real world, I use 'Mr' all the time. I run a business and everyone is 'Mr'. It's a very good thing to use when you're taking their money—keeps it businesslike. It's all too easy to get informal and laidback and suddenly it's 'Doesn't matter, I'll pay Eddie a bit later'. No thank you—when it's 'Mr', everyone knows where they are.

JV Has the 'Mr' and 'Mrs' thing gone? Not entirely. Some people are still introducing adults to children as 'Mr' and 'Mrs' and Eddie makes a good point that in business it keeps things formal. But the days of work colleagues calling each other 'Mr' and 'Miss', of all authority figures being given their titles, have passed. You need to check with people what they prefer.

WHO THE HELL IS THAT?

John: What do you do when you can't remember someone's name? I used that method where you make up a little rhyme or nickname to remember the real name but then I used the nickname instead and it was a really bad moment. I need something else.

PETER: I'm for the mandatory wearing of name tags for everybody all the time. Roman slaves had their names tattooed on them and I don't think that's going too far.

BILL: I had a mate who realised he was so bad at this that he called everyone 'John' or 'Shirley'. Once you knew him, it was all right, but it was always weird when you introduced him to anyone.

RAY: I'm pretty bad at it, so I don't use anyone's name, ever—I call everyone 'maaate'.

PADDY: I work in sales and this is a very common problem. At conferences and sales events—the sales community is very good at this—you introduce yourself at that thirty-second point when you realise that the person you are with is not going to introduce you. I often wish the broader community would take this on board and realise that we can't remember everyone's name all the time and just introduce themselves. It's absolutely fine.

ANDY: I had a girlfriend and it went on for about three weeks. I just couldn't say her name properly. I'd already asked her twice how to say it, couldn't do it again. I mean this is so bad and it's so bad for everyone. Why don't we just admit it and all wear name tags?

KIRSTY: My husband and I worked out years ago that if he doesn't introduce me to someone, then he has no idea who they are or what their name is. So I just thrust out a hand and say, 'Hi, I'm Kirsty', they introduce themselves and we're fine.

ELLA: If there're three of you, you say to the person you can't remember, 'You know John Smith, right?' and they say, 'No', and introduce themselves to him. Works ninety-nine per cent of the time!

MAUREEN: You say to the person you've forgotten, 'What's your name again?' and they say 'John' and you say, 'No, I knew you were John. What's your surname? We were just talking about family history'. With a lot of people you don't really know their surname so it's okay to ask.

JOHN: Don't panic! It's panic that drives the person's name out of your head. You meet someone you're meant to know and you can't remember their name, you panic. Don't panic!

JV Everyone has to deal with this one. We see a workmate at a social event and we can't place them, we see a parent from a school our kids went to five years ago and we have no idea who they are. There is a moment when you meet— when your eyes first glance at each other's face and recognition is meant to occur—that you can claim faulty wiring, senility or preoccupation with world affairs and you can request a reminder from the person you've forgotten; but miss that moment and you're soon covering yourself in a flurry of 'mates' and 'darls'. You've got to grab the moment at which you can introduce yourself, you have to admit to your own frailty and say immediately, 'I'm sorry, I've forgotten your name'. You can then cover yourself in a flurry of excuses; 'Haven't seen you for ages', 'Don't usually see you here', 'Confused you with someone else' and so on. But it's all in the timing.

WHAT IT'LL BE, MATE?

Graeme: I've been called all sorts of things and usually I don't mind, but I don't like everyone calling me 'mate'. From the junior on the checkout counter to somebody in a garage or whatever, they all use 'mate'. Why don't we train people like they do in America to say 'Mr' or 'sir'? I'm an older person and I find it ridiculous when youngsters do it to me.

PAMELA: I think he's taking it a bit too seriously. Women don't get called anything—'darl', occasionally—but really it's all in the tone and if it's friendly and respectful, what does it matter?

JV: We don't have a generic greeting like 'mate' for women in Australia, do we?

PAMELA: I think 'darl' is common, a little old-fashioned perhaps.

TONY: I think he's got a problem with not much at all really. I mean if someone says 'G'day mate' and gives you a smile, I think that's better than the grunt you get half the time.

JV: Should you be saying 'Yes sir' to older citizens?

TONY: Oh, I think that's a bit old-fashioned, really. I think it can be a bit superficial to be using 'sir'. I don't really see the difference between the 'mate' and the 'sir'.

HEIDE: In the past, I've worked a lot in the service and retail industries, and often when you do actually say, 'Thank you, sir' or 'Here you are, sir', they will correct you, because they actually feel older if you call them such.

JV: It is funny, isn't it? I find it really intriguing. A lot of other societies have this codified, don't they? European countries will tend to have all sorts of different names for married status and different ages and that kind of thing. Americans use 'sir' or 'ma'am'. We just don't have it at all, do we?

HEIDE: No, but what I know ladies do like is if you call them 'girls', so if you've got a group of ladies lunching, you say, 'Okay, girls, what would you like today?'. They think that's fabulous. But you've got to pick the right age group and you've got to be careful about it. Get it wrong and they hate you.

JV: What do you call a bunch of young girls, you know, 23-year-olds out at lunch?

HEIDE: Well, funnily enough, probably 'guys'. 'How're you guys doing today?' And they respond fine to that, the same as a group of mixed girls and guys or a group of guys.

SHIRLEY: I have a little story, very brief. When my future grandson-in-law, at their engagement party, said, 'And how are you, babe?', I was seventy-three, and I felt beautiful. So when I'm behind a checkout now and there's a good-looking young guy, I give him a cheeky grin and say, 'Thanks, babe'.

Graeme seems to be alone in this. Is there really a demand for formal public greetings like 'sir' and 'ma'am' or 'senor' and 'senorita' in Australia? I don't think so. At upmarket hotels or restaurants it can be fine for some and off-putting for others who don't quite trust it. Like the use of 'Mr' and 'Mrs', we probably have to make a quick judgement as to what the other person is going to want and what really suits the situation.

MR, MS, MISS, MISSUS, OTHER

Denise: I work in a restaurant as a waitress and quite a few cross-dressers and men in drag come in. I can't figure out what the correct form of address is for them. Is it 'Mr'? Is it 'ma'am', 'miss' or 'Ms'? If men are dressed as women what do you say to them? I've also worked in a

*medical clinic and the question there was do you address
them as they're dressed or as their clinical notes indicate?*

MITZI: I guess telephone etiquette is one thing, because I actually have
a few friends who are transgendered, and one of them works in a call
centre, and on the telephone she (and I refer to her as 'she' because
she's living as a she) often gets referred to as a he because obviously her
voice isn't high enough for people to recognise it as a girl's voice, and
even though she talks a little bit delicate, she still sounds like a man.

JV: Well, Mitzi, so do you.

MITZI: I do, but see I'm the drag queen variety, so it doesn't really
matter. For me it doesn't matter that I have a man's voice, because I'm
just basically a gay clown anyway. It's not so much about female imper-
sonation; it's just about gig entertainment.

JV: So if you were out, tottering up the street in your heels, in the
frock, the big wig, on your way to do your Dusty impression, should I
say to you, 'Excuse me, miss, I'm just trying to get through'?

MITZI: I guess the idea that I have a pair of breasts and I'm attempting
as much as I can to impersonate something of a slightly feminine figure,
then yes, it would be 'miss' or 'she'.

JV: In this context, where it's a restaurant, and people are coming in,
should she come up and say, 'Excuse me, ma'am, we've run out of
the barramundi'?

MITZI: Look, if somebody is attempting to gender as a woman or
something, then yes, I guess you refer to them as 'miss'. Even though
sometimes the attempts mightn't be valiant, still they should be

referred to as 'miss'—and likely the other way—because sometimes you get women who transgender into men, and that's a 'he'. And that's a whole other thing as well, because sometimes I see girls and I think, lesbians, and I start chatting away and I think, is it a man or a woman? I'm confused. I guess that's where 'darl', 'love' and 'pet' come in, or if you're straight, 'mate' or 'dude'...Even in the hotel sometimes I'm walking around in full drag and a straight guy'll come up and he'll say, 'G'day, dude, I was just wondering when the next show's on?'. And I'm like, okay, I don't know whether I'm much of a dude, but anyway. So I think generally whatever somebody's attempting to be, whatever gender they're obviously trying to be, then that's how you would refer to them.

JV: I love Denise's initial dilemma. There was the restaurant version, but she also said she used to work in a medical clinic and one of the patients would come in, in drag, but she didn't know whether to address him as his outward appearance implies or use 'Mr', as his clinical notes indicate. In a medical context that would be hard, wouldn't it?

MITZI: It would be, I guess. I guess it's whatever somebody's attempting to be. If you want to be nasty then obviously refer to them as a 'he' if she's dressed as a 'she', but if you want to be respectful of whatever it is that they're trying to do with their life, then it's a 'she'.

TIGTOG: A slightly different question on the etiquette is, unless it's a performance, surely it's not drag, it's cross-dressing. It's not really polite to call it drag unless they're putting on a performance, I think.

JV: I didn't want to get bogged down necessarily in the terms, but I think the same would apply, wouldn't it?

TIGTOG: But if a person is cross-dressing as part of normal life, it's not putting on a drag performance.

JV: No, but then the same would apply, wouldn't it? If they're cross-dressing, then they would want to be referred to as a woman, wouldn't they?

TIGTOG: Oh, of course. Address them as the gender that they're preferring to be. I have a whole other rant on binary constructions of gender but you don't want to hear that either.

JV: Look I think we'll do binary constructions of gender another day— is that all right?

TIGTOG: That's fine.

JV We never have got around to doing binary constructions of gender. But with regards to the initial problem, it's the same as anyone else. We like to be addressed as we are presenting ourselves. With some people it's obvious they want to be called 'Mr', others are going to be Bill, straight off. Here, with those opting for other than their biological gender, what's the difference? 'Yes, miss, how can I help you? And I love those shoes!', will go down a treat.

CHAPTER SIX

COLLEAGUES

A Brief History of Colleagues

Work was a hierarchy: there was an Owner—who visited the plant perhaps once a year on the worker's picnic day but otherwise knew little of what was going on or even what the plant did; there was a Boss—of whom no one knew anything, not his first name, his marital status or whether he had sugar in his tea. He was guarded by a Secretary—an unmarried woman of indeterminate age who'd wedded herself to the firm after her fiancé failed to return from the War. The Boss occupied a large office overlooking the plant and would emerge on payday to walk around with his hands behind his back looking stern. Workers operated machinery in the plant until they fell into it and died. At this point, a flat cap would be passed around, a collection made and his widow presented with seven pounds and nine pence to help with her nine children. At work, there was no communication, not even at lunchtime. Workers were given ten minutes for lunch, during which they consumed a corned beef sandwich, a thermos of tea and three Craven A's. At the end of the day they would mount wobbly bicycles and cycle home to sit grimly by the stove waiting for stew. Some drank, but this was done with both hands and conversation was limited to sport and union business.

Some worked in offices. There they sat at desks in rows with an adding machine wearing green eye shades. They could be sacked for looking up, for looking sideways, for looking anywhere other than at the columns of figures in front of them. Young lads darted among them—like pigeons in a food court—delivering messages and picking up finished work. Young lads dreamed of getting their own eye shade and joining the solemn ranks of the office workers. The eye shades dreamt of rising through the managerial ranks until perhaps one day they might have their own office and be able to pull the door open and bark orders at young lads scuttling by.

Those not in the office or in the plant were down mine. Here they laboured mightily, hewing at the very earth until their canary died, which told them they had only minutes to live. At such moments they would grunt affectionately to one another and carve a final message on the handle of their pick.

Those not involved in such honest and steadfast toil were usually travelling salesmen. In fast cars, toting suitcases of ladies' underwear and vacuum cleaners, they crisscrossed the state taking orders for their fancy merchandise. They were glib, shallow chaps who reeked of cologne, had hip flasks and thought nothing of knocking up the farmer's daughter. She was seduced by the promise of a pair of silk stockings and the vision of leaving the rabbit and mallee root-infested debt hole—euphemistically called The Farm—with Eddie the Rawleigh's Man and installing herself as mistress of a two-bedroom flat in St Kilda with a chip heater over the bath.

Farmers, of course, laboured from dawn until dusk behind the stump-jump plough planting crops that would wither in the drought, be washed away by the flood, be consumed by rabbits and locust or burnt out in the bushfires.

And then there were the unemployed. They stood, single file, heads bowed, waiting for soup, or gathered at the wharf each day to be picked to haul wool bales.

Women were banned from the workplace except as telephonists, secretaries and typists. The moment they were engaged to be married, they were sacked. The only reason they went to work was to meet prospective husbands and there was hot competition for any young lad who looked likely.

There were no colleagues, no one was a team player, there was no workplace bonding. No one went out for long lunches, except for journalists, who would phone in copy at deadline time from the bar of the Criterion where they'd spent the afternoon developing alcoholism and making up quotes.

Perhaps in law firms or among surgeons one might have had colleagues, but for the rest of the workforce, relationships in the workplace are a recent occurrence, arriving along with such things as workers' compensation, overtime, safety gear and cappuccino machines—all of which have gone a long way towards making the workplace the hotbed of gossip and wacky emails we know today.

Then: you could work with someone for decades. Now: the phrase 'too much information' comes to mind.

THE OFFICE BIRTHDAY

Stella: My friend brings a cake to work for my birthday. I don't really like the cake and I'm on a very strict diet for my weight. Do I have to eat it?

REBECCA: You have to take the cake. Insist on only a thin slice, mush it up a lot, take a tiny forkful. Use a paper plate, it will absorb the fat, and is easily and quickly disposed of with no offence to anyone.

GENEVIEVE: Oh, what is wrong with her? Take the cake. Is she some supermodel or something? It's just plain rude not to take it and to eat it.

I know this issue: I'm not a dessert eater. It's not a weight thing, I just don't eat it. I don't like cakes. I hate the cakes that turn up at office birthdays in particular. I'm always the party pooper. I'm always rejecting the host's magnificent dessert, but if I get it and don't eat it, it's just as bad. It's a no-win. You can't have your cake and not eat it too. And you must have your cake. The office birthday can be the high point of the birthday person's celebration.

NO, REALLY, I AM PAYING ATTENTION

Graeme: When you go to a meeting these days, half the people bring a laptop with them, open it up, and tap away at the computer and half-listen to the meeting and half-attend to their work. Some people think that's a wonderful gain in productivity and other people think it's very rude. It might be a palm device, the PDA; they scribble on it with the electric pen, they can get email. I think it's basically rude and I notice now that it's a bit like mobiles. People have to ask for everyone to close their laptops or their devices and pay attention to the meeting.

PETER: I think there's a difference between taking notes in a meeting straight onto your laptop and doing other business. Taking notes is okay, as long as the computer's quiet. I don't think you should necessarily judge that all open computers are doing other business and that people's minds are wandering. I mean, you don't need a computer to be distracted, you can just doodle. Maybe we should consider that if the meeting is so uncompelling that people can do something else, do we really need this meeting in the first place?

SIMON: I was at a seminar and there were people there with their laptops taking notes and other people were holding little tape-recording things in the palm of their hand. But one guy was sitting there and he wasn't making much of an effort to do anything, except he had a set of headphones on. I was wondering what he was up to, and after about half an hour he started jumping up in the air and saying, 'Go you good thing!'. And as he jumped up the headphones came out of the wireless device and he was listening to the horse races. I think that's only acceptable on the first Tuesday in November around about 3.00 in the afternoon, isn't it?

JV I'm with the 'do-you-need-the-meeting-in-the-first-place?' guy. I am blessed to work at a radio station that long ago decided that we only needed to meet at the Christmas party and perhaps three times a year to consider new ways of getting the same result. Other places meet hourly to discuss the paper clips. Try to find workplaces that don't value your input and you'll never attend a meeting again. Meanwhile, I think it's rude to tap away, text and attend to emails during a meeting, but if I were convenor of that meeting and noticed many doing it, I'd have wonder why it was interesting to play solitaire on the phone than listen to me.

BETTER OUT THAN IN

Sally: At the office I work in, some men, and it's only the men, seem to think it's okay to fart loudly and publicly. Do I pretend it didn't happen or do I acknowledge it?

MALCOLM: It is never socially acceptable except at one time during your life—and that is at the Year 7 boys' camp. If you can do it properly, perhaps do the national anthem, then you are a hero forever. If can you light it—not that I recommend that, as it is quite dangerous to a very sensitive part of the body—then you're a legend.

PAUL: For the regular flatulators, print off something or email something along the lines of 'TYPICAL MALE—ALL NOISE AND NO SUBSTANCE'.

CONRAD: It's natural. Whether it be in church or chapel, always let it rattle. It should be greeted with a round of applause. Let your wind go free wherever you may be.

JV: Have you followed that dictum?

CONRAD: Yes.

JV: Are you a lonely man?

CONRAD: I work by myself.

FRED: When my three-year-old grandson does it at the dinner table, I say, 'Did you hear that?'. He giggles and says 'Yes, that's a fart!'. I then tell him not to do it at the dinner table. I, however, am in my eighties. At this point in life we don't quite have the control we would want and so we graciously acknowledge authorship by saying something like, 'I'm sorry, but better an empty house than bad tenants'.

PETER: Best to fart and stink a little, than to bust a gut and die a cripple.

MARGARET: Buy some packets of flatulence prevention pills or medicine. And when it happens again, go up in a loud voice and proclaim, 'You poor thing. Look, this might help'. A few days later go over again and say, 'How are those pills working? Is your little problem better?'.

JV: Few problems had so many pithy aphorisms so readily at hand. The fact that we humans come with a built-in whoopee cushion is a cause for celebration. It's hard to see the evolutionary purpose, but when someone lets one go, every culture on the face of the earth thinks it's funny. However, the hilarity it can cause must be balanced with the accompanying stench—rarely a cause for laughter. How perfectly is the joy and pain of the human condition captured in this banal yet repulsive moment of anal expression? That said, what kind of sad adolescent do you have to be to let one go in the office? If faced with the flatulent in the workplace, it's okay to tell them they stink.

I HAVE TO TAKE THIS

Marty: *At office meetings, what do you do when the person you're meeting with takes a phone call and then proceeds to have a long conversation? Why does the phone take precedence?*

DAVID: That's simply rude. You shouldn't speak on the phone when someone's in your office. What I do is pull out some work while they're on the phone and when they finish, I make them wait a bit—gets the message across.

CRAIG: He's dead right. I'm constantly on the phone but if I'm doing face to face, then the phone's on message or, if I forget, I just tell them I'll return the call and apologise profusely for interrupting the meeting. When people do it to me, I just want to get up and leave. You've got to judge it, though— is the meeting more important than him being a bit rude?

NICOLE: When I go in, I make a point of turning off my phone in front of whoever I'm meeting with. When there's more than one person someone will often say, 'Okay, phones off?'. You have to. You've made the meeting in person because it's a meeting that needs to happen in person. Otherwise you'd be ringing them. If someone does it to me, I politely make little signals about the time, or let them know I'm a little anxious, or ask if I should go. That gets them off the line.

Is this office chest beating, alpha male asserting rank or simply a hangover from the days when phone calls were rare, expensive and always important (unlike today, when phone calls are as common as bacteria and usually about as welcome)? Given the number of modes of communication today— email, mobile phone, and so on—of course, if we have made a time to meet face to face, it's because we need to meet face to face without interruption. We all now have had enough time to find the divert button on our phone, to get into the habit of turning it off, of sending calls straight to message bank. If your receive a call that must be taken, then take a second to explain to the person with you what's occurred: unless you were wanting to assert that you are a powerful person who doesn't need to explain themselves to any underling who happens to be present—the common term for people like this is wanker.

I'M SO SORRY WE STARTED WITHOUT YOU

Annie: I do a lot of meetings and training. People are always late and I never know how to treat them. It's always the same people who are late and I don't know whether to fiddle around and wait for them or to start on time even if it means they miss something important. I never know what to do.

BRIAN: Put it on the agenda: 'Is there something wrong with the time of this meeting, as some of you have trouble getting here?'. You should always start on time unless you lack a quorum. Latecomers are latecomers and if the meeting always starts on time, then they are always late. If you start late it's a discourtesy to everyone who arrived on time. You do have to recap for latecomers, but as long as you're consistent, you always start on time, then you are never at fault.

RAY: We used to put the latecomers' names up on the board and have a sweep as to who'd be last. Cross them off as they come in, lots of jokes. I bet my boss a bottle of wine once that this girl would be late. My boss told her the meeting was at nine even though it was at ten just to try and win the bet. I won because she didn't even show up.

HELEN: I hate latecomers. It's so annoying. We lock the doors. People then have to knock to be admitted, and I've even made people stay back. I'm not going to hold up everything for everyone else so the latecomers can be brought up to speed. They can stay back and catch up then.

JV We all know the Dame Edna Everage technique: parade the latecomers around in front of the audience so everyone can see them and we can laugh at them. I like Brian's suggestion of making it an agenda item. However you do it, make latecomers aware that they are a pain in the neck.

YOU LOOKING AT ME?

Frank: I spent the morning running a training course and there was a guy at it with a glass eye. Where do you look: at the good eye or at the crook one? Do I look at the forehead? Do I bring it up? Eye contact is very important in training, and this was one on one. Is he conscious that I'm looking at his glass eye or his good one?

RUSSELL: I've often engaged people with wonky eyes. I've asked them straight out. I've also lost the use of one eye and mine's a different colour and you can see people looking at it. You can see the thoughts going through their head. I'd rather they ask straight out what the situation is. And you look in the good eye, make eye contact with the good eye. No point staring at my blind eye, I can't see out of it.

BARBARA: I was born blind in one eye; I need you to concentrate on my good eye and stay there. I always find people are struggling with it. Very few people are straightforward about this, but I can always see that they are uneasy. I can't believe that someone has finally brought this up. Please, whenever you meet me or anyone else, just talk about it. It's fine.

JV What Barbara says is spot on. People can see your reaction; they can sense your unease, and they know what it's about. If you ask, then you'll be in the minority; but from what Russell and Barbara suggest, they would much prefer you talked about it than kept on pretending you weren't having a problem.

IT'S A KITTEN!

Don: My wife works for an insurance company and one day she took a new kitten in to work to show her friends. The manager stormed over and told her to get it out of there. I was waiting downstairs to take the kitten home—it wasn't going to be there all day or anything. Today, someone brought a new baby in and it cried and everyone made a fuss over it and no one complained. We're not comparing a pet to a child, but it did seem a bit rough to us.

MATT: The kitten versus the baby. I have a four-year-old daughter and I'm surprised how many people compare their doggy to my daughter: 'My doggy does this, does your daughter do that?'. It's not a question of equal time for babies or kittens, pregnancy and children are a completely different thing. Workmates go through the pregnancy with the woman, she has time off, people want to see the baby; it's completely different.

NERIDA: I think it's a wonderful idea to bring the kitten in. The kitten is important, and it means both employees are valued. That's an insensitive boss who couldn't see that and what it must have meant to that woman.

GEOFF: I don't like cats. But I acknowledge that if you love it, you should be able to bring it in. Some people are allergic to cats. Some people bring in babies for a couple of hours and it's a bit long really.

SUSAN: She should change her workplace and go and work for a vet. I have a cat called Itty Bitty Psycho Kitty. I would love to take her in, but some animals need constant attention and that's not really going to work.

JV 'Fur kids' is the expression for a dog, cat or ferret that's treated as more than just a companion animal. While it may seem a little extreme to some to bring a kitten in to work to show your colleagues, I think I'm with Nerida that a little more sensitivity on the part of the boss might be warranted.

WHISTLE WHILE YOU WORK!

Jim: I want to know why we don't ever hear people whistling. Is it rude now for a person to walk along the street and whistle a merry tune? Is it because we haven't got music that's tuneful? I think we must all be getting very sombre because it's hard to whistle and not be cheerful, isn't it?

RICHARD: I work in the rag trade and I'm a habitual whistler but I often noticed if I whistled around the factory a lot of people would sort of freak out and say, 'Oh, please stop! Please don't do that'. Often they were Turkish and they had this saying: 'The person who whistles is followed by the devil'. They thought it was bad luck. I mean, I'm a real whistle-while-you-work kind of guy but at the dyeing factory there was a Chinese guy and if I walked in whistling, he'd screw up his face and say, 'Oh, shut up! When you whistle I need to urinate!'.

JV: So postwar immigration has killed off whistling. It's given us falafel, Peking duck and the Socceroos, but it's killed off whistling.

STEVE: I'm a bit of an old-timer, I'm fifty-seven years old, and I used to whistle a lot in my younger day. But I haven't done it for years, because it just seems these days not to be right. It makes you feel like a fogy, makes you look like a geezer. It's something fogies do. I haven't whistled for so long it's not funny. There used to be a song called 'Whistling Rufus' and I can't even remember how it goes now, but I think if you whistle now, it sounds like you stepped straight out of the 1950s.

JV: You may as well have the flat cap and the blazer on, right?

STEVE: It's very dating.

I'm a whistler, but only in private. Public whistling does seem to have vanished. There were songs on the hit parade that were definite whistlers. They'd have a slight martial air, a satisfying upward 'wwooop' at some point and a range of less than an octave, which is about all but Roger Whittaker could manage. I don't know why it's died out. It's satisfying, it's a musical instrument that requires no lifting and no electricity. It's cheering to the practitioner and the listener. I would argue it needs to be introduced in schools. Certainly, I would rather hear some bleachers full of Year 3s whistling than playing the recorder, which is whistle-like in tone, but with the chirpiness removed. This question has encouraged me to begin whistling in public again. I can recommend the 'Colonel Bogey' theme, 'The Simpsons' and the 'Wallace & Gromit' theme music as ideal.

CHAPTER SEVEN

FRIENDS

A Brief History of Friends

Men didn't have friends; they had mates. Australian mateship is considered to be something special, a national trait of which we can be proud. It's sometimes hard to distinguish from Belgian mateship or Saskatchewan mateship, but perhaps its most obvious characteristic is its rich and vibrant non-verbal history. How Australian men have managed to form lifelong friendships, or mateships, without ever speaking to one another has puzzled the historian and social observer for many a long year. Some posit that in the early convict years, when chained to one another for twelve hours a day, then shoved back into cells and barracks after a sound flogging, it was simply very difficult to get a conversation going. 'How was your day?' was a very poor opener as each day was somewhat the same and each convict had pretty much had the same day. Similarly, 'How do you like the new overseer? Gruel good tonight? What are you doing after candles out?' just didn't go anywhere and so convicts and their guards alike could lapse into silences which lasted for years.

It was the same for the settlers. New chums would arrive and be stunned into silence by the hopping wildlife, the endless dense bush with its infinite variations on drab olive, and the heat of December. Recovering their senses they would open their mouths to speak and immediately swallow a small army of flies. Choking, as a kookaburra mocked them overhead, they would resort to nods and grunts to communicate with the others sent to make this strange land bloom. 'Mate' itself became an utterance deeply nuanced and could be used to communicate everything from affection to hostility to 'I think the Turks have dug in at Lone Pine and me and Bluey are going over the top in the morning to make him choke on his falafel and eggs'.

Mates were mates because they were mates. If it needed explaining or had to be talked about, then you couldn't be mates. To be a mate you had to be a good bloke, so anyone could be a mate as long as they weren't a bludger. A bludger was someone who wasn't your mate because they always left the shout before it was their turn to buy a round of beers.

When mates met the correct form of greeting was to give a slight nod and to say, 'Mate', to which the correct reply was to nod in return and say, 'Mate'. You would then order a beer by nodding in the direction of the barmaid. No words needed! There was only beer and only one type of beer and what else would two mates want but two beers? Nothing would be said until after the beer arrived. Both would drink deeply and then exhale, indicating satisfaction with the brewer's handiwork. One mate would then offer an opening conversational gambit, 'Hot enough for you, mate?', to which the correct reply was a freshly coined Australian phrase such as, 'Mate, gets any hotter, you'll be able to boil the billy on my arse, mate'. And that would be enough idle chat for a half-hour or so.

But what of the womenfolk? Did the sheilas have mates? By the time an Australian woman had got up before dawn, made the damper, put on the mutton stew, fired up the copper for the washing, got her freckly brood of would-be Don Bradmans and QANTAS hosties off to school with their Vegemite sandwiches and fast-blackening bananas, washed the floors and scoured the doorstep, she was lucky to have five minutes to pop down to the Ladies' Lounge at the Criterion and shell some peas with Doreen from up the street over a pony of shandy or sherry. Australian women kept the family together and did this by organising a regular tour of cousins and great-aunts and second cousins and sisters on country properties. These were her friends and while the men stood silently and watched sausages burn on the backyard barbie, the women would be making salads of lettuce, boiled egg, beetroot and pineapple and catching up on all the latest gossip.

Then: you knew you were friends if you were on the Christmas card list. Now: people from Saskatchewan we met once send us intimate emails.

THERE'S SOMETHING DIFFERENT ABOUT YOU...

John: I'm worried because a friend of mine has recently had breast enhancement surgery and there's a real debate amongst my friends as to what to do. Do we notice it? Do we say something about it or just let it pass as natural?

JV: So how do you know she's had the work?

JOHN: It's obvious, it's very obvious, and her friends have told me about it anyway.

JV: When it's hair colour you must always say, 'You've changed your hair colour and it looks terrific', but do you do that with the boob job?

JOHN: Yes! Well, I'm not sure if it's on that same sort of level, that's where my trouble is stemming from.

JV: What if she came back and she'd had botox, would you feel as though you should say, 'That is so much smoother, that is just great'?

JOHN: I think botox is a lot less obvious than this job that she's had done.

JV: 'That lift and tuck you had over the holidays, you look terrific.' I don't know, is it appropriate to comment on people's plastic surgery?

MAUREEN: I suppose with breasts, what you could do is give them the compliment. You could say about their figure, 'Oh, have you lost weight?' or 'You're looking very good', and that way she can either say, 'Well, yes, I've had a boob job' or she can just say, 'Thank you'. And that'll let you know if she wants to be complimented or not.

JV: Yes, because I'd imagine that it's all very individual. Some people might be comfortable with it, and proud of it, some people they don't want it known that they've had this done.

MAUREEN: I had a friend who had a breast enlargement, and she went to the races and some guy commented on her legs—how good they were—and she got angry at him. She said, 'I've just spent seven thousand dollars on my boobs and you're telling me I've got good legs!'.

JV: Well, she sounds very hard to please. Maureen, that's an excellent idea, just a little side comment that invites them to tell you what's been going on.

SONIA: Of course you've got to comment; otherwise the whole point of it is lost. It depends on what you say, though.

JV: In your experience do most people want to talk about it, or do they want to keep it discreet?

SONIA: We had a lady who worked for us, and she has cosmetic surgery every so often—on her face largely. But the last time she had it done she really looked awful, as though someone had gone over it with a Brillo pad. So we didn't say anything; I mean there's a pack of women working there, and we all didn't say anything.

JV: But I would have thought it was almost getting to the level of simply having your hair done or changing your wardrobe or something. I would imagine that people are less and less ashamed of it in a way. They would just see it as: of course I have it done, I can afford it, I wanted to do it, I feel great.

MARIA: I think just come out with it, be upfront (dare I say upfront?). I'd say, 'Gosh, corker of a bustline'. That's exactly what I'd say.

JV: And have you had any friends that have done anything like this?

MARIA: I've got a dear old aunt, a maiden aunt, and she used to say to me, 'Oh Maria, you've got a corker of a bustline', and I've always wanted to say it to someone else.

JV 'Hey, you look great. Who's your surgeon? What do you pay for that kind of thing anyway? How's the sex been?' If you think you can carry it off, be my guest. And if you can't say anything nice...

YOU NEED TO UNDERSTAND...

Ralph: There's a mate of mine who won't stop arguing with you until you agree with him, particularly when it comes to political discussions. He's intent on getting agreement and doesn't understand compromise.

CLARE: I had an uncle who was so bad at political argument, was so angry and convinced of the rightness of his own view, that the only option any of us had was to retreat. We retreated so far we haven't seen him for years.

DON: With your argumentative friend, try using, 'Yes, all right, thank you very much. I hear what you're saying'. It's code for it's time to shut up now. I think most people know that and, unless he's a real dick, he should get it.

ADAM: I was a dogmatic friend until a good friend of mine tapped me on the shoulder. He took me out of the context of an actual argument and told me I was becoming a pain in the arse. He was really good, kind of gentle, but like a thunderstorm. He said I'd changed, become too assertive, and everyone had noticed. I still think I'm a dogmatic kind of person, but I'm more careful about what I say and at least know now when to shut up.

JV Everything is compromise—and I won't compromise on that. Can you tell a friend that he's out of line? It's a hard one, but Adam suggests it can be done. Take a look at yourself: are you someone who has to win the argument or do you have two goes at it and then look for some middle ground and an opportunity to change the subject? If it's life and death to you, then argue passionately. If you're out having a pleasant time, know when to back off.

HOW CAN YOU TALK TO HER?

Eloise: My close friend Susan and another friend Mary have fallen out. Susan doesn't want me to contact Mary. She hasn't said I can't but she gets very upset when I mention anything.

JV: Why have they fallen out?

ELOISE: It's a romance. They both spotted a boy, Susan thinks she saw him first, but then Mary went off with him.

JV: **Single men in Sydney—rare commodity.**

ELOISE: Mary said 'Hands off, he's mine', but Susan can't resist a challenge, so she went after him as well. It's all over now, but they're still angry. I see Susan every day, but I like Mary. It's a new friendship. Do I have to dump her?

(JV: **This is not from 'Sex and the City'—it's a real-life caller.**)

KATIE: Get as far away from that girl as possible: Susan's trouble. She's in there telling you what to do, she's going after boys who are with other girls. I know her type. In fact, I'd keep away from both of them. It won't stop here. Friends can't lay down rules about friendship, about who you can and can't see.

CLAUDIA: Loyalty takes precedence—long-standing friendship. Of course she has to support her friend Susan. Mary is new, she has to prove herself and respect the long-term relationship.

STEVE: That's just someone trying to manipulate others and control their friends. You don't need them. It's about a boy, look, that's just hormones and we can't do much about that. They should all calm down. We all have friends that other friends can't talk to or don't like much.

MARIA: Susan is the priority, but there's something about Mary. There's something about the bloke in this, too. As they've both had a waltz around with him, then maybe Eloise should have a go as well. They'd all have that in common, compare notes and it would bring them all back together. You can't direct your friends. Leave all that in the playground. More seriously, what happens to your friendship after divorce? It took a while, but my ex-sister-in-law is still one of my best friends.

JV I'm with the anti-manipulators on this one. After a while we discover that our best friend is someone who likes to control friendships. They decide when we get together; they introduce you to Mary and you and Mary feel like you're having an affair if you get together without the original friend. Aren't the best friends the ones with whom you know you can do anything and they're still your friend? Be wary of the one trying to run everyone else.

THE GROUCHO MARX QUESTION

Lizzie: At my book club, some women are proposing that we bring new blood in. How do we allow someone to visit so we can vet them? We had a situation where someone was asked to join but within a few meetings we realised they were entirely unsuitable and we had to reject them. It was awful and none of us want to go through that again.

JANITA: Host an informal morning or afternoon tea. Invite any prospective book-club members to it. All existing members should be there as well. Don't let on what's happening, don't tell people they're being vetted or even mention the book club. Everyone can have a look at them and talk about it later. That said, I wouldn't want to be a member of that book club. They seem very picky. The wrong person comes in and the whole thing doesn't work. Dear me!

BILL: I've been a member of a wine and food club and people are invited to come along as a guest. If it's mutually acceptable then sometimes the guests are invited to become members. Invite someone you think might be good along as a guest. If everyone else likes them, then see if they would like to become a member.

DONNA: Have an open night. Anyone can invite anyone they like. Just tell people this is something your book club does from time to time and it's fun. Don't let on you're vetting them, that's awfully rude, but it's okay to check people out to see if they're going to fit in. It's your night, your club. You can pick who you want.

JV That's the whole point about clubs, isn't it: like wants to hang out with like? No point having a bridge club if a bunch of chess players are allowed to join. Book clubs are a finely balanced thing, and it might have taken years to get this group working. I can understand if she doesn't want it ruined. And if you don't like the sound of this group, don't join it.

HAPPY BIRTHDAY, HOPE YOU DON'T WIN

Samantha: If someone gave me a lottery ticket and it won a vast sum of money would I be obliged to share?

JV: What do you think would be fair? Ten per cent? If you won one hundred thousand, would you give them ten thousand?

SAMANTHA: I don't know...

JV: What about one per cent, could you give them one thousand?

SAMANTHA: Oh yes.

JV: So, the going rate here is somewhere between one and ten per cent, and it sounds like a lot closer to one than ten.

RICHARD: A mate of mine's father says it's too hard to buy me a present so he'll get me a lottery ticket, and he says if I win we'll go halves. I said to him, 'What if you bought me a pair of socks, would I have to give you one back?'.

MAEVE: Oh, I wouldn't give them a thing. They're buying you a scratchy because they're too lazy to buy you a proper present and then if it's going to pay off your mortgage they want you to pay off theirs as well. Bugger that!

CHERYL: Give half back. You share it with them. If they hadn't bought it for you, you wouldn't have had that chance. It's the thought that counts.

JV: But it's not much of a thought, as Maeve was saying, is it? You stop at the newsagent and buy a scratchy.

CHERYL: It's still a gift. I would give them half and expect the same in return.

JV: I guess if you didn't do it, you wouldn't see much of that friend in the future.

RALPH: If I got a lottery ticket, and I won, I'd buy you a lottery ticket.

> **JV** It is better to give than to receive, but if you give and they receive a lot some of us would like some of it. If you win and you want to keep the friend, hand over some of the dough.

MWAAA!

Katie: How do I avoid the kiss? My husband has a friend who's very insistent on it. You get it coming and going and I just don't like it. I don't do the kiss thing with close friends, I'm not into it, and I don't know how to avoid it.

WAYNE: I don't get the kissing thing either. Can't stand it with guys—stubble on stubble. Yurk! I mean, it's not like an anti-gay thing—they can do what they like—I just don't need to be that close to some other bloke's aftershave. She should lead off with the handshake and get out of it that way.

JV: But the handshake just leads to the pull in. They grab your hand and reel you in for the cheek smack.

WAYNE: Oh, yeah, you're right. Yeah, I don't know. It's just compulsory now, I guess.

GERALDINE: I worked in France and there, they do the triple kiss thing. And when you got to work, I swear, it took you thirty minutes to get around everyone. I didn't like it. There, I just stuck the hand out or gave them a wave, they soon realised I wasn't into it and so no one insisted.

JV Haven't we all grappled with the kiss—all us non-Europeans? A generation back it was a handshake for men and a 'How do you do' for women. Now we greet one another like we're born in Napoli and raised by a black-clad Nonna making us gnocchi in a sun-drenched villa. The problem is we don't know how to do it. We don't know with whom and we don't know how many times: one cheek, two cheeks, three cheeks? At the start of a business meeting? When you meet an acquaintance at the beach? When do you start it with new people: straight away or only if you like them? Do you actually kiss, or simply rub cheeks with a little smacking noise near the ear? With friends does it always have to be accompanied by cries of 'Darling!' and little smoochie noises? And we haven't got to the central question: why does this kissing culture predominate? And can you indicate that you're not a kisser and settle for a silly wave and grin and a cheery 'Hi!'? I'd like to propose that we need a system of national referenda to determine these things. Perhaps on Election Day or whenever the census comes around, some of these questions could be included. Forget the Republic and the flag; let's find out if we would like to become a kissing nation, like Italy or France. And if so, what is the new national protocol? Otherwise, I'm afraid it's one of those social situations where the questions remain. Non-kissers can usually indicate their lack of enthusiasm for it with stiff and reserved body language and an outstretched hand at arm's length, but there are going to be kissers who will bowl on in regardless. If it's that bad on a regular basis, non-kissers will have to speak up. If it's occasional and you know it will be awkward to speak up, don't.

LEND, LOAN, BORROW;
IT ALWAYS ENDS IN SORROW*

> *Michael:* Last year I lent a DVD to a good friend of
> mine. It's a DVD I'm quite fond of, and when I got it back I
> didn't watch it for a few months but when I did get around
> to watching it I noticed that it had a rather nasty scratch on
> it. Now can I say to them, 'This was fine before I lent it to you'?
> I feel uncomfortable about accusing them of damaging it.

LEE: Well, I think when you do get them back you really need to check it
straight away. Unfortunately, I think maybe he's left it a little bit too
long. If he'd played it straight after he'd got it back he'd have very good
cause to know where the problem had started.

JV: You can flick through a book to see if it's ripped or if they've scribbled
on the pages, but a two- or three-hour DVD or an entire thirteen
episodes of a series, you can hardly sit down to check it's all okay.

LEE: You can see on the surface of the disk if there's any problem.

ROSEMARY: This guy is a really good friend of the other guy; I think you
have to weigh up the relationship. Is it worth mentioning?

JV: That's true, but if the guy is a good friend, he might be put out if
you didn't mention it.

ROSEMARY: Well, I just lent 'Angels in America' out to a friend of mine,
and every time I see her I say, 'You know you've got that, can I have it
back?'.

JV: See, it's important to you. And then it becomes an irritant between you. What I think happens is if the borrower watches it or reads it and loves it as much as you do, they think of it as theirs. And they don't want to give it back. DVDs and music, go to the DVD store, borrow it, download it, copy it, but you can't have my copy.

ROSEMARY: But you want to share good books and films with friends.

JOHN: I don't mind lending things but my pet hate is having to be the one to go and get it back. I've got to go over to their place to get the tools back and it really annoys me. The borrower should bring it back to me, I shouldn't have to run off after it.

JV *Lend, loan, borrow; it always ends in sorrow. This sounds like an old saying, but really I just made it up and it's my rule about lending stuff. If this is a book or CD or DVD that I really love, then no, you can't borrow it. On the other hand, if it's something I don't really care about you can have it. I'm no hoarder so I'm often happy to pass things on, but lending things, it never works. People break it, people lose it and people start to treat it as theirs and don't want to give it back. And as soon as you have to ask more than twice, you sound like a nag and they start to treat you like one. You have to lend without expectation; only then will you not be disappointed.*

I THOUGHT WE WERE FRIENDS

Wendy: Twenty-five years I'd known this girlfriend of mine: our children were the same age, we lived around the corner from one another, we both got divorced and we were both there for each other. She then meets this guy and I've never seen her since. I met the guy once, they went off and got married, I wasn't even invited to the wedding. I did see her and speak to her about it and all I got was this kind of blank response. I feel kind of used really—it's very hurtful. I just don't know whether I should wipe it and say that's it or really try and do something about it. It's really made me question what friendship is all about. It was twenty-five years and we really did see each other every day.

LUCY: She needs to be really straight with her. The thing that I heard was that she's hurt. She's been really hurt, but she hasn't said that. No point in making the friend wrong for leaving her out, but if she's vulnerable with her and says, 'Listen, I just want you to know that I'm really hurt. What went wrong?'. Sometimes when you're vulnerable with people they open up to you. Don't attack her, just tell her how you're feeling. Sometimes the one thing we really want to say is the one thing we're not saying.

MAX: I once saw a great piece of wisdom written on the back of a toilet door, and it said, 'If you love someone, let them go...'.

JV: Sting turned that into a song. Sting must have been in the same toilet.

MAX: 'If they come back they're yours forever, and if they don't come back, well, maybe you never had them anyway.'

JV: So, just let her go and let her come back in her own time.

MAX: Just play it cool and if she's fair dinkum she will eventually come back. If she doesn't, well, tough luck.

JV: When friendship ends, sometimes there's no way of addressing it. It's just gone.

MAX: Well, true friendships never really end. You can pick up with someone twenty, thirty, forty, fifty years down the track—and I have done this with someone I hadn't seen for a long period of time. It's almost as though it was only yesterday you were last in contact.

WARREN: Max was pretty right. I've had a lot of this happen with mates. Once they partner off with girlfriends and become fiancés and marry, you drift away. You have to become friends with the girlfriend, the new partner. New partners change your allegiances with your old friends. Then tragedies happen, divorce or worse, and suddenly the friendships change or old friendships assume new meaning. That's **life:** we reinvent ourselves as we go. The person in the new relationship probably doesn't realise the distance that has developed between her and her old friend. She's wrapped up in the new thing and doesn't realise that the old friend is out in the cold.

PEARL: Sometimes you, the old friend, know too much. You know all about them from their old life and they're trying to have a new life and they don't want all that old stuff around them. You're the keeper of the secrets and the very fact that you've helped her so much becomes kind of a burden to her. She may not even realise it, she just distances herself a little because of that. Sometimes the more you help someone out, the more they resent you for it later on. I wouldn't say anything. It'll play itself out and I think if the friendship is that strong, she'll be back.

JV Everyone's had this one. Friendship can survive all kinds of challenges and then come unstuck on something that mightn't seem like much at all. Friendship is fascinating. Some friendships are cast iron and better than family, but many are based on not much at all and can evaporate fairly quickly. It may just be that years go by and the friendship is not really challenged that much. But as soon as it is, it's gone. There's a lot to be said for letting it play out and when the time is right, that friendship will be there again. If it's not, then that tells you everything you need to know about that friend.

YOU FIX IT, WE'LL FIX YOU UP

Pam: We're renting from very dear friends and it's a long-term rental. When we moved in they said 'If you ever repair anything, we'll reimburse the cost'. We've paid for plumbing repairs, never got reimbursed. We paid for paint to fix up the fence, never got anything. We find this very difficult because they're very close friends.

NEIL: Keep the receipts and pay the rent minus the repairs. If the rent's two hundred, you've spent one hundred on the plumber. Give them one hundred plus the receipt for the other one hundred.

SARAH: Whenever you're doing something like this with friends, you have to sit down and talk about these things in a businesslike way. Make an appointment with them to discuss it. Don't try and do it when they've invited you over to dinner. Ring up and say, 'I want to come over and talk about the property. Can we do it at four tomorrow afternoon?'.

That way you're putting it on the agenda, you're making them think about it, and you're removing it from the friendship.

JV: You've thought about this.

SARAH: Been there, stuffed that up.

BRIAN: There is an unwritten law here. I'm sure she's paying less than the market rate and, if so, then you've got to wear some of the smaller repairs. If it's friends and they're doing you a good deal and you don't have to put up with the kind of things you might from a bad landlord or agent or that kind of thing, then you've got to expect to pay for the leaky tap or fix it yourself.

I'm thinking of getting 'Been There, Stuffed That Up' done on T-shirts. Business with friends is always tricky. You can't get indignant with them as you might with the real estate agent down at the shops. I think you've got to take a step back and clear this up. As Sarah says, make an appointment to talk about the house. It's their asset and they should be taking it seriously as well. I would add, don't meet as two couples either. One from each party, turn up with the receipts, a lease if you had one, get one if you don't, and talk it through. If you're worried about the friendship and the house, you're going to have to do this.

BASTARD!

Karen: I was having a coffee with a girlfriend one day, just having a chat about family and things like that, and I happened to mention that a couple of my sisters had babies before they were married. And she asked me what my parents' morals were like. I'm just wondering what some people would have replied to that. I was actually quite polite. I just said their morals were pretty good, thank you.

JV: And did this conversation take place in 1947?

KAREN: I thought I might have been back there, I had that feeling. I thought, am I in a time warp or something? I could have said lots of yucky things, but I didn't. I just said, actually their morals are pretty good.

ANDREA: As a comeback you could say, 'Well, my parents' morals were impeccable, but I think your parents' teaching of manners was atrocious'.

JACKY: I love good moral stories and my family were always very supportive of anybody in difficult circumstances when we were growing up. Perhaps her friend mis-phrased what she was really trying to ask, and perhaps we'll give her the benefit of the doubt and suggest that she might have been asking if her friend's family were going to support the daughters in this other state or had they been shunned by the family, turned away and told, 'Look, you go and look after yourselves'...I just think you have to give people the benefit of the doubt.

DAVID: Whenever that kind of thing happens, you can buy yourself some time to come up with the comeback by feigning ignorance. You say, 'What do you mean?'. You look completely confused. They then have to explain themselves and usually look worse and you've got time to come up with something good. Something like, 'Isn't it interesting how legitimate birth is no guarantee of good manners?'.

JV Nice phrasing, David. She could have thrown it straight back at her: 'Oh my parents were bastards—not literally—not like their grandchild'. Friends surprise us: we've been going to yoga together for years, we've been in the mothers' group, we've gone camping every holiday for ages and then they say something that makes you realise they have a very different value system to you. Perhaps it never came up before or perhaps you just haven't noticed. Can you be friends if you differ markedly on religion, politics, social values, views on raising children? Yes, but you're going to have to have the conversation about it and see where you are after that.

IT'S JUST ME! GOT THE KETTLE ON?

Alex: I often go and visit these friends, just drop in, but they never return it—they never drop in on me. Do I need to issue an official invitation or what? I'm Greek and we like to drop in. I might go once a fortnight or something and stay for a few cups of tea, but they don't drop back. I just want to know what's going on there.

JOHN: I'm Greek also and Alex can come over to my place any time and I'm willing to come over if he wants—and I'll cook him a good spanakopita, that's spinach pie.

JV: So this is a Greek thing?

JOHN: It is, but it seems more our parents' generation, I think, and it's falling away a bit, unfortunately.

JV: I wouldn't have thought that today in Sydney there was a lot of dropping around. If people come to my house, they tend to call first. With close friends and family it doesn't always have to be prearranged, but you'd call and say, 'We're coming over that way. You doing anything, cup of tea?', that kind of thing.

JOHN: I agree, but I remember when I was young and it often used to happen with all the relatives. They used to come over and it was like, well, what wind brought you over? That was the expression. It is something I miss, anyway. I'm willing to come over to Alex's any time. Alex should stick to it. He should not worry about them and keep dropping over if he likes to.

MICHELLE: I disagree with both Alex and John. I'm from a Greek background too, and yes, it's true, our parents' generation used to do it, but they hated it. Well, not hated it, I shouldn't be that extreme.

JV: But they put up with it?

MICHELLE: They put up with it. People would drop in at inopportune times and you just had to wear it and put off anything else you had to do and accommodate these people. And people used to talk about it behind their backs. They would just come and sit themselves down and not even ask whether or not you had the time for it.

JV: Do you think Alex is wrong to be dropping around?

MICHELLE: Well, I think, yes. I think the fact that they're not coming round, they're trying to tell him something and he's not getting the message, unfortunately.

(JV: We rang Alex back to see what he was thinking.)

ALEX: Where I'm coming from on this is, you know, it's like the thing about a backyard thing where you control what happens. Like now society's come to where the clubs, the pubs, the internet—all this stuff is taking control of people's behaviour—rather than the spontaneous behaviour of people coexisting with each other, you know. With my Greek origins, if I have to ring up and say, 'Can I come round to have a cup of tea?', I'm not going to do that. If I have to do that with a friend, I'm not going to go there, period.

JV: But that might be your approach to it. What if it's not their approach to friendship? How do you balance that?

ALEX: I agree. I just like the Mediterranean spontaneous sort of thing where there's no protocol, there's no prearrangement. Back in the village things used to happen at the drop of a hat, you know? And it was great, because there was no prearranged, predetermined thing to happen at 7 pm. I think too much technology has come into people's lives, it's stopping that spontaneous thing where I can drop around, have a cuppa tea, how're you going, you still alive? And go off again, you know. I think we've lost something when you can't do that.

I've heard people comment that Melbourne is kind of a drop-in city, but in Sydney you phone ahead. I must admit that with busy lives I can't quite see how you can ever drop in and expect anyone to just be there and available for a cuppa and a bit of a chat. Alex may well be referring to a way of living that many might consider preferable—a village where social spontaneity is in order—but in cities today, I think even among close, old, intimate friends with nothing much to do on a Sunday, you still call each other up, you never just drop around.

LOVELY TO SEE YOU

Beryl: My husband has married-couple friends. She is really lovely and makes every effort to maintain contact with us and tease up social events—dinners and that kind of thing. But I avoid them like the plague, because he is a groper.

JV: A groper—and you don't mean a large blue fish!

BERYL: Well, I think as women, we have a built-in sleazeometer. He's the only person on the planet that I have this kind of a problem with, and it's just embarrassing. I do not want to confront him. I'm sort of pushing fifty and I would have thought all of this nonsense would have been over a long time ago. When I was younger, I just would have told him to get off, but now I don't want to offend the wife. And the last time they invited us over, I hid under the doona feigning illness and my husband said there were very few wives there. And I thought, I bet I'm not the only one.

JV: You think he's a serial groper?

BERYL: I think he could be.

JACKIE: Obviously she can't keep going on the way she's been going, she'll make herself ill. So confrontation is the only way, whether it's her or whether it's her husband. I'm surprised he hasn't already, actually. And I think it's going to be curtains for the friendship, because the wife just won't be able to accept it and the groping husband will just go into denial. I was in a similar situation once and that's precisely what happened, but you just can't go on like that and not confront it.

JV: But it seems as though it's getting to that point, doesn't it, that the friendship is kind of folding anyway, because she keeps trying to get out of dinner arrangements and all the rest of it?

JACKIE: And obviously there are other friends—a similar situation must be developing with all the other friends and acquaintances, and I'm sure this poor wife of the groping husband on some level does know. She just doesn't want to admit it. But Beryl's husband—I think he's being an absolute coward about this—he should be out there with clenched fists and confronting this creep.

JV: Is there anything wrong with Beryl's husband—you ring up and say, 'Mate, we need to meet for a beer'. And then you say, 'Look, this is not on'. So the wife doesn't have to know about it.

JACKIE: But I think he'll deny it.

JV: He can deny it. It doesn't have to be that you're trying to get him to confess, but the husband just simply has to deliver the message.

JACKIE: Just to alert him that we know what's going on.

JV: That you're right out of line and this is unacceptable. Change your behaviour or don't worry about it, we're not going to turn up.

JACKIE: Well I suppose that's one thing. But why would you bother with those people anyway? Just say what has to be said and turn your back on both of them.

MARGARET: What I suggest this lady do is get out her four-and-a-half-inch stilettos, she gets close to this guy one time, does a little stumble, lands her stiletto right on his foot and swings it around and says, 'Oh,

I'm terribly sorry, was that your foot?'. And he would never do it again. I used to do that in New York when I was groped on the train. I was always doing it. But *they* never did it again.

JV I'd have to say that my chivalrous side comes out here. Surely, if Beryl's got this sort of problem and feels she can't deal with it herself, it's up to her husband to say something. But then as soon as I say that, I wonder would I really be able to sit down with a bloke and say, 'Mate, stop groping my wife'? So then I think, don't women have to learn strategies to deal with this kind of thing? But as Beryl said, she thought those days were well past. Awkward all round, but I would also suggest that this sounds like a friendship going nowhere so perhaps just let it wither away.

CHAPTER EIGHT

NEIGHBOURS

A Brief History of Neighbours

Everyone's door was always open and the neighbourhoods rang with the sound of screen doors banging as kids from up and down the street ran in and out all afternoon long. What a lovely time it was when the streets were safe for children to roam in, their only threats the local flasher, the dipso-maniac priest, the gang of local bullies, the drunk drivers on their way home from the six o'clock swill.

We lived our lives with our neighbours. Early morning neighbouring dads would walk to the train station, Gladstone bags swinging, side by side. Freckle-faced Mercurochromed children would run to school in the opposite direction, stopping only to get tetanus from a rusty nail. Mums, with hair up in scarves, would wave them both off before retiring to the kitchen, tossing aside their floury aprons, for a cup of tea and a Bex. Feet up on a vinyl and chrome chair, the mums would while away the morning, chatting and gossiping, usually about the other neighbours: 'She's drinking, you know. Smells like a brewery'; 'You know he's lost his job. They have to take in boarders'; 'She was always a slut'.

Everyone knew one another and loved to pop in whenever they could: to borrow a cup of sugar, to offer some eggs when the chooks were laying, to bring over a casserole if Mum was poorly. The kettle was always on, a cuppa always on offer. Privacy was unknown.

Neighbours were always there to lend a hand. You might top dress the back lawn or you might rip the lawn up and concrete the lot. All the dads might get together to sand back and paint a fibro lean-to needed for seventeen-year-old country cousin Elsie who was coming to stay after getting knocked up by the Shire President.

You cared about what your neighbours thought, but you wouldn't want to be seen to be keeping up with the Joneses. There were lots of rules about what you could do with the house so as to keep the neighbourhood nice. Lawns were expected to be green and regularly mowed, and 7 am on Sunday was a perfectly good time to fire up the Victa. You didn't paint your place pink; normal colours like grey or mission brown with white window trims and spouts was all that was expected.

Everyone lived in a house in a street, except for some who came back from the War and got the idea that you could live in a block of flats (or, if built after 1970 with some nice white wrought iron on the balconies, a block of units). 'There goes the neighbourhood' referred to a likely drop in property value should renters or reffos move into the street—not that everyone was as obsessed with property value then as they are now. If you paid four hundred and eighty pounds for the place, ten years later it was probably worth around four hundred and eighty seven pounds, but no one really wanted the renters or the reffos to move in.

Then: your neighbour was just like you and you talked to everyone in the street. Now: you don't talk to your neighbours; you sue them.

NICE NEIGHBOUR, BAD DOGGY!

Rob: I have really lovely neighbours, but their dog craps on my front lawn. How do I approach them about it? I'm worried about spoiling the good relationship we have, but I really hate their dog poo.

ERICA: You wait until the neighbours are asleep, scoop up the dog poo and put it back on their **land:** put it back where the dog sleeps regularly. Dog rolls in it or sniffs it and recognises that it's his and that it's come back. You only need to do it once—this really works. See, you don't have a problem with the neighbours; you have a problem with the dog. Talk to the dog, deal with the dog. Always best to be subtle with neighbours, never direct.

SASHA: I had a barking dog problem and whenever it started up, which was often late at night, I would get around the streets and find out the address. I'd get the phone number from rates or wherever and ring them up and start barking down the phone.

(JV: Make sure you have a private number before you try this.)

GEOFF: Do the plastic bottle thing. Half-fill some bottles with water, upturn them and stick them around the yard. It doesn't work but it allows you to instigate a conversation with your neighbour, who will inevitably ask, 'What's with the plastic bottles?'. You can then say, 'I've heard it keeps dogs from pooing on your lawn. It may not be your dog, but there's some dog who does it every morning'. It's a gentle way of telling them to check what their dog's doing and where.

MIKE: A neighbour's dog loved my front lawn: every morning a lovely present from her. So I went to my local council and got a copy of the Dog

Act. I put it in an envelope and gave it to my neighbour one morning with a couple of plastic bags. 'Thought you might find some of this interesting,' I said—nothing aggressive. She came back a couple of days later, apologised and thanked me. We've been great neighbours ever since.

> **JV** Forget for a moment that it's about the dog. Look at how much thought people put into dealing with a problem with their neighbours. Never go in angry, half-cocked or at the wrong time. Sit back, take a week or two. Think about what you're going to do and what this is going to mean. You and your neighbours are together for years.

LET ME SEE YOU OUT

Roger: We live in a high-rise, and I'm not sure what to do when guests are leaving. Do you say goodbye at the front door or do you say goodbye at the lift door or do you ride down in the lift with them and say goodbye at the lobby door, or do you walk out to the street?

JV: Have you tried all five?

ROGER: Well, I just say goodbye at the door and press the lift button for them as a courtesy, but sometimes it feels like I should ride down with them. I mean when we lived in a house we'd walk up the front path to their car.

MICHAEL: I lived on the seventh floor of an apartment building, and I just feel each time to take a person to the lift and then let the lift disappear is very impersonal, and lacking in couth. I like to go down with them into the front foyer and take them to the front door, because that virtually is your front door in the building. And there's the added point of security. You don't know if they know how to get out of the building, and if they can close the door so that the security business will function correctly. But I just think it's very impersonal to put them into something like a vertical coffin, like a lift, and send them hurtling down seven floors.

VICKY: I have lived in a block of flats, and when people would leave, there would be the yodelling up and down the stairs: 'See you later!' 'Goodbye'. So I'd suggest that they should go down to the front door and say goodbye.

JV: But if it's a big building with a lift, you're not going to get the stair yodelling.

VICKY: You still get the lift lobby yodelling.

JV: So, I see, in fact going down is quieter, because they go all the way down, they get out the front door and they do it there.

VICKY: That's right, cuts out the yodelling.

JV We could do another book just on apartment living—and ninety per cent of it would be about noise. How to deal with the one inconsiderate fellow flat-dweller is always a challenge, but the solution usually involves the body corporate, some notices in the lobby and something which doesn't point back to any particular individual.

WHAT IF SOMEONE SEES ME?

Andrew: Is it okay to put my rubbish into someone else's wheelie bin? On garbage night, I go out with one bag that just won't fit into mine, and I sneak around feeling like I'm doing something really bad. Why is that? Am I breaking the law?

DAVID: I can't stand people putting garbage in my bin. I have a sign on the lid that says 'DO NOT PUT YOUR RUBBISH IN MY BIN'. I put the bin out and sometimes I go out later at night to put more in and it is now full.

JV: Can't you go and put yours in someone else's?

DAVID: I am not going to sneak around the street putting out my rubbish in someone else's bin. It's simply not right.

PAUL: Well I rang up my council when I had too much rubbish once, and they said you could put it in anybody else's bin. Originally the bins were supplied by council, they were council property. And I don't think you've got to go and bother people and ask them. Once the garbage bin leaves your yard and is placed in the street it belongs to the street. You can't sneak around people's backyards filling up their bins, but when they put them out, it's fair game.

JV Although there are only two responses here, this was a three-day debate on the radio. There were only two views: 'How dare you put rubbish in my bin?' and 'What's the big deal?' There are some councils who fine you if you have excess in the bin—you can't stick a bag on top or alongside—but all councils say that they don't care whose rubbish is in whose bin, as long as it's in a bin.

HANGING OUT YOUR CLEAN LINEN IN PUBLIC

Ben: I'm a painter, but it probably could happen to any tradesman. Sometimes you can be on the job out near the backyard or something, and in the mornings a lady will put her washing out on the line, and that afternoon, a big storm rolls over. Do I take the washing off for the lady or do I just leave it? People don't like you touching bits and pieces sometimes.

JV: I would have thought anybody would be so grateful if you got it in ahead of the rain.

BEN: Yes, but I've questioned a few people on it, and you can see some of them don't think much of the idea.

CHRISTINE: If it was a trusted tradesman, I wouldn't mind. If it was somebody I didn't know, yes, I think I might be a little offended.

KATH: Well, I think he should. It recently happened to me. We had some builders around the place and they needed to get access to where the clothesline was attached to the house, and they took the washing off, and I was very glad they did.

JV: I think it's a question of some people being embarrassed by their own undergarments.

KATH: As long as they don't run around the garden with them on their heads.

JV: That's right, as long as they're not doing anything that they can be arrested for.

PAUL: Well, I'm a tradesman, so I would say if they know the customer well, yes, they can bring the washing in. And usually they're able to do it in a big pile—as if you've done a very rushed job helping out—and don't fold it up because people don't like to pay tradesmen's wages for folding up washing.

JV I think if you're a tradesman, you should know if it's okay. You should have a fair idea of if this is the sort of client who would want you doing that, or it's the sort of client who'll give you a hard time and suggest that they're not paying you to bring in the washing. I often find tradesmen who work with different households and clients every day of the week are quite good at getting people quite quickly. If in doubt, leave it out.

MY HOME IS A TEMPLE

Rachel: *We're pulling up the carpet and putting new flooring down. What's the etiquette for shoes? I want to tell people to remove their shoes when they come inside. Do I ask them, model it myself, do I have to give them little scuffs like on aeroplanes? I asked everyone at dinner the other night and there was real resistance. Someone said that many people would be embarrassed about their socks or the stink of their feet, so I'm in a real quandary.*

EMILY: I enforce it. I went to Japan, and everyone takes their shoes off. So we started doing it at our house and there's a sign at the door, 'Please remove your shoes', there's a box there to put your shoes in and no one has any problem with it. I like the ambience of it, it's relaxed and it makes people feel relaxed. Some of the older ones baulk at it, like my father-in-law, but then I insist and off the shoes come and it's fine.

PAULINE: She thinks everyone's fine with it, but I bet she made that poor father-in-law totally uncomfortable. The floor is made to be walked on. If culturally expected, that's different, but we don't have that culture here, so people turn up with odd socks or the toes out of them. I think if she wants it that much she should supply scuffs for everyone, but really, what's more important to you, people or floors?

JV Funny how all new things can't be scratched, but then all new things get scratched a little and it doesn't matter. And all new things—shoes, cars, floors—only seem to get scratched a certain amount and then they don't get scratched any more. Although many homes do have a no-shoe policy—particularly with kids—I think it's hard to enforce as such. Does it really matter if one or two wander through fully shod?

PLEASE SIR, CAN WE HAVE A DIP?

Jan: We put in an above-ground pool a few months ago at our place. Now I've got a thirteen-year-old and a ten-year-old and a seven-year-old. And next door have about the same age group. And we're on good terms with the folks and all the rest of it. Occasionally they'll come and swim in our pool, but sometimes you just want it to yourself on a Sunday. The next-door kids pester us to come and have a swim. They hang over the fence, they keep asking or they just hang there and stare. I'm not sure how to approach the neighbours to get them to rein their kids in. I'm desperate.

ELIZABETH: I had friends who had four children and a swimming pool, and very popular they were. But they decided that they would make Sunday a family day so they had some quality time together. And all the kids told all their friends and all the neighbours that no one was allowed in the house or the yard on a Sunday. And it worked really well. This was a country town, so the message got out much more quickly. They had Sundays that were totally free, and it was just family. Nobody could even set a foot over the threshold unless they were part of the family.

JO: They should put in a flagpole. When the flag is up, the neighbours are welcome; flag down, stay at home. This means they can go next door, talk about the whole thing and deal with it then.

LINDA: Well, I don't think these people are seeing the whole picture here. What we did is we—'cause Christmas was coming up—we went to one of those department stores, and you can buy for under a hundred dollars, really cheaply, a two-foot swimming pool. That's two-foot high and it's like a couple of metres across. You wrap it up, you put it under the next-door neighbour's Christmas tree, and you say it's for the children, and then they've got no excuse coming over. And if the kids are looking over the fence, you just say, 'Oh, what about your own pool?'.

That's an interesting approach. Supply the missing infrastructure for your neighbours. The only problem here is if you feel as though you can't talk to the parents about it. Then you could try talking to the kids themselves and give them a definite rule. Risky!

WHAT'S EIGHT PER CENT OF TWO DOLLARS?

Greg: *If you're having a garage sale and you put the signs up and you've done all the work, but your neighbour starts bringing their junk over to sell—are you entitled to the sale proceeds? If they don't help with the garage sale, if they just dump their stuff and then disappear, do you keep a percentage for promotional costs, labour costs, and so on?*

JV: Well you've got your signs, haven't you? Thirty pieces of A4 paper, you've got half a roll of sticky tape, you've got an hour and a half walking around the neighbourhood sticking them up on telephone poles.

GREG: And then we've stood there all day from 7 am, we've put the folding tables out, they've done nothing.

JOHN: I've had this happen. A neighbour dropped a TV at our garage sale and he thought it was worth about fifty dollars. I sold it for five. He was pretty angry, but what was I meant to do? Haggle for him? Then I've had others who've said, 'Look, I'll drop this here, if you can sell it, great, keep the money'.

SCOTT: I don't have a big problem with neighbours bringing stuff over. I've got a bit of experience with art galleries, and I'd suggest charging a commission as they do, anywhere between forty per cent and sixty per cent.

JV: Yes, well I reckon Greg has done all the work, he's set the whole thing up, he stands out there from seven o'clock in the morning till five in the afternoon, I think a sixty per cent commission's pretty reasonable.

SCOTT: Exactly! Overheads directly resulting from representing the seller as their agent and a commission is the way to go.

BRIAN: I had a mate bring over a set of golf clubs and I let them go for five dollars when he wanted fifty. He wasn't happy, but what am I meant to do? Sit there haggling with people? They weren't worth fifty bucks.

JV Difficult! I'd have lawyers standing by at 7am when the neighbours started seeing you as a hard rubbish day alternative. Does anybody ever have a communal garage sale? A few houses, a whole street, an apartment block? An annual event, could be a lot of fun.

CAN YOU KEEP YOUR SWEAT TO YOURSELF?

Matthew: I live in a block of units where we've got a communal sauna, spa and pool, and there's a sign saying 'Please sit on a towel when you enter the sauna'—but it's largely ignored, James, and I can't go in there. I can't go in and sit in pools of other people's sweat. And I just don't know how to approach them.

DANIEL: I think it's an absolutely repulsive habit. It's the same as sweat on gym equipment, and you should just say something straight away, because not only is it repulsive, but it's dangerous: it's unhygienic, disease-ridden. You'd have to say something...

JV: But it's very difficult, isn't it, because it's one thing saying it in a gym—where you're coming and going—this is a block of flats he's got to live in. He turns around and says to one of his fellow residents, 'Look, can you just use a towel?', and it's an incident.

DANIEL: But it's an incident that you have to go through once so it doesn't happen again, because it does pass on diseases. It is not clean, and you don't want to be sitting in a puddle of sweat. I can relate exactly. I was on my honeymoon recently and we were at a swimming pool in Bangkok and there was a lady actually hawking up phlegm and spitting it in the swimming pool. And after that you're not going in the pool, and you don't want to have your enjoyment of the sauna or the spa ruined. You just have to say, 'Listen, it's not hygienic, it is dirty, and please don't do it'. And if they don't like it, well, maybe they won't come back and you're winning on all sides.

SUE: I think he could just discreetly put a flier into everybody's letterbox in the unit block, telling them how unhygienic it is not to take a towel into the sauna.

JV: It always looks good in the brochure, doesn't it? Beautiful apartment building: an unrippled pool, free of swimmers; a spa with a lithe-limbed couple, six towels each folded neatly nearby; a sauna with an attractive model pouring water on the hot rocks, tucked into her towel with another turban-like on her head. Move in and it probably only takes one afternoon with sixteen kids thrashing about in the pool, a sighting of a fat hairy slob pulling himself out of the spa, and the discovery of a large pool of someone else's sweat in the sauna to make the area seem not as welcoming as it did in the publicity. The difficulty with all apartment issues is that you may be right in wanting others to behave differently, but you don't want them to know it was you issuing the orders. So the flier is good, I would have thought. Large, new signs with the rules clearly stated would also help. It's not me complaining about your lack of towel, it's just the rules.

BUT IT'S MY MUSIC, RIGHT?

Julie: I've always lived in a house and I've moved to a flat for the past year, so I don't know the etiquette. I've always been quiet, I know my neighbours, all of that, but last Tuesday it was my birthday, right? And so my nephew, a twenty-year-old who plays drums in a band, he came over and we proceeded to play music and sing two-part harmonies.

JV: Nice...

JULIE: Very nice. I thought it was nice and then the police came knocking on the door.

JV: Now what time of the day or night was this, Julie?

JULIE: It was ten to one.

JV: What, in the morning?

JULIE: Yeah, it was a Tuesday.

JV: Ten to one at night—you mean am—you were singing?

JULIE: But I don't get my neighbours. They had to send the police. Couldn't they just come and knock on the door?

JV: Was it loud?

JULIE: Well, we were singing along with records.

JV: So the record player's up loud, and you're standing in there going, 'Nah, nah, nah...', at ten to one in the morning and you're upset the police came.

JULIE: One of my neighbours couldn't just come up and say, 'Excuse me...', instead of sending two policewomen over?

JV: Have you spoken to the neighbours since?

JULIE: No, I just smile at them.

JV: And they haven't said anything about it.

JULIE: No. Is that flat etiquette, though?

STEPHEN: I don't think the question is whether the police should or shouldn't have been called. I think she probably concedes that, but whether they should have put the dressing gown on, got out of bed and come round to her door at nearly one in the morning. Who wants to get up that late? Just call the cops on the phone right by the bed, that's much easier. I think it's a question of ease, that's what's going on.

JV: I wonder whether we should check with the police. Do the police want to be called to that sort of thing? I've got a vague sense that they do, because they don't want a situation to get out of hand where someone's gone to try to interfere and often at that hour of the day alcohol's involved and it can get a little worse, but I'm not too sure on that.

SUSAN: Why should the quiet neighbour have to, as Stephen said, get out of bed, put on their dressing gown, go down the hall and knock really loudly on the door, and probably not even be heard?

JV: Do you think Julie's well out of line here, taking any umbrage at all?

SUSAN: Oh, I think she is. I think the question **is:** why doesn't she look at the clock and just turn it down a bit?

JV: That's right. At ten to one, whether it's your birthday or you've just turned fifty or whatever it might be, a block of apartments on a Tuesday night...

SUSAN: Yeah, I've had neighbours say the same to me, and I say I'm not going to climb out of bed at 2 am and crawl around the neighbourhood and knock on the door and you're not going to hear me.

JV: But I've had the circumstance where I've had to go in next door and bang on the door, and I've got—it's not abuse—but it's been very confrontational and it hasn't stopped a thing.

SUSAN: Exactly. You know that you're going to have a confrontation.

JV: If anything it's escalated it.

SUSAN: And you're just trying to get some sleep, and you think, ugh, I'm not going to do it. I've been the noisy one too, and I say it from both **sides:** if the police come to me when I'm noisy, well fair enough.

DAMIEN: I think they're right to protest, and I think the lady should have shut up at ten to one in the morning. But for goodness' sake, stand on your own two feet, get out of bed and go and see her. The police aren't our servants. If you have a butler, send him, but the noise is next to you, it's your house, go and see about it yourself, don't go to the police.

JV: That's why I wondered whether it would be worthwhile checking with the police, do they actually want to be called or not.

DAMIEN: Well, I think you can use your own judgement there. They obviously knew who the neighbours were—well, you'd have a fair idea who the neighbours were—and if you're afraid of getting a punch on the nose, well and good, call the police, but it's just a couple of people singing to records, it's not like it's a rave party going on. But people call the council and they call the police—anything but face their own lives themselves. Get out there and do it.

On this one I'd thought I'd check with the police. They have no trouble about being called out to this sort of incident. They want you to call them. I have on several occasions tried to intervene and it doesn't do anything. The party continues, it gets louder, people abuse you for turning up and asking them to be quiet at 2 am. Let us remember that if you're being loud at 2 am, there are often drugs and alcohol involved. Though I perfectly understand the view that says you should deal with your own neighbours yourself, I wouldn't do it again and would always ring the police to deal with issues of noise.

WHAT DON'T YOU GET ABOUT DRIVEWAYS?

Richard: I live near a medium-sized shopping centre. People constantly park over my driveway, all the time. There're signs up, it doesn't help. And then people get aggressive when you tell them off.

BARBARA: I have a disability sticker. I had so much trouble with people parking in my space I got some pre-printed sticky labels. They read, 'You're in my parking spot, would you like my disability too?'. I stick it onto their windscreen so they're shamed while it's on there and they have to try to get it off. Sticks in the mind.

JV: So 'You're parked in my driveway, would you like my mortgage too?'.

BARBARA: Maybe. I'd worry about aggression. When I do it, they're not there and they can't tell where I might be, but it's clearly his driveway and so he might cop it worse.

MALCOLM: I used to be in this situation and, seriously, I let people's tyres down.

JV: But that only works on that individual and it blocks up your driveway for longer.

MALCOLM: Yeah, but sometimes you don't care. You just want them to be held up and annoyed like you. I don't know, he should buy a big four-wheel drive and just go straight over the top of them.

KAREN: It's a bit of a nuisance, but he could park his garbage bins or get some witches' hats or something. At least that would cut it down to only the most determined who were prepared to get out and move the bins. It puts you at the advantage then when you catch them, because it's clear they had to move the obstacle to park there. They are doubly in the wrong.

JV I find it hard to believe that people would be so stupid and inconsiderate as to park across someone's driveway, but they do. It's even illegal to park across your own driveway in your own car. Unfortunately, all solutions are likely to get an aggressive response. Considerate people don't do it in the first place. Perhaps some further obstacle will at least cut down the instances.

CHAPTER NINE

LOVE AND MARRIAGE

A Brief History of Love and Marriage

For many generations love and marriage occurred only between men and women—and it had little to do with the couple themselves. Two fathers would get together and arrange the matter. The father cursed with a daughter would be relieved that someone, usually a much older man of fifty or sixty, would take his daughter off his hands so long as the father supplied six good milking goats. The daughter would become the man's wife, attaining a status somewhat lower than that of a good milking goat, but higher than any daughter she may subsequently produce. Love had not yet been thought of.

In recent centuries, in some of the more frivolous societies, it has become acceptable for men and women to deal directly with one another. However, there were many rules to ensure that no one married above or below themselves. It was also important that each party remain entirely ignorant of sex until the wedding night. If a young man wanted to get to know a young lady, then he would put brilliantine in his hair, call on the family on a Sunday before Evensong and request permission of her father to 'step out with her'. Stepping out, a slang expression discouraged by the Church Elders, included perhaps a walk along the towpath by the canal, a visit to a local monument for fallen soldiers or being allowed to walk together to Evensong two steps in front of the parents. Any of these activities in combination meant that the young couple were engaged and they would be married as soon as Lent was over.

The wedding was a riotous affair for everyone except the couple. The entire village drank all night, banged saucepans and waited for the husband to hang a bloodied sheet out of the bedroom window, at which point the village would cheer and go home. The couple would finally be left alone; a precious time during which they could find out each other's first names, and a little about one another: she's a brooding hysteric; he's subject to fits of violence.

Once married, it was forever. Divorce was something Americans did and for Catholics there was no such thing. You were allowed to die, however. There were Widowers—whose young wives had usually died during childbirth—who would wait a respectable interval, perhaps a week or two, and then marry the spinster sister of their dear-departed wife. There were Widows, but it was considered to be their fault when their husbands died in the War or in an industrial accident or of syphilis. They were encouraged to wear black until they themselves died, lest they turn into temptresses for wayward husbands. They were never invited out again.

A confirmed bachelor was a man who lived with his mother and worked as a floorwalker or buyer of women's dresses in a large department store. He loved the theatre and perhaps kept a small pied-à-terre in town. He was always very neat, drank sherry, and the women in the family adored him. He knew actors by name and had conversed with them. He was definitely homosexual, but the word had not yet been invented. Men were sometimes found in compromising positions with their valets, but that was put down to years of inbreeding in the upper classes and could be treated by sending the offender on a tour of Europe. Some classics professors knew of the habits of the ancient Greeks, but those texts were kept locked up in the college library and were only shown to post-graduates after a glass or six of port.

It had occurred to no one that women might form a liaison of any kind. Occasionally two women, spinsters, would share a house and a cocker spaniel for many years, but that was just for company.

Then: marriage was largely a property deal. Now: things have become quite loose and it won't surprise anyone if soon it's acceptable to marry your pets.

WHEN EXACTLY SHOULD I CALL YOU?

Stephen: Boy meets girl; girl gives boy phone number. When does boy ring back? Monday seems too keen, Tuesday a bit wishy-washy, Wednesday downhill run to the weekend, Thursday too late and Friday you're off to meet another phone number.

JV: In what you say there's never a time to call back.

STEPHEN: Well, you call back and the women sometimes act as if it's weird. It's like you're some kind of desperate guy who calls women back. If you were any good, you wouldn't be calling. Can you call on Sunday or is that just out?

LIZZIE: The faster you call back the better. If you like a woman and you've got the number, the quicker you call back the more likely you are to get what you need. Can't call too **soon**: Monday's great, makes them feel special. Monday's a great day to call.

JANE: Not Monday morning, nine o'clock though. Let them have Monday to chat about it with the girls, discuss whether you're going to call and whether she really wants you to call. Then you call Monday night about eight o'clock and you've got an update for everyone the next day; Tuesday, before midday, at the latest.

HILLARY: Ring back on Monday night, and if you don't get the vibe, let it go. Make a suggestion of getting together, but keep it low **key**: a movie, a movie on Thursday or on the weekend, like on the Sunday, not the whole Saturday night thing.

MONICA: If he hasn't rung by Wednesday: next! You have to call by Wednesday to set up the weekend. They need to know what they're doing, but don't try later than Wednesday, that's desperate stuff.

PETER: He's got it all wrong, he's calling back with intent. Call back on Sunday, not with any purpose or scheming, but just to say thanks: 'Thank you, it was a great night, great to meet you, I just wanted to see how you were and say thank you'. It really takes the wind out of their sails, you can have a straight ahead conversation and the next meeting will either flow out of that or it won't. You ring up with the date in line and it's awkward.

JV I've seen several films recently where there's been the number exchange and, of course, now it's mobile phone numbers that are exchanged. The characters in these films both rang the mobile almost immediately, as they were in the cab going home, as they were walking down the street still in view. Very romantic and silly and moves straight over the whole 'When do I call?' thing. It's no longer a problem, you already have called, now you're in a relationship. Again, it's interesting how mobiles are changing these issues all the time. You don't have to call, you can text anytime: witty little message; respectful thanks. So it's not quite 'The Phone Call', it's keeping in touch, it's seeing if there's anything there or was it just the daiquiris talking?

SO, DO YOU HAVE TWO HEADS OR WHAT?

Robert: I was internet dating and I included my photo, and I'd been chatting with a few people or messaging a few people, and it got to the stage where I asked one particular person for a photo, *please. And she got really quite annoyed. She said, 'Why do you guys always insist on a photo?'. So I guess my issue is if one person puts up a photo, is it reasonable to expect that a lady would also put up her photo and not get too anxious about it?*

BRENDAN: I think there're a couple of protocols. First of all, the photos have got to be there, you've got to ask quick, got to insist on it and, secondly, there must also be telephone communication before you meet up—they were basically my rules. I put my photograph up and hid it. You can put it on and you can have it hidden—basically because I work in the medical business and I didn't want potential patients of mine coming and saying 'Oh, I saw your photo on the internet'. But once I had engaged with someone over the email, and I can see that there is at least some potential for some kind of conversation or relationship, then photos are revealed one-on-one, but nobody else gets them.

JV: And so you shouldn't be offended—you're not offended if someone says 'Could I see a photo?'.

BRENDAN: No, not at all. Obviously with women, of course, the image is such an important deal and you might be getting along famously until the point of the photo and then they're worried that as soon as the photo goes up, the guy will lose interest. If that's the case, then the guy would lose interest when you sat down next to him at a coffee shop anyway.

JV: Yes, I suppose, but you also feel as though perhaps your personal presence can overcome photos, people don't necessarily photograph well.

BRENDAN: Sure. Even if that's the case and that's what the guy is saying, well, maybe he's not the guy for you anyway. So stop flogging a dead horse.

JV Internet dating has evolved so quickly. When I first started 'The Form Guide' internet dating was a new thing and people were very uncomfortable about it. Now, the qualms are gone. If you're someone who doesn't like the photo exchange thing, then I'm sure there's a site out there where you can meet like-minded people. A friend of mine took an internet date to a dinner party with old friends of hers. The question came up during the night, 'How did you two meet?'. The friend said it never occurred to her that she would prefer not to admit at this point that they were cyber buddies. The date smoothly said, 'Through mutual friends'. They're still seeing each other.

WAS I THAT BAD AT THE HEN'S NIGHT?

Suzie: Something strange—well, I think it's strange—happened to me. I was invited along to some friends' engagement party, I was invited along to the hen's night, but then missed out on an invitation to the wedding.

JV: Wow! How many were invited to the engagement party?

SUZIE: There would have been about thirty or forty people.

JV: And at the hen's night?

SUZIE: Hen's night—probably, I don't know, fifteen girls.

JV: So you're in the top fifteen.

SUZIE: Well, I thought I was, but I've obviously missed out on the big occasion.

JV: And do you know how many people got invited to the wedding?

SUZIE: There were probably sixty or so. And I was told that there were a lot of relatives or more senior people, that sort of thing, but I haven't been given any apology or any reason why.

JV: And when you were at the engagement party and the hen's night, was the conversation that, you know, oh, the great day's going to be terrific and I can't wait to see you and it's all going to be exciting? Was the general assumption that you were all going to be there?

SUZIE: Yes, exactly. And then some other people I know got an invitation and I was waiting for mine—but it never came. And there was never anything said to me along the lines of 'Oh, well, sorry, you know, there were too many people', or anything like that. And I asked a few other friends and they said, 'Oh yes, that's normal for people to have a bigger engagement and a smaller wedding'. And other people were thinking along the same lines as I **was**: that no, it's generally a smaller engagement, bigger wedding.

JV: I would have thought you'd have been invited to both, particularly if you were in the last fifteen on the girls' night out. If you're in the top fifteen friends, I would have thought you'd get a go. Have you had any contact with the bride since?

SUZIE: I have, not a huge amount, but she was all very nice and I think she was just trying to avoid the issue really.

JV: And you feel a bit hurt about this.

SUZIE: A bit confused, really. I don't know, I don't think I've done anything wrong. I thought I took a nice present along to the engagement. And I paid for everything and did all that sort of stuff, so I don't think I've done anything to offend anybody.

I thought this was an interesting problem, because—like a lot of the wedding questions—you realise that virtually everyone has a slightly different idea of what's expected. Even though weddings come down to the same fundamental events, everyone's got a slightly different interpretation. Suzie's expectation is that if invited to the engagement party and, in particular, to the hen's night, you're going to the wedding. However, many people called in to say that that's not the case. Often now, the pre-wedding celebrations are for those who aren't invited to the wedding. The wedding might be small, only for the family and the most intimate friends, the engagement party or hen's night is a big bash for all. Suzie feels as though she was a close friend and should have been invited, but that may not be what the bride-to-be was thinking.

REALLY? MY MOTHER AND HER MOTHER WILL HAVE A SAY IN THE WEDDING?

David: A couple of weeks ago I got engaged. And I guess we've got a fair bit of planning to go ahead with at the moment, but I was wondering what level of involvement my future mother-in-law and possibly my own mother should really have in this whole event.

JV: You're planning a wedding and you're curious as to what level of involvement to expect from your mother-in-law and mother. What do you think they should be doing?

DAVID: Well, I'm not really sure. I think they should do a little bit, but they are doing a fair amount at the moment—and I'm a bit worried...

JV: So at the moment they're suggesting venues...

DAVID: A couple, yes.

JV: And they're suggesting dates...

DAVID: Yes, and having to see them and all that sort of stuff.

JV: Having to see the venues? Oh, so if you suggest a venue they want to come and see it—you know, Rose Bay Yacht Club or whatever it might be. We'd love to go down and have a look, Rooty Hill RSL, let's go over and check it out. And so you're finding this surprising?

DAVID: Well, both my fiancée and I are the first children in the families, so we haven't had any experience of this.

JV: Who's footing the bill?

DAVID: The two parents are splitting the bill, pretty much down the middle.

JV: Right! And you're surprised that they want to know what's going on.

DAVID: Yes.

JV: David, I would take the level of involvement that they have now and just draw one of those graphs that go sharply up towards the date of the wedding. It'll just escalate like that, I think. Exponentially I think their involvement will increase as the date of the wedding gets closer, but let's see what others think. Are you looking for strategies to try and minimise their involvement?

DAVID: Oh, look, we're up for any help.

JV: But what you actually want, you'd like their involvement to be a little less?

DAVID: A little less, yes.

PETER: We're going through the same experience at the moment—our daughter's getting married in July—and I think he ought to take some good advice from both mothers.

JV: So, you're the father and the father-in-law, and what you're suggesting is that there's good advice to be had here.

PETER: Well, yes. We've been to some weddings lately where things haven't been organised properly, like people forget to arrange cars to pick up the oldies, or there's not enough food at some of the functions we've been to and half the kids are going down like ninepins 'cause they've got no food in their belly and they've had three glasses of champagne. I'm serious! It's a little bit easier for us, because we're wholly and solely footing the bill, which means it's not being run by a committee. So he's got some problems there, but he should take some good advice.

JV: It's true, isn't it, the young people, they think they know everything, don't they?

PETER: Well, my wife says that everybody these days wants to have a non-traditional, laidback wedding, but my wife said to me yesterday—we got married in '77 and we were the same—but she said, 'I regret not having a traditional veil and all that sort of stuff'.

JV: But I reckon that every wedding I've ever been to, four months before, it was a non-traditional, laidback wedding. And when I got there, somebody in white was coming down the church aisle.

PETER: Yes, you're quite **right:** the scale is going rapidly from one side of the pendulum to the other.

JV: But also, one of the things about a wedding is that everybody thinks, 'Oh no, I'll do it differently', and then you say, okay, you're going to have eighty people, there's got to be a service, actually the bride does want to wear a wedding dress, and so on. And it just multiplies into—guess what?—you're having a wedding.

CHARLIE: My suggestion to David is take as much advice as you can, 'cause I know it can get a bit much sometimes. So just pay them lip-service, but as long as he stipulates at the end of the day, it's his and the fiancée's day.

JV: You've got the final say over an event being paid for by the parents.

CHARLIE: Exactly. Because in the end it's their day, not the parents' day, and the parents just want to give them their day, that's why they're donating the thousands of dollars.

JV: This is always an interesting one, among other wedding things, someone at some point always makes this statement: it's their day, not the parents' day. But in actual fact, I'm sure that someone's about to ring and say, 'You know, it's not just their day; it is the parents' day', you know, like their child's getting married.

CHARLIE: It is the parents' day. Believe me, I know—coming from an ethnic background and marrying a different-yet-similar culture—you learn about weddings the way you don't want to. But you've just got to put your foot down at the end of the day, I've found, and say, 'Look, it's my day. I'm happy that you're paying for it, but I don't want this at the wedding'.

MARY: Yes, I think that's right. And as for the wedding, look, you might like to think it's your wedding—it's not. The wedding's not for the bride and groom; the wedding's for the family and everyone else. And traditionally the mother of the bride organises the wedding because usually it's the bride's parents who pay. But as there are two sets of parents who are footing the bill, he who pays the piper plays the tune. However, I would recommend they write down a wish-list. Give them a brief of what they want, relax, and let the parents organise it. Because in the end, that day goes very, very quickly, and most people can't even remember what happened, what with the excitement and the Champagne. Just chill out and let some others do it, but give them your riding orders.

MICHAEL: When there's a wedding there're going to be mothers: toss 'em in early, let 'em do battle and they'll wear it out, and just enjoy the wedding on the day. There's no way of getting out of it.

JV

When David asked his question in such a sweet innocent tone of puzzlement, I felt a paternal inner glow. Ah, David, I wanted to say, you remind me so much of myself. You have no idea of weddings, do you? I too had ventured into the wedding area with the expectation that we'd book a venue, find a church and hire some suits. So young I was and, like David, so ignorant of what lay before me. So, I took his question, knowing that the callers would soon set him right, with the rich satisfaction of the older man taking the younger under his wing and introducing him to the rituals of the tribe. In a way, all wedding questions have the same subtext. Is the wedding for the happy couple? Or is the wedding for the family and friends? Is it really a public ritual in which the happy couple simply have to play the part of the bride and groom and everyone else must be satisfied? I would venture to say that almost all happy couples start off by thinking it's their day and their wishes will prevail, but by the time she's walking up the aisle, they've found out that what Great-Auntie Maude thinks, how much Dad can afford, which day the bridesmaids and the reception centre are available, and the current fashion in cakes and veils, have somehow managed to dominate in a way that was not anticipated at all. A wedding is an excellent test for any couple. Any couple that can survive a wedding has a good chance at surviving a marriage.

DARLING, THERE'S SOMETHING
I HAVE TO TELL YOU

Charles: I'm getting married. Five or six years ago I had a fling, a one-nighter with my bride's younger sister. I've never told her. Should I assume that the girls have talked about it? But as the wedding gets closer I'm really getting churned up about it. Should I tell my fiancée? Should I talk to the sister?

CHERYL: Don't say anything at all and always remember that sister's birthday.

VINNIE: Deny it. Lie. Even if caught in bed, deny it; it's not what you think. He's joining the family, the sisters are going to be talking together for the rest of their lives. Don't bring it up, don't mention it, forget about it and if it ever comes up anywhere, deny it ever happened.

LINDY: It depends when he had the affair. Was there any overlap?

DAVID: He should watch 'The Bold and the Beautiful' for a week, he'll know exactly what to do. It wasn't him with the sister but his long-lost twin brother who's about to fly in from Acapulco to help him out.

PAUL: All successful marriages are built on trust so there's no better way to start than with a big lie and a cover-up. He's going to have to talk to the younger sister, and tell her never to mention it. If she already has, and his bride hasn't said anything, well then just leave it alone.

JV: But then it just sits there, ticking away. It's hardly clearing the air, is it?

PAUL: Yeah, well, maybe marriage is just a bundle of things you're too afraid to bring up.

DENISE: You can't talk to the sister because then you're colluding with her. He's got to go now, straight to the fiancée, and tell her. Life is long, there's so much time for this to come out and if he's worried about it now, in a few years time he'll be making excuses not to go to the sister's house and all sorts of things. If the relationship can't deal with this little blip, then it can't deal with much at all.

JV — I thought that in any relationship that got close to marriage there was a moment, usually during the period when sex is better than food, when in a laughing, loving way, the couple disclosed all former paramours and peccadilloes. If that happened and our groom didn't mention the sister, then he's in big trouble. If that moment hasn't happened and it's still to come, he's in big trouble. If he never tells her and one drunken Christmas Eve years down the track the sister says, 'I don't know what you see in him. He did nothing for me', he's in big trouble. Our thoughts were with this caller, and he elicited the deepest sympathy.

POPPING THE QUESTION

*Michael: I'm going to propose: tomorrow.
Do I have to have a ring?*

SALLY: Do people still propose when they're unsure? Doesn't everyone know now and the proposal is kind of a little mock ritual?

Have a little box and put a little plastic joke ring in it, and then go together to choose the real ring; much more romantic.

LEANNE: Perhaps just a smaller piece of jewellery, a lovely necklace which, when she wears it, she'll remember his lovely proposal. But I think you shop together for the ring now.

GREG: Big ask turning up with the ring. Do you really know what she likes? Do you have the faintest idea about diamonds and rings? And he hasn't got it by now, right? Big ask. He's getting married. It's risky enough as it is, don't ruin it by getting the ring wrong. Bad start!

With twenty-four hours to go, Michael is ringing a radio talkback helpline for advice. I get the feeling we're going to be hearing from him a lot as his life and marriage progress. Here's a typical situation where things have shifted: perhaps once if you could afford it you always had a ring there at the moment of proposal, but now mortgage often precedes marriage; there may not be a real moment of proposal; a bride might like to choose. There are many reasons why, when on bended knee proposing a life together, a man may not have yet troubled his jeweller.

THIS TIME OUR LIST IS AT...

Stella: *I've been invited to a work colleague's third wedding in fourteen years. The invitation came with a gift registry list at David Jones. Surely you don't have a gift list at a third wedding? And is it compulsory? Can I just buy some flowers or something?*

SAM: Should she have to give back the presents from the previous two? It's obvious what the problem is **here:** she's been cleaned out by the previous two weddings, needs to get started again. I would get a nice silver frame and print off a list of family lawyers. Sounds like it should be kept handy.

GORDON: Go to Dymocks and get a book on how to save your marriage and make it stronger over the years. I think you could also probably turn up with nothing and I don't know if anyone really notices. There's so much fuss around weddings that by the time they get around to opening the presents are they really going to check who brought what?

JV Well, for the thank you notes.

GORDON: Oh yeah, well, do the old switcheroo: take along your own card, rip one off a present and stick your own on in its place.

JV: No, I've got a better one than that: take a pen and, when no one's looking, just add your name to someone else's card; 'Love and Best Wishes from Amanda and Simon', and then you write, 'and Gordon'.

GRACE: It's going a little far wanting a list for the third wedding. But at any stage the bridal registry isn't compulsory. You should look at it, but if there's nothing there you want to give or you can afford it's perfectly all right for you to give something else.

ROBERTA: I agree with Grace, but I support the registry idea. My sister got married, this is back in the seventies, and didn't even think of a bridal registry and she got eight candle snuffers—it was the seventies!

JIM: Treat it like a maintenance operation. If you were at the first couple's and you got them a dinner set, ring her up and ask her is anything broken? Is the gravy boat still there? Do you need a couple of extra plates?

JV Wedding presents have become a difficult area. The days when a blushing bride would gush over four or five toasters, six travel rugs and eleven fruit platters at her family home are well gone. But a bridal register for someone who changes husband—do you need to buy a present for someone who changes husbands about as often as they change their car?

ARE YOU WORTH THE TRIP?

Daniel: My wife and I have been invited to a wedding this year: it's my wife's niece, who is a Sydney girl, and the young gentleman in question is from some remote NSW country town. So you would think that the choice of venue would be either Sydney or the country town, but, in fact, they're taking it to a resort island off the coast of Queensland, which means that there's expense involved for everyone. Accommodation is expensive on those islands, the flights there and back... It looks like it's going to cost us around two to three thousand dollars. Is it reasonable of them to do this or am I just a curmudgeonly old skinflint?

EMMA: I'm getting married in Bali in October, and anyone who doesn't want to go or who feels obliged to go or anything like that—honestly, I don't expect them to go and that's fine.

JV: And how did you indicate that in your invitation?

EMMA: Invitations are going out early, we've given everyone a verbal six or seven months' warning, indicating that it's going to be in Bali and to keep an eye out for great deals if you see any in the paper. If you feel like a holiday, feel free to join us. I don't expect anyone to go, but if they do I'll be more than happy. With your caller, I sensed the tone...I don't want anyone at my wedding who's feeling like they don't want to be there or anything less than excited about it.

JV: Can most of your family and friends afford this kind of thing?

EMMA: We've given everyone warning. We've sort of sussed out there're some great deals to Bali. You could basically go for a long weekend for less than a thousand dollars and we've definitely tried to find out if most of our family could.

JV: Do you expect a present as well?

EMMA: No.

GREG: No, I think that's completely wrong. You've got to have a wedding where it's somewhere reasonable that everyone can get to. That girl doing it in Bali, she doesn't get it. She's getting married, she's all excited, no one can say to her, 'Hey, I'm not coming' or 'I can't afford it'. It's her big day, they don't want to spoil it. And even if they are saying it, I bet you she's not hearing it. I think it's wrong to expect everyone to troop off wherever just because you're getting married. It's not just the cost, look at the time commitment.

PAM: I have been in this situation, where a dearly loved relative chose to have their wedding in Bali and expected everyone to go. We were the only family members who couldn't go because we had several young children and it was just beyond us. So we missed out on the whole shebang.

JV: I can hear Emma's excitement about wanting to do this, but surely there are going to be people in her life who miss out.

PAM: And we would have loved to have been there, and we really feel like we missed out on it; but the attitude was, well, if they couldn't be bothered saving up for it, that showed that they didn't really care. And that wasn't the case. They could have had a fantastic honeymoon and invited people who wanted to come with them to go and do that. We would have loved to go, but in reality, there are going to be people who you want at your wedding and who really want to be there, but they're not going to make it. I think it's a bit presumptuous to expect that everyone can get to some tropical location for your wedding.

As observed before, the wedding questions lead us to ask, 'Who exactly is this wedding for?' (see 'Really? My Mother and Her Mother Will Have a Say in the Wedding?' on page 194). Several callers organised weddings offshore because they didn't want family and a lot of fuss. The grumpy old uncle doesn't have much choice; he married into that family thirty years ago and the deal hasn't finished yet.

JUST THE CASH

Eve: A couple of weeks ago my parents got a wedding invitation and it said at the bottom of the invitation, no gifts, envelope preferred. I was just thinking, is that right, and how much money should you really give?

JV: I suppose, in general, you're meant to tuck into the envelope what you otherwise would have spent on a toaster.

EVE: It's quite hard, though, because they know who it's from, your name is on the card, so really it's a representation of you. I'm not sure what they're actually going to do.

JV: You think it's bad form to have the envelopes, to have the cash?

EVE: I think a lot of people think even having a registry is rude, but I think having a registry would be much more useful to someone—and much more polite than asking for money.

SALLY: This has been going on for ages. At my daughter's twenty-first we had a travel registry and people gave what they could afford to the travel agent and she's been off in Italy now for a month having a great time. Cash is fine. In Europe they pin money to the bride's dress. I think we're just a bit behind in that. Let the people have the money if they want it, and as far as the money goes, again, err on the side of generosity if you're in doubt. If you'd buy them a one-hundred-dollar gift then give them one hundred dollars.

JV: And you think people need to get over the whole idea that cash is somehow rude as a wedding present.

SALLY: Yes, I do, because we're different now. Often we've already set up our homes and we want other things in life. We want a holiday or we want to buy an updated car or pay money off our mortgage.

PAUL: Cash at the wedding, it's okay, but I think, once again, it's the height of rudeness to *ask* people for cash. I'm old-fashioned.

JV: We *have* moved on. When my parents got married they would have been setting up a house and that would have been quite literally setting up a house. They would have needed a set of cutlery. When I got married, I already had a set of cutlery.

PAUL: So did I, but I got a very good set of cutlery when I got married.

JV: But I had a good set of cutlery. You know what I had? I got given a set of silver cutlery at my wedding—it's still in the box. I don't need it. I don't use silver cutlery. It's very nice, but I've got a perfectly good set of cutlery that we use anyway.

NICK: Where I come from to give money is very common. Often what happens is a lot of the time the couple can't afford the wedding that they want, so they take a loan.

JV: So you're actually paying for the wedding.

NICK: Basically, what you do is, if they get catering for the meal, then you know that catering for you at the wedding will cost them about one hundred dollars. So, if you want to help them, you give them one hundred and fifty dollars.

ANN: My daughter and her fiancé have been living together for twelve months. They already each had a flat of their own, so they don't need extra toasters, etc. You put the money in an anonymous envelope and there's no real embarrassment.

JV: You've seen this done before?

ANN: We went to a wedding where they had a letterbox in the middle of the table and people put their envelopes in.

NICOLETTE: The cash, well, I'm Greek-Australian, so it's quite normal for us to give money. And as you said, you tend to have to give a bit more when you're giving cash, so you can't just give one hundred dollars, especially if a whole family's been invited, you almost have to do one hundred dollars a person.

JV: And do you understand that the gift is to pay for the wedding?

NICOLETTE: Well, it depends, I think. Things have changed. Years ago you bought presents because people literally needed the help to set up house, which is what would have happened when my parents got married. But now everyone's got everything, so people don't want the presents, they want the money. Now, that could be going to pay for the wedding, or it could just possibly be going to a deposit for a house, or it could be going to anything—could be going towards their honeymoon.

JV: So you think the minimum in the envelope is not one hundred dollars, it's more like two hundred dollars.

NICOLETTE: Oh definitely. We've got a family of six. There's absolutely no way you could put one hundred dollars in an envelope for six people.

JV: If all six of you were going to the wedding.

NICOLETTE: You'd almost have to give a minimum of three hundred dollars. But I like the other lady's idea about anonymous envelopes, because that way you can actually sit down and say, well, this is what we can afford...

JV There's a cultural background here. European cultures are perfectly happy with the whole cash thing. In many cultures, the community, the friends are paying for the wedding or the collection of cash is seen as a way of the couple getting their own place together. As usual the British middle class lot saw it as very insulting to suggest that the family couldn't pay for their daughter's wedding and instituted a set of strange rules about great-uncles buying silver cutlery sets. Today, when many are mortgaged before being married, giving a couple cookware and blankets could well be redundant. Interestingly, many still find the registry list at a major store a little off-putting, even though it's very common. I think that may be something to do with price. When there're lots of five-hundred-dollar items on the list and not enough fifty-dollar pepper grinders people get grumpy. But cash is definitely in—our happy couple may already have HECS debts and be locked out of the housing market because they're paying off the Barina—and a couple of hundred in the kick is far more deeply appreciated than an oversized fruit platter.

THE YOUNG MAN AND THE SEA

Brian: I need some help here. It's to do with my future son-in-law. I took him out on my boat fishing. It was a get-to-know-you fishing day. We went out with another guy, there were three of us. We were about a kilometre off Sydney Heads and he became violently ill and asked if I'd take him in. And at the same time we started catching fish. So I forgot about him underneath in the cabin, vomiting.

JV: What were you pulling in?

BRIAN: Trevally. We were on the trevally and we just couldn't help ourselves, so we forgot about Paul and he was actually dry-retching inside the boat. So what happened was we didn't bring him in. I actually put him on to a mate's boat who was going in, and he ended up in the hotel with the mate, 'cause the mate always calls in at the hotel on the way back. And, to cut a long story short, this story often comes **up**: should we have brought him in or should we have stayed out? Now the other friend...

JV: But he ended up at the pub, had a nice afternoon at the pub with your mate.

BRIAN: No, he got into trouble there, too, actually, James.

JV: What was his trouble at the hotel?

BRIAN: Well, he left his wallet on the boat, and there was four of them and they were pubbies and what happened was that he got into a shout with them, and it got round to his shout and he said, 'Oh, I don't have any money', and in the end my wife had to pick him up at the hotel. And I got a call from my wife abusing me. I got a call from my daughter abusing me and the problem is, James, my daughter's marrying this guy and I know this whole fishing trip incident is going to come up.

JV: So you want to know if you were an absolute bastard for not taking poor vomiting Paul back in to shore? Or was Paul an inconsiderate wuss who should have kept his head down while the trevally were running?

BRIAN: Look, he ate two of the trevally that night and had four beers at the pub, he couldn't have been that bad. He did have concussion though.

JV: Concussion?

BRIAN: What happened was that at the boat ramp, putting the boat in, we didn't realise it but Paul slipped over down at Putney and he hit the back of his head on the boat ramp. And half of his problem I think was concussion, thrown in with the... If I'd known he had concussion, we wouldn't have taken him out.

JV: Gee, it's a complex story now, isn't it? Anything else you think is relevant?

BRIAN: Well, I'd only known Paul for about four weeks, the trip was a getting-to-know-you day, and my mate David said, 'How do you like him?' and I said, 'I don't really know him' and he said, 'Well, that's it. Let's stay here. He's not the boyfriend for your girl'. So I must admit that influenced my thinking, but the main reason we didn't take him in was the fish.

MICK: He did the right thing, but there's another rule of the sea that he should have followed: if you've got a mate and you're out fishing, the fish are running, and he starts dry-retching, he goes overboard for burly.

JV: So, is the rule of the sea if the fish are running, we're not leaving? Doesn't matter if he's concussed, he's down in the hold dry-retching?

CHRIS: I think you may as well call the wedding off.

JV: I think he's lost any chance at being a grandfather. I don't think little grandson's going to be down there learning to bait the hooks with grandpa, but did Brian do the wrong thing?

CHRIS: Right from the beginning and all the way through he did the wrong thing.

JV: I'm hoping at the wedding they might serve trevally.

SHANNON: It depends on the type of fish. The trevally is not something worth kicking out for. If it was snapper or kingfish, well, he could die in the cabin.

JV: So you're saying they made a very poor judgement on the type of fish. Mick said if the fish are running, he didn't say the type of fish. You think the type of fish matters?

SHANNON: Absolutely. Trevally aren't worth it, but if it was snapper or kingfish or something good, well, then you can definitely stay out.

JV This is a short version of something which had epic qualities to it. It took Brian around twenty minutes to tell this story and as it unravelled it got worse. We continued to receive much communication on Brian's story, all revolving around the same few issues. First, Paul could have died in the hull of the boat from dehydration—absolutely irresponsible to leave him unattended in such circumstances. Secondly, the fish are running and that's it—first rule of the fishing trip. Thirdly, risking someone's life for trevally is irresponsible, but for snapper perfectly understandable. These are areas well beyond my comprehension.

IT'S NOT MY MAIDEN NAME, IT'S JUST MY NAME

Leanne: *I've been married now for eighteen years and I never changed my name when I married. Banks, people who've been sending us Christmas cards for years, continue to send things addressed to 'Mr and Mrs Smith'. How can I get them to use my surname? I'm not Mrs Smith, I'm Leanne Jones. I've tried to tell some friends not to do it and they make excuses like it takes too long or they just drop the surname altogether. Is it that hard?*

MARK: I get addressed all the time as 'Mr My Wife's Surname', say 'Mr Brown', because she kept her name and she does all the business things. So, the mechanic or the bank rings up and says is that 'Mr Brown'? Well, it's not, but I don't really care about it.

JV: I guess it has to do with whether you're the one making the point; perhaps you have a strong enough sense of identity or whatever that it doesn't really matter to you. It's slightly amusing.

MARK: And it is hard today to keep track of who's done what. You've got friends in blended families, remarried friends, friends who've taken the partner's name, friends who haven't. It can become a bit too hard to keep track of, and maybe the recipient shouldn't get too offended. And when you're sitting down at Christmas writing out a hundred cards or something, it can all be too much.

PAULA: I think she should send out two separate cards, one from herself and one from her husband. That way her friends will get the message that she is her own individual person.

JANET: My husband always tells people that he wouldn't allow me to have his name. That's his standard joke, but otherwise, just go with the flow. You can't be making the point every time, like when you check into a hotel or something and they say 'Mr and Mrs Smith'. Just go with it.

PAMELA: I kept my own name and my theory is that a lot of women see this as an insult to them. It's like, well, we changed ours, why didn't you? They think you're a bit uppity and they think you think less of them because they didn't change their name.

KATE: Leanne's in good company. Queen Elizabeth is Elizabeth Windsor, and her husband is Philip Mountbatten. And if you ignore the other titles and you are addressing a letter to her, you wouldn't insult her by calling her Elizabeth Mountbatten because her name is Elizabeth Windsor.

JV: What about Charles and Andrew and Anne? Are they Windsors?

KATE: Yes, because Elizabeth Windsor's children, all her children were named Windsor. Their surname is Windsor. So it's Andrew Windsor and Edward Windsor and so on.

It's an interesting moment: here're people trying to make a point and trying to change how we operate to underline that a woman is not a man's property when married, but the society around them hasn't shifted. To make the point they have to insist on being called by their own original name, but then everyone else doesn't see it as a big deal and just ignores it. Do you persist and be an irritant? Do you give up despite your principles? It's definitely up to you, but I find most women in their forties, who were feisty about this in their twenties, can't be bothered battling it every time.

I'D LIKE YOU TO MEET MY, UMM...

Tim: I plan to marry a woman that I'm in love with. We've discussed this, although she's married to another man. They're separated, but not yet divorced. Can I call her my fiancée? Is she my fiancée if she's married to somebody else?

HANNAH: I managed quite successfully to be engaged to someone who was officially and technically married up until the week before our wedding.

JV: And did you describe yourself as a fiancée?

HANNAH: Yes, and I had the ring and all the appropriate bits and pieces. Nobody knew that he wasn't divorced, because from the moment he was separated he described himself as divorced and, being your typical disorganised bloke, it never actually quite happened. So the week before the wedding was slightly stressful.

JV: And you don't think 'fiancé'—I was wondering whether 'fiancé' is a one-off term?—you could only use it for your first bride or groom.

HANNAH: It doesn't seem to be a problem.

JV: So it's reusable. Should this happen again, Hannah, do you think you'll describe your next partner as a fiancé?

HANNAH: I'm rather hoping I don't get to that stage, but why not?

KATE: I think the word 'partner' should apply to everyone because it reminds me of when I was nineteen, people used to be going out with

'James' and then all of a sudden it was 'my fiancé'. You lost your name and then it's 'my husband'.

JV: I always find 'partner' so—it's just a little businesslike, don't you think? You have partners in business and tennis.

KATE: Or 'my love', then. You don't say 'my de facto' if you're not married, do you?

JV: I always liked 'my de facto'. I think that has a certain technical charm to it.

KATE: I can never understand why people get married twice anyway. Didn't they learn the first time?

JV: What do you think on this specific problem, if still married, is 'fiancé/e' reusable through multiple marriages and, if still married, can you describe someone as your fiancé/e?

KATE: Technically, I guess. Call her 'my betrothed'.

JV: I like betrothed.

MALCOLM: On the marriage issue I think there was—it might have been English—a turn of phrase, people were often introduced as the other person's 'intended'.

JV: My intended. I always like to say 'We've posted the banns'. I think that's got a nice Thomas Hardy feel to it. She's still married, can he describe her as a fiancée?

MALCOLM: I don't think so. I think 'intended' is safer.

JV There is at this stage no official tag for unmarried partners. Everyone has their own concoctions: Person To Contact In Case of Accident is unwieldy though accurate and Love Puppy makes others vomit.

I DIDN'T MARRY YOUR PARENTS!

Nikki: Every year my English in-laws come and stay. They stay for five weeks. They want to be entertained every day, but there's not much they get excited about. I dread it for twelve months. This year I've said, 'Enough!' We've just had a baby and I've told my husband he's got to tell them. They can stay a week at the most. He doesn't want to, but when they're here, he starts going to the pub and working Saturdays and leaves me alone with them. Am I being unreasonable?

CORINNE: Some little fridge magnets reading, 'Guest are like fish. After three days, both should leave'. That's terribly hard, family don't see themselves as guests. How can she tell her in-laws, 'You're wearing out your welcome'?

JV: I sometimes think there're only about two people in the entire world that we can bear to spend longer than three days with. If you find them, you should marry them.

CORINNE: Sure, but check their parents first.

CAROL: Same situation with my grandparents who are always coming to stay, but we organise things for them—some trips away, that kind of thing. Make the most of **them:** have a weekend away yourselves, use them as babysitters.

JV: Can she tell them not to come or to come and stay for only a week?

CAROL: No. What she can do is address the husband. He seems pretty slack in all this. He's going to the pub and working Saturdays—forget that. She should tell him to pull his weight and that she's going away with the girls for a weekend. She's going to the movies every Thursday night. This is a good chance to get some good things in place.

NICOLE: She's got the perfect excuse: brand-new baby. It's a perfect excuse for everything. You say, I'm sorry, the baby's very difficult, not sleeping, waking up all the time, so just for this year, we've rented a unit for you, just nearby, it'll be better for you, you won't be interrupted, and it's a bit hard for us with the new baby and everything. Perfect!

JV: Nicole, it's genius what you're suggesting; however, they could well be the kind of parents who respond 'Oooh, love, don't you worry about us. We don't mind the baby. We don't want to stay somewhere else, we'll be absolutely fine'—you know what I mean? What if they don't get the hint?

NICOLE: Insist until they do and, if they don't, do it anyway.

> **Standing up to the in-laws; always easier said than done. Sometimes, though, you've got to do it so that both parties can find new ways to enjoy each other's company rather than grinding on, saying nothing and everyone ends up hating one another.**

DO YOU TWO WANT TO SIT TOGETHER?

Jennifer: *I'm holding a dinner party for all of my family. My youngest brother has recently separated from his wife, but is still living in the same house. They've got two young kids. My brother said not to invite her, it would be too uncomfortable. But I feel really bad about it, and I know she's really hurt that I haven't invited her. It's all new and I don't really know how to handle this kind of thing.*

KEN: I think Jennifer should invite the ex-wife. Separations are primarily problems between the parents, and at the end of the day they're still her nieces and nephews and it is a family dinner.

JV: At what point then are you excluded from the family dinner because of divorce or separation? I mean the young brother is the original family member, doesn't he have the right to say 'No, I don't want you to invite the ex'?

KEN: Oh no, it's not his party.

GEOFF: James, I don't think she should have invited her, and I feel that quite strongly. I had a bit of experience with that situation, and I think a separation, even though they're under the same roof, is a fairly definitive statement of what the situation is. There needs to be a recognition at some stage that they're going to go their own separate ways. So I think she should be quite comfortable about not inviting the partner and respecting her brother's wishes on that score.

JV: The couple can break up, but often the various in-laws will stay in touch with one another.

GEOFF: That's right. I don't think that not inviting her is a statement that they'll have nothing to do with each other anyway. She can remain friendly with the sister-in-law, even though she hasn't invited her to the family lunch under the circumstances.

JV Divorce and separation create myriad different issues for all of the surrounding friends and families—the grandparents, the sisters-in-law, the kids, the cousins—it's ripples-in-the-pond stuff. Negotiating it in the first months and years is going to be hard and there's no general advice available: it's case by case.

EX AT THE PARTY

Paul: What happens if you're at a party and your ex-wife turns up? Is there an etiquette about which one should leave?

JV: So it's ex-wife—and how long ago were you together?

PAUL: We were together eleven years and then a separation of about six months when we turned up at the same party. I'd been invited, not knowing that she'd been invited by somebody completely different, and it just ruined it for me.

JV: So within the first year of your separation...

PAUL: But she knew that I was going to be there, and I didn't know. I just said, 'Look, what are you doing here? I just don't think it's appropriate, particularly as you've taken me to the cleaners!'.

JV: So who do you think should have left—you or her?

PAUL: I ended up leaving...I thought she should have left, but she didn't, and I found the whole thing distasteful. The event was actually a surprise birthday party for me. And I said, is this a part of the surprise? To her, I said, 'Do you want to talk to me about something?'. 'Oh no,' she said, 'I just thought I'd come along and enjoy it, 'cause I know all these people as well and I haven't seen them for a while'. And I thought, the woman's got more hide than an elephant.

WILLIAM: I think it's quite simple. I think the clue lay in the fact that Paul told us that the host of this surprise party hadn't invited the wife. So I think it was up to the host, seeing Paul's discomfort, to play the role of the host and quietly say to the uninvited woman, 'I'm sorry, but you're actually not invited to this party, would you mind leaving?'.

JV: You're right: it was his surprise birthday party that he ended up having to leave. And whatever the circumstances of their break-up and whatever she might think...

WILLIAM: It's all irrelevant. She gatecrashed a party as an uninvited guest.

JV: Yes, or was invited by one of the other guests was the sense I got.

WILLIAM: Yeah, but that's an uninvited guest, sorry.

JV: No, I'm with you, and I think that's an excellent point, that perhaps the etiquette was for the host to do something about it. Do you think, in general, that people need to be sensitive about this in the first few years of their separation?

WILLIAM: Absolutely! And of course, you're right, they're going to have friends in common. And equally, their friends—it is sad that people have to be divided up into her camp, his camp—but your friends in those situations have to be sensitive to it as well. In that particular case, it all boils down to the host.

WILLIAM 2: About the divorced guy, I reckon he ought to get over it. I've been divorced since 2001, and we go to the same parties. And we thoroughly enjoy ourselves.

JV: So you're able to be at the same event and just ignore one another.

WILLIAM 2: Yes. Get over it.

JV: If it was fairly fresh, like this is in the first six months...

WILLIAM 2: Well...one of my sons, he had a party, we were at the same party, we just did it that way. I suppose we didn't have any fighting over who was getting what, we didn't do that.

JV: So would you describe it as an amicable divorce?

WILLIAM 2: Yes.

I would rather stand between a hungry lion and a tethered goat than come between any divorced couple and offer advice. I've had callers who say they've been able to divide their property with no rancour, but fight horribly every year over what's going to happen with the kids at Christmas. I've had people dealing with issues for decades. All mention of divorce brings a torrent of calls from angry men and regretful women. It's always deeply personal, very particular and although we can put up general ideals, such as putting the children first and trying not to fight the emotional issues through the practical matters of property and access, every single issue is loaded with history and hurt and makes the Middle East look easy.

CHAPTER TEN

CHILDREN

A Brief History of Children

Everyone's childhood used to be the same. Girls had pigtails; boys had tadpoles. Girls had one rag doll; boys had a cricket bat made out of an old fence paling. Girls sat in the kitchen and played with dough until sent down to the pub to bring Dad home; boys ran barefoot through the streets torturing cats and throwing stones at each other until sunset when Mum stood on the back step and bellowed for them to come in.

Mum wore an apron, cooked, scrubbed, operated a mangle and during times of war worked at the munitions factory. Dad was a mysterious figure who disappeared early, returned home late and on Sundays dug up the potatoes. Mum and Dad would have been married at nineteen after a brief courtship involving a dance, a night at the cinema, a picnic rug, a bottle of Dinner Ale and a pregnancy scare. A year later they had their Eldest. They would continue to produce children every year or so, including Big Sister, Little Brother, the Middle Child and Baby—and any family with less than four or five children was not taken seriously. Only Children were pitied and were always spoilt and plump.

Families lived in three-bedroom houses. Boys had one room, girls the other and no one was allowed in Mum and Dad's room ever—unless it was clear they were dying of the croup. There was a formal parlour, to be used when Grandma and Grandpa came over, a kitchen, and some lucky families had a glassed-in back verandah, which was usually occupied by a boarder with the DTs; if not, it made a marvellous playhouse for the youngsters or a terrific separate bedroom for the Eldest when he began to inspect himself for hair.

All families had the same rules: you sat at the table at dinner time; there was no talking with your mouth full and it was illegal to place your elbows on the table at any time. In some families talking was banned altogether until all had finished eating. At that point, Father would sometimes read from the Bible and test the children on the scripture they had memorised.

All families had Uncles, Aunts and a dozen Cousins. Uncles and Aunts would come around often, and one of the Uncles, at least, was always incorrigible. He'd turn up with a bottle of beer at inappropriate times and bring sweeties for the children. One of the Aunts could be relied upon to make tactless remarks along the lines of 'Your Eldest looks pale. Is he playing with himself?'. Cousins were a tribe who were there to provide light relief and to lead the younger children astray. They kept ferrets, were allowed to send away for X-ray glasses from the back of the comics, and would lead expeditions into town for a little shoplifting and light vandalism of the old railway sheds.

Grandparents came in two varieties: the Spoilers and Smotherers or the Harsh Victorians. The Spoilers always had cake, suffocated younger children in capacious bosoms and allowed the boys to drive the tractor. The Harsh Victorians corrected speech, rapped children on the head with thimbles, and spoke only in proverbs.

Internal relationships within the family were complex. The two boys, the Eldest and Little Brother, would be locked in eternal rivalry, never realising that Dad didn't care much for either of them unless they were opening the batting. Big Sister would baby Little Brother and ignore the Baby, turning one or both homosexual. No one cared about Middle Child but there were always high hopes for Baby. Incest was common, as can be evidenced by any celebrity biography.

Family values included not getting caught, never dobbing on anyone in the family, and being able to eat any amount of boiled cauliflower. If you misbehaved you were thrashed. Rolling pins, wooden spoons and Dad's belt were kept at strategic points around the house and could be used by any nearby adult if a child so much as thumbed their nose or fibbed.

Childhood lasted until you were fourteen, when Eldest was expected to join the workforce as an apprentice fitter and turner, Big Sister to stay at home and make gruel for the parents as they lost their faculties. Additional daughters were to work in shops until pregnant.

Then: children were as lean as whippets and a clip over the ear fixed everything. Now: they are as fat as hippos and we're afraid of them.

VOTE MUM OFF

Donald: *I've got two grand-daughters aged four and five. Their parents are separated and I realised that their mother lets them watch 'Big Brother'. The mother's our daughter-in-law and we get on quite well, but I was a bit taken aback that this was what they were watching. When they're with us they watch 'Play School' and the real kids' programs. Should I say something to her? I can sense she won't like it, but I really feel as though it's wrong that kids of that age are watching this sort of thing.*

SANDRA: I don't think it's a particularly good idea. I'm wondering if it would not be better for the grandfather to raise this with his son and then for his son to raise it with his ex-wife. I think the reaction that he is going to get is 'Keep your nose out of how I raise my children'. And obviously he doesn't want to alienate the relationship he has with his grandchildren nor what seems to be a fairly harmonious relationship at this stage with his ex-daughter-in-law.

JOHN: The problem is that what would get heard is not, 'I'm worried about the TV they're watching', it would be, 'You're not a good mother'. That's the message she'd hear and it would be on for young and old—big family barney. I mean, I think that is what he's saying.

JV: I don't know that I got that sense. I think he's just a bit bewildered by this particular choice, just as you might be. Look, she's a great mum, but, boy, they go to McDonald's twice a week.

JOHN: That is a very good parallel, but all you can really do is raise it with your child, the son in this case. Say, 'Look, I wouldn't have let you watch that sort of stuff at their age, why do you think it's okay?' and don't make a big deal out of it. Just ask and try to have the conversation.

JV This is one of those ones where you have to weigh up the relationship. Do daughters-in-law like fathers-in-law questioning their choices? Are they able to talk about these things? Do you want to put the daughter-in-law offside over a bit of stupid TV? Children seem to survive watching all sorts of rubbish. The world is currently being run by people who consumed way too much 'Mr Ed' and 'F-Troop' and they seem to be doing no worse a job than a generation who sat by the wireless and became Argonauts. TV-watching, like food, is one of those instant-guilt areas for parents and Donald's comment will spark instant-defensiveness from the mother.

WHO PAYS THE FERRYMAN?

Jack: In shopping centres with those two-dollar rides, a lot of them now have space for three and four children. Now, my daughter just likes to sit on them and I don't put money in them. What I want to know is, if someone comes up and puts their child on, and then puts two dollars in, do I have to take my daughter off, do I have to offer half, or do I just let her be a free rider?

JV: Are we getting to sort of 'ride rage'?

JACK: No, we're not getting ride rage, but I always feel a bit funny because they fish around looking for the change, and I might have two dollars in my pocket; I don't want to encourage her to want it every time.

JV: So you're pretty scungy about the whole ride thing then?

JACK: Well, yes—they're just a total waste of money, they don't actually do anything.

ALISON: I've got a little boy who's eighteen months old and I follow the same philosophy as the other dad; I never put money in the machine because it just seems like a waste of money and too much hassle. But I think if his child is on the machine, on the ride, and another parent comes along and puts their child on, they're being quite rude themselves for taking the ride from the first child, and I don't think he's obliged to put any money in. He's had his ride gazumped.

JV: So you think that the one who's going to pay the two dollars has a right to say 'Look, I'm renting this now for the next minute and a half, do you want to move your child?'.

ALISON: Yes, I think so. Because how do they know he's not got a pocketful of two-dollar coins that he's saved up to stick in for his child?

TANYA: Yes, I don't have a problem with it, I'm one of those parents who does put the two dollars in, but only for my three-and-a-half-year-old if he's helped me with the shopping, so it's a reward thing. And if there's another child playing on it, I let them ride. My child enjoys the company.

JV: I use the reward system as well. You go into the supermarket, and they say 'Can we have a ride?'. 'Right, on the way out, if you're okay, if we all survive the next hour.'

TANYA: And I'd rather spend the two dollars on that ride than on some disgusting chocolate bar thing that will make him hyperactive for the afternoon.

JV: That's right. I mean, I think Jack's the cheapskate here, quite frankly. Jack, who can't come up with two dollars because he reckons his kid won't remember it. He is starting a pattern that worries me for the future.

JANE: I'm rather caustic about all these tight people. I think being tight about the rides in the supermarket is really sad. My daughter is thirteen now, but she loves those. We spent a bit of money on them, and it was well spent.

JV There's often a reaction to this kind of question which usually involves the phrase, 'Get a life', as though, unless you're dealing with your sister's crack habit or the Taliban has taken your village, your problems aren't worth worrying about. However, this is the very essence of 'The Form Guide'—matters which aren't obvious and that might trouble someone. It might seem odd that Jack would seek resolution to such a slight issue on a talkback radio program, but when you're a first-time parent of a toddler, things like this can be odd and confronting. I think Jack could loosen up a little on the ride. He might think there's nothing much going on when that Wiggles car rocks back and forth but when my daughter was about two, I fired up a Postman Pat van and she was terrified. I had to take her off. Now, that's two dollars wasted!

HEY JUNIOR...BEHAVE YOURSELF

Lorraine: What do you do with other people's children who are staying in your house? Kid comes over and behaves like a little *monster. These are boys in their early teens. Do you send them home? Do you correct them? I had one boy who came over and he was picking on my son. I had another who was just unbearable one night. I told both of them off but I felt awkward about it.*

JV: I have children younger than that and it's fairly easy at that age. I think they're so used to grown-ups coming and telling them what to do that they barely distinguish between them. I always think it's my house, my rules, I'm responsible and you'll do what I say, but I'm sure it gets harder as they get older.

LINDSAY: I have no problem about disciplining other people's kids in my house. I think when they come over, it's fairly normal that you have some understanding of the perspective of where the other parents are coming from and what sort of standards they have. And particularly on a sleepover; you'd only do that if you were comfortable with the family and that would mean the discipline and standards were kind of the same. In general, kids need boundaries, I think, otherwise you're going to lose it.

CAROL: I have a ten-year-old boy and we often have lots of boys over. We had one who was mucking up a bit, and afterwards I told my children that he wasn't allowed to come back again because of his behaviour. It was the boys who put the pressure on him. We'd been planning an ice-skating day and they told him, 'Mum's not going to take you 'cause you don't behave'. He turned right around. He was great. When he turned up I sat him down and said, 'Are you going to behave?' and he said, 'Oh, I'll be really good'. And he was as good as gold. The kids know where the line is.

JV: Good work, Carol! Come to my place anytime and sort my kids out. I think by ten or twelve, kids know that there are rules in all situations and they know the standard kind of stuff and they know that there's variation. Different rules at school or at church or at Saturday sport. So, even if you're a bit harder than their parents, say, it doesn't matter. They understand that.

CAROL: They're also a bit sneaky. They think they can get away with something at someone else's house that they won't get away with at home. But as soon as you pull them up, they're dreadfully embarrassed and they realise they've got to behave or they're going home.

JV It's hard enough knowing what to do with your own children let alone anyone else's. Plenty of people suggested don't do anything, but don't have the kid back. Most felt that you have to step up and lay down the law: your house, your rules.

HEY JUNIOR...PART TWO

Dave: My little boy, he acts as if he's naughty all the time, to other people, 'cause he's actually got autism. So it's very hard to go out in public with him—even though in our eyes he's being a good boy, to other people he's being a little bit of a ratbag, you know.

JV: What sort of things happen? Let's say if I'm standing near you in the supermarket, what might I observe your boy doing?

DAVE: I knew you were going to ask me that question. His communication's pretty poor. We try and get through with a bit of humour and we often refer to him as that guy Bobcat in the *Police Academy* movie, so there might be a bit of yelling and things like that going on...

JV: So I'd notice. I'd look at you and think this is odd.

DAVE: Well, the problem is...he's a good little kid, you know, he looks just like his brother, he's normal and everything like that.

JV: And what sort of reaction have you encountered from other people? What's the problem that you've encountered?

DAVE: Well, what made me think about it last week was I gave his mum a bit of a break and I took him and his brother to a show, and he was fine, but then I said to him, 'Look, we're going to leave and go and see Mum, go and pick her up'. And in his mind, once you tell him you're going to do something, you can't change it in any shape or form. But then I had to take him to the toilet, and he started to yell that we had to go and pick up Mum. So when I got him in to the toilet he was screaming his head off, and a gentleman said to me, 'Mate, looks like you've got to give him a bit of a smack on the bum'. And I came back with—which I never do, because it's sort of not my style—I said, 'Look, mate, that's the way it is when you live with autism, you know'. And his face went pretty red pretty quickly.

JV: That doesn't sound like such a bad response. Did you feel uncomfortable doing that?

DAVE: Yes, because I don't like to be rude to people, but at the same time the longer we live with it, you just get fed up with people who want to give you the solution to the world in two minutes, and they don't even know his last name. In general I would probably tell some other kid to stop it myself. But then...until you know the situation, sometimes you should give it five minutes and just have another look at what's happening.

JV: Perhaps what you're looking for are ways you can tell people what's going on without embarrassing them or yourself or your son.

DAVE: Yeah, the autism societies actually have like a little business card that they print, and you can give it to people, but you just can't do that every time. I think people just have to be a little bit more aware of different disabilities nowadays, because, as I said, he looks fine...

MARGIE: I guess the first thing I want to say to Dave is to never be embarrassed by your child because they're beautiful children with wonderful souls locked in a world that is safe for them. But the world that *we* live in, to them is very frightening, very scary. They need structure and they need routine. When I was working at a school for autism we'd take the children out on community access, and, yes, there were some interesting incidents. But truly, once you tell people that these children have autism, it really gets to the better side of them and they just tune in to you and talk to the children and use the language that we use, which is very minimal language, of course.

JV: So Dave's response should be, perhaps just in a quiet way, to say, 'Look, mate, thanks very much, I understand, but just so you know, he's autistic'.

MARGIE: Absolutely. And it's nothing to be ashamed of, because they're beautiful children.

JV: And is that general advice that's given to parents, what we just described then—is that the general advice that's given?

MARGIE: Yes, absolutely, because basically there's nothing to be ashamed of. Your child has a disability. Autism is nothing to be ashamed of because these children are actually quite clever in a lot of ways. They need structure. What I advise mums to do is take your child out shopping, have the visuals, get them involved in the shopping, have a routine so they know what's coming next. They'll know that after the shopping there's something exciting like 'I'm going to the park', or 'I'm going to have McDonald's'. And then they can see an end to it, and that helps them to self-manage their behaviour, and never to be ashamed.

MICHAEL: In relation to the autism: I used to teach them swimming and they're lovely kids. Don't be embarrassed by them, treat them as normally as you can, and if someone does take the time to say something, just respond in kind. Say, 'I'll make a note of that when the autism wears off'.

JV: That's similar to what Margie's saying, just be upfront about it, let people know. I think I might have suggested he was embarrassed, but I don't think David is embarrassed about his child. But you can see the difficulty there. We all find it difficult if our child's standing out in any kind of way. We all find that difficult, don't we?

MICHAEL: Absolutely, but I think the more he gets out and about, it'll just become second nature, and they are very, very special people. They're amazing people to associate with. You get a lot of joy out of them.

CHRISTINA: Well, I say something dreadful if people are really being awful about how my child's behaving. I say, 'Look, he's autistic, that's why he's badly behaved. What's your excuse?'. And I know that that's not very nice, but then they're not being nice.

JV When people say the world today is ruder and no one has any manners, I think of this kind of example. There was a time when there would have been no tolerance or understanding of David and his child. Now David has organisations he can turn to, the rest of us are far more aware and accepting of autism or mental illness or disability or difference of any kind than the generation that easily used terms like 'slow', 'spastic' and 'retard', and would have had little patience or support for parents whose children weren't 'normal'.

AND I WANT AN IPOD AND A
PHONE AND A CREDIT CARD...

Marie: We have a twelve-year-old son who's an only child, and he still believes in the Tooth Fairy, the Easter Bunny and Santa Claus. And I'm just wondering how to break it to him that they don't exist.

JV: Wow. Has he been to school?

MARIE: Oh yes, he has.

JV: Are you sure he's not putting one over you?

MARIE: Well, maybe he is.

JV: Is it you who believes in him believing in the Tooth Fairy and Santa?

MARIE: It could be. Many years ago we used to say, 'If you don't believe, you don't receive'. And maybe he still remembers that. But I'm just wondering if we should break it to him or just leave it for a few more years.

JV: Wait until he goes to university perhaps or meets a girl? You've never tried to talk to him about it?

MARIE: No, in fact a tooth fell out last night, so we went through it all and he was convinced that the Fairy would come and leave the money.

JV: And by this stage, what does he want, about twenty-five dollars?

MARIE: You're not far off actually.

JV: So he leaves his VISA under the pillow. What, do teeth still fall out at twelve?

MARIE: They do. We're up to the molars now, the molars will be the next ones.

COLIN: I think the lady should nurture his eccentricity. I think she should go the other way. When he gets home from school, get dressed up in a bunny suit and say, 'Hey, this is great, this is great fun'. This kid could end up being anything; he could be the Prime Minister of Australia, an engineer, he could be doing anything.

JV: How astonishing is it that he's able to resist what, all media, all the rest of his peers? It's like he's been vaccinated against peer pressure.

COLIN: Well, I think he obviously knows that they don't exist, but he just loves the fact that it was possible. But if we had a world full of eccentrics like him running around, I think it would be a better place.

INGRID: I have a fourteen-, a twelve- and a ten-year-old, and I'd just like to say the Tooth Fairy still comes to our household. My husband still nurtures the belief; the world's pretty harsh out there, so why not maintain that and nurture it.

JV: Is Santa still coming?

INGRID: Santa still comes, yes, and I think it's worth their while to maintain the belief. The ten-year-old still brings his tooth to school, shows it to the class and no one says anything; I mean, he's convinced, so I guess he convinces everyone else.

JULIE: Yes, we had the same thing happen. We decided to have a word with our daughter when she was ten, and still believing very strongly. We decided perhaps she might get ridiculed at school and I had a word with her but she just told me I had the whole thing wrong and that she was just going to go ahead with what she knew to be correct.

JV: So she said, 'Look, Mum, are you kidding? How else do all the presents get down the chimney?'.

PRUDENCE (five years old): Well, Percy said that Santa, the Easter Bunny and the Tooth Fairy weren't real but I can prove that it is real. Well, my friend when she lived here got a note from it, and it came out just how it was, she left the tooth and got a note.

JV: So your friend's got a note from the Tooth Fairy?

PRUDENCE: Yes.

JV: Have you lost any of your teeth yet?

PRUDENCE: Yes.

JV: Did the Tooth Fairy come?

PRUDENCE: I've lost four.

JV: And the Tooth Fairy came?

PRUDENCE: Yes.

JV So there's no question.

PRUDENCE: Even if you're in France.

JV Anyone who's had their six-year-old turn around and say, 'Whatever' with a perfect sitcom shrug, who's tried to buy clothes for their daughter and been surprised to see their eight-year-old looking like Paris Hilton, who's been horrified at what their boys can Google up, would love to have a twelve-year-old who's excited about Santa.

HELLO JJAISEENTAE

Justin: I'm in a real quandary. I've got a two-year-old and a four-year-old, so I'm constantly meeting a lot of other parents with children. And I no longer know how to respond when they tell me their child's name and it's some made-up, in my opinion, stupid name. Now I used to do the old, 'That's nice, that's different, that's unusual', but since 'Kath and Kim' everyone knows that's just a euphemism for 'That's ridiculous'.

JV: You mean Kayeela…?

JUSTIN: Yeah, or Kaneeka or Tennis, or, you know, normal names spelled differently, like with a ph instead of an f, or a k where a ck used to be, and things like that. And look, I know I'm passing value judgements, because I've taken traditional names, but it's just—Oh, it's really become a thing.

ANDREA: I have four children all with unusual names…

JV: What are they?

ANDREA: They're Bede, Jaydon, Freya and Cale. And they're all sort of Welsh and Gaelic. I love them and they really suit the kids. When I tell people my children's names, I'm not expecting them to make a comment on them. Just like when I hear other people's names and think, bloody hell, that's a boring name. I don't think he needs to make a comment. You just say 'How do you do'. You don't have to make any comment.

MARGARET: He could keep his opinions to himself. I just had another thought. I know I've tried this in the past if someone has unusual name, I straight away talk to the child, not the parent, and I've said, 'Oh well, hello, Piana', or whatever the child's name is, and spoken to the child. And that sort of takes the focus away from the parents.

JV: He's got the two- and the four-year-old and, as he said, he's meeting children and parents all the time, so this is not going to be an unusual situation. He should just now simply be able to swallow whatever's thrown at him. This is Kaeela, and you say, 'Hello, Kaeela', and you wipe any reaction from your brain.

GARY: The only thing for him to do is to get into a time capsule and go back twenty years, because it's the guys called George and Bill that are the weirdos now. Everyone's called Tiegan and Jacinta and if Jacinta is spelled in the normal way, you're lucky. It's usually got three y's and two i's and a z.

JV I noticed when we had our children that no one could resist commenting on the names we'd chosen. They were not that startling, but it was like everyone felt they had a right to express an opinion on them. After a while I encouraged this because I felt we may as well get the reviews in first, and if there's a big negative reaction it's not too late to change it. However, once the kid is out there wandering around with whatever name attached to it, no one's much interested in anyone else's opinion of the name.

FAMILY VALUES

Robyn: I have two children and they've been asked to stay at another family's home with two children they know and play with a bit. The problem is I don't like the children and I don't like the parents. They're bad-mannered and foul-mouthed. All of my children's foul little ditties come from them. They're the kind of kids who never have to go to bed. And then, am I meant to reciprocate?

JANE: It only gets harder. Wait until you've got sixteen-year-olds and you don't like their friends—nothing you can do there. Say no to your kids; direct them into other friendships. It's okay at that age, do it while you still can. Say to the other parents, 'We don't do sleepovers', or explain that your kids behaved badly last time and the punishment is no sleepovers. If you've got a gut feeling about the kids and the parents then go with it.

MIKE: Parents are way too worried about this kind of thing—life's rich tapestry and all that. It's a chance for her children to see another family and then you can use that to point out what an excellent job you're doing as a parent.

GRAEME: I often say no to my daughter about sleepovers. Sometimes you just don't know the parents well enough. Better a daughter who's a bit upset with you than a daughter who's exposed to something you don't like at all. I told a parent once that I was sorry, we don't know them well enough, come over and let's be better friends and see then. We're the parents, it's our job to be watchful.

JV Short of sending the children to stay with axe murderers, are parents too worried about this kind of thing? We want every moment, every bit of school, every bit of life to reflect and enhance our values? Can't they be questioned and challenged? This is one where I wonder if we should be a bit more like Mike—let 'em go. The hardest part of parenting is not the holding on, it's the letting go. At some point they have to cross the road on their own, they have to take the car and they have to go and decide for themselves what's good and bad. It's not easy.

THE PERILS OF SOCIAL MOBILITY

Alison: We live in a small cramped flat and my eight- and nine-year-olds happen to go to a school where a lot of people live in beautiful houses with in-ground swimming pools and tennis courts and the works. My kids get invited to go and play at those houses all the time and I feel too embarrassed to ask the other kids to come back. But I'm also feeling embarrassed about never having the other kids back for a play date.

JOAN: Organise a trip to the park. Every now and again invite them over but make it a day in the park or at the beach. Be the mum who's happy to take four or five kids to the movies on a Saturday. And make the other parents aware that this is you reciprocating their play dates and I'm sure it'll be okay.

JV: You have to reciprocate, don't you?

JOAN: If you accept the invitation in the first place, there is an obligation to reciprocate. I have a small two-bedroom house on a main road; I absolutely identify with not wanting to have the kids back to my place because it's very cramped. Often having two extra kids in the small space and the stress that's involved for us makes it really not worthwhile.

JV: Do those with the larger homes, with the pool and the tennis court, do they tend to accept that their place is going to be a bit of a centre?

JOAN: I think they do, because I have a sister who has a wonderful home, and I tend to take my kids out there and use her pool and so on. And yes, they deliberately bought a place like that so that their daughter can invite her teenage friends over—there's that expectation. But I don't think that their daughter expects everything that she's got at home to be at her friends' houses.

JOHN: Our children went to a private school and we lived in a very ordinary house because we couldn't afford both the expensive education and the expensive home. So what we used to do is whenever we invited other kids over was get them in the kitchen and cook. I used to make them homemade Monte Carlos and scones with cream and all the things that kids love, and it got to the stage where all the kids with the pools and the tennis courts all wanted to come to our place all the time. The mums and dads were ringing me up for the recipes, their kids won't eat their food any more, they want to eat our food.

JV: This is what happens, isn't it? You make a sacrifice for your kids to go to that kind of school and it throws them into a different world from yours; they're with the rich kids.

JOHN: Exactly, but I'm happy with the outcome of the whole exper-iment. My son is now thirty and he lives in a beautiful big house, and I still live in the grey little old house I had when I sent him off to school.

JV: Well I guess that's what you were hoping would happen.

JOHN: I was.

JV I found this one quite touching, and I loved getting a call from someone who could tell me how it all worked out. We all want better for our children—and that will bring some social cost and difficulty along the way. I also liked the simple practical solutions: be the mum who takes them to the movies or the park; get them over for cooking or board games. Kids can be cruel and judgemental, but they just want to have fun and there're plenty of ways of doing it that don't involve owning significant slabs of real estate.

WHAT HAPPENED TO A CARD
AND SOME ANZAC BISCUITS?

Bill: It seems increasingly common—and I have to say at the private schools—to buy a present for the teacher at the end of the year. One parent collects thirty dollars or so from everyone else, and then buys a seven-, eight-hundred-dollar present: a weekend away, grand final tickets, that kind of thing. What do I do if I don't want to be part of that? And is this all starting to get a bit much?

HELEN: When this came up at my daughter's school I said that we'd already done something. The first year it was fifteen dollars and then it was twenty-five the next. It doesn't reflect our values. If my daughter or I want to do something, I want it to be on a personal level. Perhaps I make something or go out and buy something myself. But I think the child should be making the gesture as it should be about the relationship that's built up there, not just some automatic thing.

CHEZ: Say no to the present thing. I'm a teacher and I love it if I get a gift from one of my children, but only if it's heartfelt and a little gift out of their pocket-money. It's beautiful. Some obligatory gift from all the parents, well, a weekend away is nice, but it's not the same thing.

MARK: Happens in cricket **clubs:** all the players combine on a birthday, one of the parents goes around and buys a present. Everyone forks out fifteen dollars—that's three hundred—and then they buy him a bat or something. It's team spirit, it's bonding; quite expensive bonding, but bonding nonetheless.

RUSSELL: I like the present. Our boy's in Year 4 at a private school on the North Shore, ten dollars per family for Christmas. I jumped at the idea; hard to buy anything decent for ten dollars. Amalgamate and you can get something decent. And let's face it, we're pretty busy this time of the year. I don't mind outsourcing the gift-buying.

JV I swear he said 'outsourcing the gift-buying'; I would have thought it kind of defeats the purpose. And in schools what teacher wouldn't love a bunch of little presents that look like the child had bought them or made them themselves?

247

MEMORIES

Simon: At the school concert or the ballet night, I've got a real problem with the other people videoing the thing. If someone pulls out the tripod and stands up and blocks your view for the entire show, then you can tell them what to do, but parents don't do that. They pull out the little video camera and flip out the little screen. Now in the dark, it's a real distraction to have this little bright screen in the row in front of you. I find it hard to relax.

SADIE: I agree and I think the school should see it as a revenue opportunity: do a video and sell it to the parents; ban everyone taking their own cameras. I think even when there's just a few doing it, it's a distraction. Everyone should sit there and be an audience, not jumping up to get a few shots.

GRAEME: At our childcare it's forbidden to photograph the class unless you have the consent of all the other parents. Get a pro team in to do it properly. I don't want to seem too paranoid but I'm always a bit concerned about someone I don't know shooting a video of young kids.

BILL: Look, all those people who are so intent on capturing the moment instead of enjoying the moment make it like at sport or at concerts, give them a little media pit. They can all huddle in there and get all the shots they want without annoying the rest of us.

CHRIS: It's getting a bit rough when you can't a take a video camera to your own kid's event and take a few shots. You can't get in anyone else's way but when the professionals do it, it's just a big wide shot, your kid is just one of the dancing fairies up the back. When I do it, I can get right in there and all I've got is my kid. Relax, what's the big deal? Proud dads with cameras are part of the event.

JV Oh no, it used to be proud dads with cameras; now it's the entire audience with camera phones holding them up, snapping away and emailing photo files to cousins in Slovenia. Soon you'll be providing a live-feed of the ballet concert to your website, audio and video-streaming the event in real time via the Blue Tooth connection stuck on the side of your head. Oh, you can do that now? Perhaps future ballet concerts should be held in television studios instead of church halls so we can all get the lighting right. This is one of those where it's not really a big deal if someone is videoing the ballet concert in front of me, but it is annoying to have this little screen between you and the stage. Could all would-be video-graphers be a little more considerate of everyone sitting around them?

I'M NOT A NATURIST, BUT...

Barbara: I've got two little children and it's just suddenly dawned on me: I'm not sure at what age or what stage does it start getting a bit creepy for them to see me in the nude? My two boys are three and five now, so we still have a shower together and a bath and that kind of thing, but when does the line get drawn?

JV: Do you feel uncomfortable?

BARBARA: No, no, not now, but I'm just wondering, there will probably come a time when it might be a bit embarrassing or they might say things to their friends at school or something.

KEN: I guess it's probably around about three and a half. The reason I say this is that my three-and-a-half-year-old grandson at a restaurant recently stated that, 'My mum can't see when she does wee, because she doesn't have a penis'. So I would suggest probably at about three and a half they seem to notice this sort of thing.

GRAHAM: I'm sort of in agreement. I think she's going to have to leave it up to the kids to give her a bit of a pointer. They're going to start making comments to her and generally they're not going to be encouraging comments about her body. I've got two boys, fourteen and seven, and I still wander around in the nude. The fourteen-year-old keeps his distance, the seven-year-old's still okay but he did—it was at around three and a half—he started to make comments. He said things like, 'Daddy, you've got big tentacles', and stuff like that, and you don't want that at the dinner table.

JV: No, you don't need that, you're quite right. But you're on to the essential thing there—the kids will let you know. The kids will be telling you. You'll know when they're uncomfortable, that's for sure.

CYNTHIA: They certainly will. I've got a twenty-two-year-old who comes in to visit me in the bathroom. He'd knock first, but certainly he doesn't stand back having a chat with me while I'm behind the shower screen.

JV: And you're still comfortable...?

CYNTHIA: Very comfortable. And this has certainly been something that we've done at home. And I also use this sort of philosophy—I'm an early childhood teacher—and certainly I think it's really important to support children's sexual development.

JV In matters like these, you can't tell other people what they should or shouldn't be doing. In general, on sexual matters, most advice tends towards being direct and honest with your children whenever the questions arise. Give them as much information as they need, that you consider appropriate to their age and that you are comfortable disseminating. As to walking around nude, I think the day the kid points at you and says, 'Oooh, gross me out', is probably the day you'll buy a robe.

IS MY EATING DISTURBING YOU?

David: I was at a big shopping centre the other day. I'd just bought some lunch and sat down outside on a bench and a father came up with a baby and right on the bench next to me he changed the baby's nappy. It was disgusting! They have a baby changing room and everything but he's doing it right under my nose. I mean, he's probably a very proud father and proud of everything his child does, but I didn't need that while I was eating.

KATRINA: In a neutral kind of way, the guy having his lunch should have said, 'Oh, did you know there's a nappy changing room in the shops?'. Maybe the guy didn't know. I'm the mother of two babies and I've had to change them in all sorts of places, but you always try to be discreet.

STACEY: I'm concerned for the privacy of the child. I'm no prude and I'm not paranoid, but a bit of dignity for the child I think is right. Don't just strip them off in public.

JV: So, this is a little different to, say, the breastfeeding in public issue, right? This is about bad smells and the privacy of the child.

STACEY: I think so. Breastfeeding is different again; it can be done reasonably discreetly and shouldn't really impose on anyone, but changing a baby's nappy, it's all out there, isn't it?

JV: Usually, at some point.

STACEY: Unless you've worked out a new way to do it.

AHMED: We have just moved here to Australia and back in our country a lot of people change babies' nappies everywhere.

JV: Where are you from, Ahmed?

AHMED: We're from Iraq, and it doesn't matter that much. People, they know it's a natural thing, and as it's a natural thing people just don't care and they don't whinge.

JV: So in other words, you're thinking that David's perhaps a little bit uptight about it?

AHMED: He worries too much, no need to get worried this much. It's just a natural thing; he would have done it when he was little. These things you can't help, and it's better than having the baby smelly all day.

> **JV** Look, I love to have an Iraqi on the program telling us to relax. In general, baby changing should take place in the parent room or somewhere private. No one really needs to share a parent's pride in the contents of their baby's nappy.

But also, let us remember that we have all been caught short—a screaming baby, an appointment to get to, a nappy that must be changed—pants off and job done. Life, like shit, happens.

DOES YOUR DAD HAVE A SHOTGUN?

Jane: My teenage son, who's not eighteen yet, brought his sixteen-year-old girlfriend home to stay the night. I was worried about the Ukrainian parents banging on the front door and I was very unsure what to do. It's one of those things that you know is going to happen, but I wasn't expecting it that night. It was right in the middle of his HSC exams and bang, he's there with his sixteen-year-old girlfriend. I don't know if her parents know she's there, it was very difficult.

JV: How did you handle it?

JANE: We had a long discussion, where I was told that I lived in the fifteenth century, and there was lots of brouhaha, if you can imagine. In the end, I said, 'Well, I'm relying on her parents to tell me it's okay, and until I hear that *I* won't be okay with it'. And so the solution he found was that he went and stayed over at her place.

JV: I guess that means the parents were okay.

JANE: Well, I think they're about as confused as I am, but I'm going to talk to them, although it's all a bit after the horse has bolted.

PATSY: I think you should stick to your old-fashioned guns. I did. I'm a grandmother now. When my daughter came home with the man who is now her husband and wanted him to stay the night in the same bed in my home, I said, 'No way!'.

JV: So you have a sense that you should set up from the word go that this is the rule and it never deviates.

PATSY: In my home, yes, my rules. That's the way the world goes round.

TONY: I'm with the last caller: just say no. If it's impossible and she has to stay over because she can't get a lift or anything, well, they sleep in separate rooms. My daughter was seventeen and she wanted the boyfriend to stay and I said, 'Well, he's on the couch'. The reaction was hostile, but it's a great way to get them to leave home. If they can't play, they go somewhere else.

JV: Had you ever talked about it before that point? When she was fifteen, sixteen?

TONY: I can't remember, James, but it would have been along those same lines. But I think she was just challenging me, that's all, by bringing the boy home and probably thinking to herself, well, he's here now so Dad won't say no. And I did. And of course he was embarrassed and she was embarrassed, but I wasn't.

PAUL: We've got teenagers and my view would be that I would be quite happy for them to stay because I see it this **way**: that if they weren't doing it at home, they'll be doing it somewhere else. And the main thing I would be trying to tell them is to make sure they're protected. I'll give some comments on the other if I may. Keeping them safe is the most important thing. I've had boys and girls, a sixteen-year-old girl can walk out the door, so be careful, she can just go and you've got no way of protecting her then. If you want to talk to them about it, go for a drive. They can't run away. They hate it, but they can't walk out the door. The main work is done while they're growing up. They've got your morality and then they'll make their choices.

JV This argument divides along the same line as alcohol consumption and young people: they may as well do it at home and then we know where they are; or not under my roof and not while you're underage. There're no rule. People's religion, their morality, the maturity of their kids all come into play. There're many, however, who say if you haven't talked about sex with your kids the whole time, it may well be too late to start when one of them brings a friend over for a sleepover and they haven't brought their jimmie jams.

THE ROSE OR THE CHINESE DRAGON?

Anneliese: I told my sixteen-year-old daughter that she could have a tattoo for her birthday. She's come back to me wanting a Celtic armband, and some enormous symbols on her shoulder and her back. I had in mind something a little more discreet. I'm wondering if I went down completely the wrong path here.

SALLY: How about a henna tattoo, which is not permanent...I think henna lasts a few months.

255

JV: Does it sound weird to you that a mother has offered to buy her daughter a tattoo for her sixteenth birthday?

SALLY: Well, it does, really, but I didn't want to sound rude. Go for henna. When my daughter wanted to cut and dye her hair, I bought her an expensive wig. She wore it for a couple of months and decided she didn't like the look, and then she had her long hair back. It was expensive, but it was worth it.

NICOLETTE: I personally think it's a bit young, but then as she's started the ball rolling, she's basically then got to say, okay, well, you're sixteen now... If she's given her the okay to get a tattoo, then it can't be on her terms. She's opened the can, and if her daughter wants something big, then that's what her daughter wants.

JV: I suppose, but that's a little bit like saying we're going to give you a car, and she says 'Well, I want a Mercedes', and you say 'Well, we were thinking of a Barina'. She said she thinks it's appropriate for her sixteen-year-old to have, say, a little butterfly somewhere and this daughter wants huge Maori symbols all over her.

NICOLETTE: She probably should have clarified and... If you make an open statement like that without sitting down and actually talking about it, this is what happens...

There is a legal issue here. In all states of Australia, you can't get a tattoo if you're under eighteen years of age without the written consent of a parent or guardian. Check your local Department of Health and you'll find it spelled out in some such off-putting legislation as the Skin Piercing Act of 1992. But what about the offer? I think the mother should be thinking long term: I'm not referring to the permanency of the tattoo, I'm simply referring to fashion. If something which was once seen only on sailors and ex-cons is now so mainstream that mothers offer it to their daughters, then by the time the daughter gets it done it will be as old-fashioned and outré as a permanent wave. The mother needs to stop trying to be her daughter's best friend and become more of a mother and save her from the embarrassment of being a cliché of her generation. When soldiers who've survived battle have their battalion inscribed on their skin, when winning Olympic swimming teams ink Olympic rings onto their ankles, I get it. When sixteen-year-olds get dolphins on their bikini line, I think it's idiotic.

BOYS WILL BE BLUE

Darren: I actually wanted to make an apology over the airwaves, if anyone's listening who might have been in this situation. Football game, rugby league boy. My boy is in a sixteen-year-olds team and at the end of the game—they'd just won by two points—they had a victory song. And it was as blue as you could imagine.

JV: Sixteen-year-old boys singing a blue victory song...

DARREN: Extremely. Now the other side and even some people on our team were very offended. I unfortunately—well, not unfortunately—got lumbered with the manager's role this year. I didn't realise this was the sort of thing that was happening in the football team. We actually ended up having a team meeting yesterday. They have all signed a letter of apology and stuff like that, but the thing is, I found out later on that day that the guy who was the previous manager was quite okay about the whole sort of thing and is a bit peeved about this. What do I do? I'm actually using your show to be able to say, listen, I'm really, really sorry about this and blah, blah, blah, but my dilemma is that there's a number of people in the club who think that it's quite okay...

JV: This is boys' own fun, this is normal, what's wrong with you, mate? What was the tune?

DARREN: It was that US army chant thing. One guy instigated it and the others follow on.

JV: 'I don't know, but I've been told...'

DARREN: Yeah, exactly, the whole thing. At the time I'm listening to all this, and I just stood there. And I didn't stop it. And me being the manager, I should have done this, but I just was sort of dumbfounded.

JV: You're saying there's a culture among parents, former coaches and that sort of thing, that says this is okay, and how do you confront it?

BOB: If he's uncomfortable with how they're **going: walk!** If they don't conform to his standards, he should leave. If he's the manager and he's uncomfortable with what's going on, they should toe his line.

BRIAN: I think it's a matter for the club itself. I think Darren chickened out by not jumping on them straight away. In most rugby league associations—I can only speak for mine—it's frowned on very heavily and can involve fines and disciplinary action on the team, including loss of points, etc.

JV: So Darren should be looking at, what, some of the rules and policies around junior league?

BRIAN: Yes. I'm sure they're in there, because it's frowned upon because we don't want them giving the sport a bad name...

JV: Okay, there're the rules there and, yes, you've got to be a bit assertive, but Darren's in that position where he's a dad, he's taken on just looking after the team. And suddenly he finds there's something of a culture that he's got to confront. And it doesn't matter, this is a culture that's prepared to flout the rules in a way.

BRIAN: The only way the culture could be changed is if people like him stand up. If there's an element in the club that condones this sort of stuff, well you need to get that element out. But most clubs are pretty strict on this too. It's something that happens; give a friendly warning and then if there are upset parents, get them to write to the association.

GREG: I think he has to show leadership, and he has to put his foot down straight away, and he has to say, 'I'm the manager. This is what I want you blokes to do, because we're only playing sport, and you have to adopt certain ways of behaving'. Because when they become adults, if they're not shown the proper way to behave, then it's going to reflect badly on them.

JV: I think in a way we're slightly missing the problem that Darren's got here. I think he believes in it and he's not afraid to lead the kids, but he's got a problem with the other parents and a general culture that actually says that that behaviour is all right. The boys being a bit blue, the boys misbehaving, boys will be boys. How does he deal with that?

GREG: Right. In that case, if I was him I would write a letter to all the parents and say this is how I see it, I don't think it's acceptable and I just want to bring it to your attention.

JV: Could be a good way to go, but I don't envy him. I know we've had this kind of conversation here and in other programs when we talk about parents' involvement in junior sport. And you go along just to help the boys out and to manage the team and to get them through the season, you don't expect to suddenly have to deal with this kind of thing, do you? You're perhaps not all that well equipped for it.

LIZ: I actually don't know how [Darren] can confront that problem, but as a mother with three boys who play rugby league—and I'm starting to come up against some of this culture—I would like to encourage him to do his best and to hang in there. It's good to think that there are coaches who have a bit more of a conscience and a bit more of a high ideal about these things.

KATHY: I don't know about rugby league, but I suspect that there would be a code of conduct for parents, players, coaches, managers and everybody involved.

JV: I'm sure there is. But isn't the dilemma here...

KATHY: Well, I think what he should do is get hold of the code of conduct, speak to the coach, send a copy of the code of conduct for parents to the parents, get the kids to sign the code of conduct for the players, and tell them that if they don't adhere to it, they'll be benched.

JV: There is all of that which I'm sure is correct procedure. But your real problem is that you've got parents who think he's going over the top by doing that.

KATHY: Well if that's the code of conduct from the governing body, it's not him saying it. It's the governing body. He's just implementing it. And I don't think you can change it...

JV: But would you want to be in that position, Kathy, if you were coach of a team and there are fifteen parents involved and ten of them think you're a raving idiot because you're going down this path? How would you feel?

KATHY: I wouldn't feel very good about it, but how do you change it? I think you have to do this kind of thing to change the culture and to make people aware.

JV What I thought was interesting in this one was that it was difficult to get the real nature of Darren's dilemma. Yes, there might be rules and procedures he could follow and, yes, he should stand up for the values he believes in, but how many of us do, or more accurately, how many of us ever really have to? Darren is just a dad helping out with the local team. He's already ahead of a lot of us who drop the kids off and run and are lucky to be found flipping a sausage on a fundraiser night. He's made a commitment to the boys for an entire season. Now he finds he's not only got a problem, he doesn't have much support from these boys' parents in dealing with the problem. From sporting clubs to police forces, we are always discussing how you get rid of a culture—a culture of aggression, of sexual predation, of corruption or whatever. The answer is no easier for Darren simply because his problem is small and on a local level. I don't think in this case we found an answer for him except to perhaps distance himself by invoking procedure and the ruling body of the sport. But I felt a great deal of sympathy for him and, unfortunately, it's a perfect example of why people don't take on these roles: too often you get more than you bargained for.

CHAPTER ELEVEN

SHOPS AND SERVICES

A Brief History of Shops and Services

There was a time when going to the shops was a leisurely activity involving a train trip, a string bag and a level of obsequiousness from those serving to rival a courtier. Sir or Madam would have the door of their preferred emporium opened for them. Inside the lift was a genuine returned soldier, driving the machine and informing Sir or Madam of what was available at every stop. Lift doors would part, and there would be a manicured floorwalker wearing a beautifully tailored suit, smelling slightly of lavender, and with a neat carnation in his buttonhole. Every query would be answered with a slight bow of the head and a small yet gentle smile would form underneath a perfectly clipped moustache. 'Manchester, madam? Certainly, right this way and Mrs Rochester will be pleased to help you.' (Floorwalking and window dressing, along with the Opera and the ABC were the only available employment for homosexuals.)

Sir or Madam could buy something and know it would last. A kettle, a pair of gloves, a refrigerator; you were making a purchase that you did not expect to repeat inside of twenty years. To have an account with such an establishment entitled Sir or Madam to levels of being fussed over that would have been familiar to minor royals. The purchase would be securely wrapped in brown paper and string and if not carried to the car, entrusted to the delivery service, which would arrive at the appointed time and install the item at no extra cost.

For daily items, the woman of the house went to the local grocer. Here she stood and waited to be served. 'I'll have a pound of potatoes—and none of that green muck you gave me last week, Mr Cartwright, if you please—half a pound of sago, some split peas and some oatmeal.' And then it was off to the butcher. Here you could purchase mutton or bacon. Beef was considered unhealthy and chickens were for laying eggs—they were only eaten on Christmas Day, and they didn't mulch up their beaks and turn them into nuggets for the children!

The streets were filled with travelling salesmen, icemen and rabbitohs. Rabbitohs came by two or three times a day. Rabbits existed in plague proportions and so rabbitohs would catch them in one street, skin them as they turned the corner and sell them in the next. Many a fine Australian grew strong and tall on a steady diet of 'underground mutton'. Rawleigh's men went from door to door selling Rawleigh's products. These included hair grease, chilblain balm, castor oil, worming tablets, and a floor polish that doubled as any of the above. Rawleigh's men were rakish and considered 'fast'. They were not homosexual and fathered many children to many a bored housewife easily seduced by the promise of a new thimble.

Milkcarts plodded by and a milkman, who was also the local football umpire, would run up onto the verandah, drop off a pint or two and run back to the horse and cart, which had plodded on to the next stop. The manure from the horse was highly prized and sons anxious to please their fathers would gather it up in the wheelbarrow and leave it in a steaming fresh pile by the vegie patch. Bakers delivered bread, the post came twice a day and the postie blew a whistle as he dropped the letters off, and day or night, doctors would come to your home if your child was a little spotty.

Then: the customer was always right. Now: the customer can't escape the phone prompts to complain about the service that doesn't exist.

VIRAL MARKETING

Brian: I have a pet hate and that is young children—below ten, basically—riding in the main section of shopping trolleys. It doesn't matter what shopping areas you go to, you see mothers using these trolleys as an enlarged pram and these kids—one doesn't know where they've been—their feet, their backsides straight in the shopping trolley, where my food may go.

JV: You're taking me on here. I head to the supermarket and I'll have two children under ten, and bang, they go into the trolley. It's part of the fun. It's part of the game. For us it's a Saturday afternoon outing. We're going to go ride the shopping trolleys, and you're suggesting that my unclean, filthy brats may contaminate your pumpkin at some later date.

BRIAN: Yes, your brats in particular, mate.

JV: Yes, probably mine in particular, that's right. You see, if it's a Saturday, they mightn't have had their bath the night before. So is there a health issue there? Do the trolleys ever get cleaned?

BRIAN: No. You watch those trolley guys out in the parking areas, they just pick them all straight up from those big trailers, and...

JV:...haul them straight back up...

BRIAN:...and hurtle them off again.

JV: And that's about it. And you're worried about a little bit of bacterial matter.

CLAYDON: I'm outraged, if not almost speechless. I'd like to ask Brian if he has children? And also if he's ever gone shopping with children, especially a wee little toddler, and been able to convince the toddler to sit in the seat when they don't want to? It can't be done. I mean, what's going to be infected? You wash your fruit and veg. Most things are packed. The risk of infection is minimal.

JV: E. coli bacteria are not going to crawl through the outside of your Coco Pops, are they?

JANE: I can't believe it. I don't quite understand what he thinks the kids are going to give him, and whether it's coming off the kids or their shoes? But he actually needs to be more concerned about the supermarket trolleys themselves. There was a study done that showed they were the germiest things ever, particularly the handles: people sneeze all over them. So my only solution would be home delivery or take a giant plastic bag or, in these politically correct days, paper bag, and line the trolley. Then you don't have to worry about the kids. And quite frankly, he's more likely to get knocked over by a rampant child in the actual aisle and do damage to himself that way than he is if they're contained in the trolley.

Some people are worried about infection in all sorts of areas. I've had a caller who thinks that fruit handling should be banned. Sure, but can't you wash your apple when you get home? Is there really any risk of infection from a shopping trolley any more than just being in a supermarket with lots of people? And anyone who wants to go to the supermarket with young children and not use the trolley as a source of entertainment and transport is welcome to take mine any day they please.

TIPPING

Monica: *The other day I was in the city outside one of the really big posh hotels and a man came out of the hotel to get into a taxi, and following behind him was a hotel employee, loaded down with bags and suitcases, the whole shebang. The man didn't even carry his own briefcase—the employee carried the whole lot, loaded it into the car for him, and the fellow just hopped into the car and sat there. Then I saw him lean out and hand to the employee a dollar coin. And that made me so angry, I wanted to jump out of my car and give the young guy some money myself...I know it's his job to do that, but it doesn't matter.*

JV: What do you think would be an appropriate tip?

MONICA: Five dollars. Whatever I'd had, loose change or whatever or if I had a five-dollar note or something like that, that's what I would have given him.

JV: The few times I've stayed in the hotel—I don't suppose I ever have that much luggage, just like one case—so I tend to carry it out myself. I always find the tipping moment very uncomfortable.

MONICA: I don't think you need to do a tip for that, but this young man—there were two suitcases, another bag and a briefcase, and a suit bag. And he did it properly and he packed it in gently and put the boot lid down. He did a really good job, a proper job.

JV: So he'd earned the tip.

MONICA: Well, I think he did. And I think a dollar—I mean he took it with good grace, thank you very much—he was quite lovely about it, but, oh, it made my blood boil.

KYLIE: I worked in the hospitality and hotel industry for near on five, six years, and I felt really uncomfortable taking tips off people for doing my job. Okay, you might have a trolley full of bags, but that's kind of what you're there for, to me.

JV: Was that the general attitude among the staff?

KYLIE: For the most part, yes, it was. We were in a corporate space hotel and it was. I had one gentleman come in from overseas trying to give me a fifty-dollar note for taking two bags upstairs. And I just sort of went, you don't need to tip in this country. It's not compulsory to tip.

JV: Oh, come on Kylie, it was fifty dollars...

KYLIE: But that's the point, he was over here trying to find work, and it was just the wrong time for that kind of money. It was two bags that weren't heavy—and on wheels.

JV: So, if you're in the restaurant game, tipping is part of the salary, pretty much, isn't it? But in the hotel game, tipping's not part of the scene.

KYLIE: It's not, even in restaurants. It's compulsory in places like America, but their wages are worse. I did get tipping in the hotel restaurant, but again, I said to people that you only tip if you think the service was good enough.

JV: I think a lot of people still have that attitude. I wonder if we're

moving more towards the global perspective on tipping, which is, kind of, you tip regardless.

GREG: I spend a bit of time in these five-star hotels with my wife, and I used to tip—stupidly, I felt—and I thought, well, hang on, they're just providing a service that they're being paid for on an hourly basis anyway.

JV: What would you tip for all of the luggage, you and the wife? You've got the three bags, the makeup cases, the sports bag and whatever else—what would you tip for that?

GREG: Nothing. What about the guy out the back slaving in your back garden doing all this work all day in the hot sun—he just gets paid. These guys get paid. Same with the restaurant: they get paid to serve out the food and pick up the plates.

JV: Do you never tip in restaurants?

GREG: Occasionally I do when I think it's been a really exceptional night and I want to express that gratitude, but ordinarily no—and my wife sort of bolts for the door in embarrassment. But I just say, well, bugger it, these guys are being paid. We aren't in America here.

JV: This has been the traditional Australian attitude to tips, hasn't it? If it was great you'd get a tip but it's not standard. You don't tip the hotel valets and that sort of thing. You might tip in the restaurant, but only when it's good. Is that where we still are?

SUE: I have an opinion: tipping, no. And I think we shouldn't be talking about whether we should be tipping. We should be putting our energies into making sure that in Australia we all still have decent wages so that we don't have to rely on tips.

BRAD: I'm a bellman at a hotel and, as far as it goes, international people do tip a lot, which is great. Why not, if they want to show their appreciation, and we're all for it? We don't earn that much money, so it does help. But we do find that Australians don't tip, and, to be honest, there can sometimes be, I guess, a negative way of looking at them whenever they come into the hotel. So, of course, we enjoy it, and I think if someone wants to show their appreciation for a job well done, then fair enough.

JV: Is it factored into your wages?

BRAD: It's not, no.

JV: So they don't say, 'We're giving you ten dollars an hour, but don't worry, there'll be tips'.

BRAD: No.

JV: So are you being paid a decent wage?

BRAD: Some of the boys are getting paid all right. It's just under thirteen dollars an hour, so it's minimum wage.

JV: The Australian view is that you're being paid and you're being paid okay, so I don't have to tip you? Is that view acceptable?

BRAD: It could be, but when you look at the US, they only get paid, what, eight dollars an hour, nine dollars an hour, and they expect to get tipped. It all depends. Obviously some people are going to give you fifty dollars; other people are going to give you five dollars. But at the end of the day it all does help. I'd walk away at the end of the day with four hundred and fifty dollars in the hand if I didn't get tipped, so, of course, living in Sydney, it does help.

JV: I think we've got a problem with tipping in Australia: it's the money. In the US it's dollar bills. You can peel off a couple of 'em, and it feels all right, but to give you a dollar coin or a two-dollar coin, I feel like I'm telling you to go and buy an ice-cream.

BRAD: Sometimes you do get that. Some people will give you three dollars and say, 'Go and buy a beer', and you feel like turning round and saying, 'Well, hang on a minute, where do you buy your beer from?'.

JV: That's right. I'm not a member of a leagues club nearby.

BRAD: But it goes for everything. It goes for restaurants, too. I think if you get good service at a restaurant, why not? I always throw ten dollars on the end of the bill or something like that.

JV Tipping is a very vexed area. There are plenty who only want to tip if the service is terrific. There are others who tip as a matter of course. That's in restaurants. When it comes to cab drivers, pizza delivery and big hotels, no one has a clue. We've all seen it in the movies where the sophisticated (usually) male reaches into a pocket, the five-dollar bill is all ready to go and they press it into the palm of the concierge and the transaction goes off without a hitch. In Australia, when Australians are served by Australians, they don't like tipping them. And I do wonder if it's partly the problem with the coins and the money. Five dollars seems too much for taking my bags to my room. But a two-dollar coin seems condescending. Mainly, however, it's just that we don't have a culture of tipping. It's not built into the wage system, and into our minds. We expect that people are well paid and will do their job. And more seriously, neither do we have a culture of corruption; where we have to grease the palm of everyone to get the car parked or the application approved.

DON'T MIND ME

*Simon: I run a liquor store and I can't believe how many
people come in now and purchase wine and beer and keep
talking on the mobile phone. I try to be friendly and polite, but
it's very hard with someone who's completely ignoring you.
They put the EFTPOS card down and when I ask them, 'Which
account?', they act like I'm interrupting them. It makes me feel
like some kind of servant and I get to the point of wanting to
throw the change at them.*

SHARON: I think it's to Simon's credit that he is such a polite
shopkeeper. I'm not a shopkeeper myself, but I'm very appreciative
when people show breeding and politeness. And I think that he should
rise above the rudeness of others. I really admire him for continuing to
be polite to people. And I think that he should continue to do so, and
really bring into relief other people's rudeness by continuing to be polite.
I don't think he should lose that. It's a very valuable feature of his
personality that he should keep...

JV: Sharon, I think you've hit on something essential there. Isn't that
what manners and etiquette is about? You'll have a code of
politeness and decency and compassion for your fellow human
beings and regardless of what they do, you will stick to it.

SHARON: Simon should not be discouraged when he's faced with rude
people. There are people out there like myself who really appreciate his
politeness. There will be others in the shop who will observe the
rudeness of the mobile-phone customer but they will also observe
Simon's reaction. I think his courtesy will show up the distinct rudeness
of the mobile-phone user.

LEE: I think he should have some little signs down underneath the counter and you could bring a sign up that says 'Hi' and another one 'How are you today?' and if he doesn't get a solution from that, another one, 'I can see you're too busy to say hello'...

JV: I love the idea of signs, because to me it just—I'm just seeing Wile E. Coyote: 'Bye bye...' I love that image.

JOHN: I'm going to go against the grain, I'm going to go against the trend. I think that Simon's missing a fundamental point of his reason for what he's doing. He's in business, he's got customers, his livelihood relies on selling grog. And I think he either needs to put up with it and accept the money that goes towards his lifestyle or move on into another business. There are two fundamental rules in customer service. Rule number **one**: the customer is always right. Rule number **two**: if the customer is wrong, refer back to rule number one. Business is business.

JV Does Simon need to be split? No, he maintains his unflappable courtesy in the face of the appalling rudeness of those who would talk on their mobile phone while in the shop and he keeps in mind that he's running a business. If they turn up to buy their wine from him, what does it matter how they behave? I think the moment their credit card is rejected, he has every right to say loudly enough so that whoever they're talking to can hear, 'I'm sorry, that card wasn't approved. Do you have another you wish to try?'. A little vengeful embarrassing is good for the soul.

DON'T LET ME INTERRUPT YOUR WORK

Libby: I was in the bank holding a sleeping toddler—she's very heavy—and there were three tellers on duty. One was talking on the telephone, and the other two were busy with their Lotto entry. I stood there for ten minutes, and nobody looked up, nobody said anything and I was the only one in the bank—I was the queue. I didn't say anything, but I've been wondering ever since if I should have made more of a fuss.

BOB: I've got two possibilities for her. She could have stood there and just said very loudly, 'This is unforgivable, get me the manager now'. Or if she's the quiet type, she could walk over to one of the girls doing the Lotto and say 'Would you please get the manager so he can tell me why your Lotto is more important than my banking?'.

NEIL: Banks have got cameras in them. I reckon if she approaches them straight away, they should have it on footage for a week or two, and the manager would be able to see actually what happened. I think it would make the point a lot better.

It's interesting how often we put up with something rather than make a fuss. Make a fuss!

THE RULES OF ENGAGEMENT

Pat: I was at a garage sale the other day and I picked up an item and a woman called, 'I saw that first!,' as though she had some sort of claim on it. She indicated that I was to put it down. Is that some sort of garage sale rule?

(JV: Many people's ideas of social interaction remain close to the playground. 'I saw it first'—she should have claimed 'dibs' on it or 'bagsed' it. Perhaps the other claimant should have said she was on 'bar' and so all dibs were off. Then they could have played 'scissors paper rock' for it.)

PETER: Well, 'Whoopee poopee', I would have said, 'I've got it now!'.

(JV: See what I mean about the playground?)

PAUL: It's a hands-on **rule**: you've got to have a hand on it, then you have dibs. I do a lot of shopping for old LP records at garage sales, and it's yours while you have your hand on it, and someone else's as soon as you don't.

(JV: The caller genuinely said 'dibs'.)

GARY: I'm just fascinated by the way every garage sale looks the same. It's always the same rack of droopy clothes, three broken appliances, two dozen books, a couple of kids' toys. They're called garage sales for a reason: it's because whatever you buy there is going straight into your own garage. We've got garage-sale junk floating through the community like space junk orbiting the earth.

(JV: Gary has moved well beyond the playground.)

AREELA: Would it be acceptable if they both wanted an item for the garage sale owner to conduct an auction?

JV I love Gary's analysis of garage sales: the quality *is* dropping. The garage-sale item is something that is not bad enough to put out for council pick-up, but not worth taking a digital photo of and putting on eBay. What does that leave, considering that people seem happy to take a photo of a broken trike and put it on eBay? That leaves a lot of stuff that can't be worth fighting over, surely? But at garage sales, Boxing Day sales, and book fairs possession is ten-tenths of the law.

HEY, YOU!

Sharon: I'm a midwife who works in one of the major city hospitals and when I'm at the desk doing stuff too often somebody comes in looking for a patient and just says the patient's name. They don't say please, or hello or excuse me, they just make this rude demand. I feel like if they were my kids I would say, 'Not until you say please'. Is there an appropriate way to tell an adult to ask more politely—to say, hello, or excuse me or please?

CATHY: I think if they just walk up and say 'Ruth Smith', you say, 'Hello Ruth Smith, how can I help you?'. And then they have to spend much longer explaining what they want. And if it's a bloke, and you say, 'Hello Ruth Smith', that'll really get them going. I just think people are bloody rude and that's a good way to get them to say something.

ROBIN: I think for the midwife, it's all in the tone. I think she should just look up, raise her eyebrows and say, very politely, 'Excuse me?'. Then they'll probably say they want to see so-and-so, and if they bark at her again, she should just go back to her work and ignore them.

JV: It does have a lot to do with your own force of personality, doesn't it, whether you can carry that off?

ROBIN: Yes, I think so, but it doesn't take too much to just very calmly look at them, raise your eyebrows and say 'Excuse me?' or 'I beg your pardon?'. They can take it that you may not have heard them, and I think most people under those circumstances would get the hint.

MELISSA: I've worked in a hospital for twelve years and I think it's terrible how people are so rude. So I think, kill them with kindness. They come up and just say in your face, 'James Bloggs'. And you say, 'Hello, how are you? Good afternoon...'. And if it's about a baby, say, 'How exciting—is this your niece?'—that sort of thing. It's terrible. I think she has every right to demand politeness.

JV: That's an interesting approach. It makes you feel better; you're not joining in on the same level of surly aggressiveness. What were people's reactions when you did this?

MELISSA: Well, if you say, 'How are you?' most people answer, 'I'm well, thanks, how are you?' without even really thinking about it, so that you've almost forced them into being polite.

JV: Well, I suppose you've also just given a practical demonstration on how to communicate.

MELISSA: That's right.

JV: When you work in a situation like that where you see dozens of people all day, you can form a dim view of humanity. You can end up thinking that most people are rude. Do people just walk in, they may not be rude in any other situation, but they just are in that kind of thing?

MELISSA: Well, I think you have to be very easy on people, though, when you work in a hospital, because they are in a situation that isn't normal to them. Hopefully, it's one of joy anyway, if she's in the maternity section...but if you're dealing with people that are in a stressed situation, you have to give them a certain amount of leeway.

JV: It's true, a lot of people are uncomfortable in hospitals, and there could be a lot of stuff going on—the birth might have been very difficult, you know.

MELISSA: That's true. They might be very stressed because something horrendous might have happened. So I think you've got to give them a certain amount of leeway, but still, common courtesy is very nice.

JV No wonder we love nurses and midwives. In the middle of life and death, underpaid, overworked, and still you can get a Melissa who has the breadth of compassion to see why you might be being rude. Hello, Excuse Me, Please. They don't appear to mean much, but they stop wars from starting.

WHAT'S WRONG WITH HIM?

Kristy: When you're going to visit someone in a hospital, is it polite to look into the other rooms at the other people in the hospital as you're walking along the corridor?

JV: You find it irresistible?

KRISTY: Yes, just a bit curious.

JV: I'd draw the line at opening the doors.

DONNA: I think Kristy should become a nurse—I'm a nurse and we're in dire need of nurses—then she'd be able to get behind the scenes and find out exactly what's going on.

JV: Do patients find people looking in their rooms distressing?

DONNA: Oh, where I work most of the patients are too out of it to realise what's going on. They don't notice but the relatives do. People shouldn't look in, but then again, maybe if seeing some sick people prompts them to look after themselves a bit better, maybe it's a good thing.

DI: I've been a nurse of long standing and I think it's quite despicable the way people peer in. I wonder if she'd like people looking in her bedroom when she's vulnerable and cannot react or there's no one there for her or anything. You're sick and ill and people are staring into your room. Isn't it obvious that you shouldn't do that?

JV: I think so, but she was describing that irresistible human curiosity to peek at misfortune.

DI: You go to the desk, you find out where your patient is and you walk straight there. People walk into hospitals and treat them like shopping malls.

JV Does anybody actually think it's okay to look in other people's hospital rooms like it's a live version of 'ER'? Why not go in, pick up the clipboard and have a look at their chart? Hospitals are hard places. Hopefully we don't go there often, but when we do it's because someone we know and love is sick. Keep in mind that everyone who works there is doing an incredible job that you wouldn't want to do and everyone they're looking after is someone else's loved one. Best behaviour!

CHAPTER TWELVE

TOILETS

A Brief History of Toilets

Of course, there is no history of toilets before the late-twentieth century—toilets were simply never mentioned. It would no more have occurred to a gentleman or lady to mention their bodily functions than it would for them to have spat on the Queen. In fact, if it were not for a spate of racy memoirs from chambermaids and valets, we would have no evidence that any of the middle or upper classes had a bladder or bowel whatsoever. The lower classes of course were permanently scatological and lived knee-deep in excrement. In their fetid tenements and terraces, their tiny cottages in twisted streets, they expelled their waste into the rivers from which they drank.

In a scene often cut from *Henry V*, Falstaff and Hal drink pints of sack far into the night, before Falstaff issues this challenge, 'Can a King piss no higher than a clownish knave? Fie Hal, your piddle would lose Northumberland, your drips stain the ermine and see all England drown in France's pot'.

Although most (see writers as diverse as Laurence Sterne and Daniel Defoe) revelled in it all, finding the body at once hilarious and repulsive, the great proto-satirist Jonathan Swift was so disgusted by his own bodily functions that he regarded humans as irredeemably filthy and suggested they should be drowned in 'grate pooles of their own shyte, and therebye provydde at least some goode as fertilliser for the Tree'. The Swiftian view was that only plants lived a truly moral life, producing—in accordance with the science of the day—'no waiste more than an aycorn'.

But others had stronger stomachs for the waste products of themselves and others. Boswell was rhapsodic in his description of Johnson's stool. 'We arrived in the Outer Hebrides and dined on hideous combination of sheep stomach and peat washed down with fermented malt. The next morning, I observed in Johnson's chamber pot a prodigious stool as long as my arm, deep brown in hue and firm as the great man's opinions'.

And of course Pepys looked around him and behind him: 'After attending to some business at the Navy stores, I went home stopping only to cavort most eagerly with Widow Oats. Once home, I sent for my pot and observed that my movement was quicker than normal. I sent for our Maid Jane, played with papes and sent her out for bran'.

But by the time of Jane Austen, it seems that no one is troubled by their bowel or their bladder. (Does Mr Darcy ever have to go to the little gentlemen's room?) Despite the comic and dramatic potential, Dickens creates no one who is flatulent—'Frederick Fartbottom, Perfumier, sir, at your service!'.

All of this charts a course from a society where chamber pots were emptied from a third-floor window onto any passing head to a world where the body was a mystery below the chin. But you might expect by the twentieth century that in Steinbeck or Hemingway, DH Lawrence or Kafka, you'd think somebody would be wiping someone's arse, but nope, not a poop out of any of them. It's really only recently that the toilet has come back; I think as bathrooms multiply in homes—often outnumbering the occupants—we're now happy to talk about it again.

Then: no one had a sphincter. Now: we discuss colonic irrigation with strangers.

WE'RE REALLY QUITE EFFLUENT!

Ruth: Is it appropriate as an assiduous water-saver to leave one's toilet unflushed when one has visitors? I have thought about putting out the wee verse that says, 'If it's yellow, leave it mellow, and if it's brown, flush it down', but when people arrive and the toilets are unflushed it seems wrong, and then it seems weird to be running around the house flushing the toilets when I see someone walking up the drive—and it defeats the purpose.

JV: When people have a septic tank, they often have a sign up explaining the procedure, don't they? Would this be any different: it's house rules?

MARY ANNE: I think it's just a family thing really. You can't have a house full of unflushed toilets if visitors come over. What, bits of toilet paper and everything? I think that rule really only works overnight with the family.

But in these dry and thirsty times we should be impressed by a display of other's effluent, shouldn't we? As long as they haven't been eating asparagus. I think as a house rule it would be a hard one to support. You would feel a need to explain house policy on this matter whenever anyone came around and, as Mary Anne points out, would anyone be that comfortable in someone else's toilet with a bit of someone else's by-product hanging around?

I CAN MULTITASK YOU KNOW

Sadie: I started going out with a guy recently and I thought it was acceptable to go to the toilet and continue talking to him and he thought it was completely unacceptable. At what stage in a relationship is it acceptable to go on in and continue the conversation? I think it's okay after about five minutes.

SARAH: Never! My husband and I have been together for twelve years and we wouldn't even talk through the door to have a conversation. We discussed it about six months into the relationship and I said something like, 'Friends and I were talking about this, what do you think?' and he said, 'Never!' and I said, 'Absolutely agree'.

JV: Isn't it good you found one another?

SARAH: That's right. We're very like-minded.

SIMONE: I knew I'd met the right man in my life when I could sit on the toilet and do a number two and he didn't even blink and just kept on shaving.

JV: And how long into the relationship did that take?

SIMONE: About two days.

SUE: My husband believes it's incredibly personal, it's sacred, you shouldn't go in there ever...I think men use it as private time just to get away from the family. My father used to call it the Seat of Power, the Place of Learning.

JV: It's a time when men withdraw to consider their next strategy.

SUE: Yes, that's how my father used it.

BRENDA: I remember Barbara Cartland saying that once you've shared a bathroom with your partner, all romance is gone.

DIANA: The only time in a relationship that it is acceptable is when you march in and announce that you are leaving and you've got your suitcase in your hand.

JV: You actually did that?

DIANA: Yes, he was on the toilet and I marched in and said, 'I'm leaving you', suitcase in my hand. He was quite vulnerable at that point.

 I think in most relationships, this issue will find its own level.

THE RULES OF POWDERING THE NOSE

Jennifer: My sister and I went to the theatre. At interval we went to the ladies together. I waited for her outside the toilets in the lobby, but she was waiting for me inside the toilets outside the cubicles. She got very annoyed and said that I was wrong about where you wait for one another. She called through the door to someone who wasn't me and found the whole thing very embarrassing. I don't agree—you wait outside, don't you?

JOSIE: If it's big enough inside the toilets, well, yes, that's where you wait. You can do your hair, wash your hands. It's part of the experience. Women have more to say to one another. We don't want to break the conversation. It's nice to check on one another. Your make-up's okay, you've haven't got your slip showing, that kind of thing.

JV: If guys did that—did a fly check, for example—it could get very ugly.

ALEESHA: I get annoyed at the whole gaggle of women in the toilets having a chat. I go by myself. I can check my own butt to make sure there's no toilet paper.

JV: How did you get this extraordinary independence?

ALEESHA: You know on all the tests, I score right in the middle. I can read a map, I like the footy, that kind of thing.

KATE: We go in for a gasbag. In a pub, it's sometimes the only quiet place you can have a chat.

CHARLES: With blokes it's straight back to the bar; you can't wait outside the toilet at interval. In a theatre it's packed. And if you were a bloke hanging around waiting inside the toilets, that would be very off-putting for everyone else. You're waiting for a friend? Oh, right!

MALCOLM: I hate it when the girls go to the toilets; that's where I get knifed. You're talking to some girl at the bar, it's going great, her girlfriend comes up and takes her off and you know that in the toilets, the girlfriend's knifing you—what are you doing with him? Don't talk to him—they come back, you're dead.

JV I have so few insights here. Why women need to go to the toilet together, yet men can go alone, is an eternal mystery. It says so much about our essential masculine and feminine nature, but quite what it's saying, I really don't know. Where should you wait? That seems to be determined by the size of the crowd, the arrangement of cubicles and basins and the size of the ante room in the toilet. Perhaps women need to fix a meeting point before entering to reduce any chance that they might lose one another for even a second during this event.

HEY, PIG BOY!

Reg: My brother-in-law is not a handwasher. I was taught to wash my hands in the loo no matter what I did. He goes in and comes out and contaminates all my Monte Carlos. I know because there's no basin in the toilet, so he comes out and sits back down at the table. I want to confront him about it, but I'm not quite sure how to do it.

ROSEMARY: When I was growing up there was often a little hand-painted tile in the loo with a funny poem on it. Perhaps he could make up one about washing your hands...

JV: No matter what it is you do, you must wash after the loo.

ROSEMARY: Yes, that's the kind of thing.

JV: Be you friend or family or my best mate, I'd rather you don't contaminate.

ROSEMARY: Oh, that's perfect!

JV: I think it needs some work, but if you are the kind of guy who doesn't wash his hands, are the you the kind of guy who's going to pay attention to some twee little tile?

ROSEMARY: Yes, but it allows the host to say something. 'Can't you read? Didn't you read the message in the loo?'.

ALAN: I think a sign in the toilet is fine. And maybe you make it more for children—'Children, don't forget in this house we wash our hands. Adults, see children'—same kind of thing, a bit funny, but a way of making your house rules clear.

GERALDINE: Oh stop mucking around, give the brother-in-law a bar of soap and a towel and tell him what it's for. You've got to live with this pig forever.

JV Every family needs a blunt great-aunt and Geraldine shows terrific potential there. A blunt great-aunt sits on the couch crocheting and when her great-nephew emerges from the toilet she speaks to him like he's seven years old. 'Go and wash your hands, Geoffrey!' And then spends the rest of the day telling the rest of the family and anyone who drops by that Geoffrey had to be told to go and wash his hands after toiley. In the absence of a blunt great-aunt, the difficulty is sorting out whether it's worth telling him off. Is he going to resent that, is it just going to create further tensions in the family? It's hygiene, it's your house, you should tell him what you want.

WHEN YOU GOTTA GO...

Robert: I'm a plumber and when I'm working on the toilet, do I need to go and ask the owner if I can use the toilet? It feels really weird to go and do it, but I don't want to be busted because I was busting.

JV: When you're on the job, can you be on the job?

DEAN: Most plumbers I know would pee in the sink or out the window. Fix it first, then use it. You could say you were just giving it a test run. I think any owner would think it was great if you asked. In fact, I'm so impressed I want that plumber to work for me.

BOB: I know this problem. I had a plumber out fixing a toilet and the client came up just as he was doing his business and wanted to know why the door was locked. It was awful. Of course, he should have asked, just to let the client know what's going on.

JV: Is this covered in their TAFE course or during the apprenticeship at all?

SIMON: It's a glaring omission. Look, number one's okay, number two's out of the question.

JV: Do plumbers use the terms number ones and number twos?

SIMON: No, they don't, but we're usually not on the radio. Look, when you're fixing a toilet, you usually have to flush it numerous times and wait for it to fill and in between you get the noises in the pipes and you can usually get a number one in and no one's any the wiser but number two, you can't shut the door and stink the place out.

JV: What are the other questions of etiquette that plumbers have to deal with?

SIMON: So many, so many. I always struggle when the problem is sanitary napkins that have blocked the sewer. How do you tell the lady of the house?

JV: What methods have you used?

SIMON: I always ask the husband to tell her—and that's bad enough!

It's a funny relationship between homeowner and workperson. Homeowner (HO) needs work done; wants workperson (WP) to do it. HO resents paying WP to do it, even though HO doesn't or can't do it themselves. HO assumes WP is going to try to rip them off, do a shoddy job or leave muddy boot marks on the polished blackbutt floorboards. HO needs to calm down, keep an eye on WP, but make him a cup of tea as well. WP needs to remember they're in someone's home not on a worksite. For further advice see the movie Kenny!

CHAPTER THIRTEEN

CELEBRATIONS

A Brief History of Celebrations

There were public celebrations and private celebrations. When Sevastopol was relieved or the wily Boer beaten back or a coronation occurred in Mother England, men and women would throng into the streets, throw their hats in the air and issue three loud 'Huzzahs!'. The upper classes would retire to the Town Hall and spend the rest of the day making toasts. A glass of claret or hock would be raised to 'His Majesty' or 'Our brave lads!' or more abstract notions like 'Courage'. By the early evening, those remaining would be toasting their hounds, their hats and increasingly abstract notions such as 'Kismet!'. The evening would conclude with the women going home and the men departing for a brothel. The lower classes would remain thronging, guzzling gin and pork pies before fornicating briefly behind an aspidistra. Such events were countenanced in the interest of growing the nation.

Thronging also occurred when a much-loved figure, such as a boxer or a racehorse, died. For some reason, this usually happened in America.

The much-loved figure would return packed on ice in a cargo ship. His body would be carried through the streets to a funeral service at St Mary's or St Andrew's and the entire population would line the streets, hats doffed, to see him pass. Once past, the gin and the pork pies would be passed around and there'd be many fevered attempts to grow the nation.

At home, celebrating was frowned upon. It smacked of frivolity and enjoying oneself, and nothing good could come of that. It was normal to take a switch to anyone who laughed or skipped gaily. Birthdays, however, were marked. Among adults, a wife might say to a husband, 'I believe it's your birthday, my dear' and present him with a new pair of kid gloves. The husband would smooth his moustache and murmur, 'What's all this then?', while affecting not to be moved by his wife giving him a peck on the forehead. That evening he would celebrate at his club before retiring to a brothel. It was not expected that a husband would remember the wife's birthday at all.

Children were allowed a birthday party. A candle would be placed on a plate surrounded by treats like candied fruit or raisins. How their little faces lit up when Nanny brought it in. They would tear impatiently at the wrapping of their present and squeal with delight when they found a new pair of brown boots or a hoop. Many a happy hour was spent rolling the hoop around the courtyard in front of the stable. The kindly grandfather would slip a penny into their hand to be spent on boiled lollies, Father would come into the nursery and, if the child were the boy, ruffle his hair in a particularly affectionate way while pretending he couldn't remember how old the lad was this year. Actually, he was pretending to pretend. He had no idea how old the boy was and wouldn't until he was twenty-one. If it were a girl, Father would have no idea either. It was up to Mother to keep track and inform Father when it was time for the girl to 'come out' into society and be married off to someone with five hundred a year—or, if plain, a vicar in a poor and distant parish.

Christmas was the one day of unbridled celebration. After a four-hour church service, children would scamper home to see if Santa had put anything in their stocking. A stocking doesn't hold much, so they were thrilled if there was a striped candy stick or a wooden thing that went clackety-clack. All would sit down to lunch and eat until Grandma fell asleep face down in the brandy butter. This was the signal for the ladies to retire, for the children to go and play with their hoops and for the men to go to their clubs and thence to a brothel.

Then: we could mark the most significant event by sharing an orange. Now: party on dude, coz, like it's Tuesday!

HIP HIP?

Mark: Birthday parties! Who starts singing 'Happy Birthday', but more importantly, who says, 'Hip hip...'? I'm a caterer and quite often there's this chasm, and is it okay for the caterer to chime in and do the hip hip?

JV: So you often feel this yawning void at the end of 'Happy Birthday'. Does somebody else usually pick it up?

MARK: Not always, but what is the hip hip hierarchy?

STEVE: The hip hipper, well you don't have to worry about the hip hip because it's very unhip. What you do, when they've finished singing 'Happy Birthday', is you start singing 'Why was he born so beautiful...'

JV: I hate that song. I must admit I despair, once you get through the hip hip, if someone starts the 'He's a jolly good fellow', and then if someone does 'Jolly Good Fellow', you always know someone's going to do 'Why was he born so beautiful?'. Can't we stamp it out?

JONATHAN: The hip hips are entirely superfluous and shouldn't be initiated, particularly by someone that's not there for the birthday person. That's just totally disingenuous and interfering. If the person clearly doesn't deserve it, then far be it for the hired help to initiate it. Absolutely beyond the pale!

JV: People may be very happy that he's started the hip hip.

JONATHAN: They may be stuck with him because he's family. He may not deserve a hip hip.

JV: Or you just think that some groups are hip hippers and some groups aren't. You can't force a hip hip.

JONATHAN: I think it depends on the birthdayee, whether he or she deserves it.

DAVID: I'm not actually going to say who's going to start with the hip hip, but my sister-in-law's family—she's an American—they have a little tradition, which I think is unique. They launch into a version of 'Happy Birthday' which is sung to the tune of that Russian death march that the old communist premiers used to get when they died...'Happy birthday...Happy birthday...Horror, war and despair, people dying every-where...happy birthday'. They all sing it—it brings a sense of perspective to the birthday.

JV: That's fantastic, isn't it? No one wants to do a hip hip after that.

RAYMOND: I think it's okay because I don't think anyone notices actually who the hip hip hoorayer is. They're all so focused on the cake and the person. I think 'Happy Birthday' just isn't long enough to sum up the moment, that's the trouble. It should be longer. So you sing that and you've run out of steam after about ten seconds and you—I feel the need, anyway, for it to go on a little bit longer. I'm enjoying that moment. And then it all kind of peters out and you get on with the cake.

JV The consensus from others was that they like the hip hip, they don't mind who starts it and it's always funny when someone does 'Why was he born so beautiful?'. It's only me who finds it annoying and up there with singing 'Twenty-one today, twenty-one today...' at birthdays for seventy-year-olds.

STRICTLY LIMITED OFFER

Lulu: At a kids' birthday party, say for five-year-olds, what am I meant to do about parents who turn up with other siblings? Does that child get included in pass-the-parcel? Am I meant to have lolly bags for them? I mean, some people at least ask, but others just turn up and kind of expect that their three-year-old can join in as well.

DEBORAH: It's up to the parent who's brought the sibling along to hold them back from the pass-the-parcel and to explain to the child that it's not their party. On the other hand, if I were the mother hosting, does it really matter if there's one extra trinket from the two-dollar shop? An extra snake in a lolly bag or two? I'm always amazed when parents hang around. I drop my kid and run for my life.

AMANDA: They're all crazy. What's wrong with these people? The more the merrier—relax, enjoy, be hospitable. Good god, what's another lolly bag and another pirate hat? Gee, is that a budget breaker, that extra hooter! Be open, your kids will be open and no one's going to worry. And with the parents, when they stick around, well, there's some extra help, another to make sure no one gets whacked in the head at the piñata.

BOB: If she's happy to have them then fine, but she should feel equally free to say no. When the kids are little you've got to accept that the parents are going to come, and often if you've got a four-year-old, you've got a one- or a two-year-old as well, so what are they going to do? But once at school I think you can say on the invite, or when they ring to RSVP, come and collect your child at 4.30. Be grateful they've had the courtesy to ask.

JANE: We just had our five-year-old's **party**: three separate parents left uninvited siblings while they took off. One father brought an older daughter along, threw her into the party while he sat down and read the paper. He didn't even try to talk to us or help or anything. And you know, lolly bag time is a feeding frenzy and if you don't know how many are coming, some kid's going to miss out and they don't understand. It's awful. I just say to any parent, have another half dozen lolly bags ready to go, because you don't know who's coming really.

JV Of all areas of inquiry I get most about children's birthday parties: twenty-firsts, weddings, funerals, barely a concern. From the time the Spiderman invitations go out until the curled up fairy bread hits the bin—nothing is certain and no one knows what to do. Toddler gatecrashing is rife through the kids' birthday party scene. All parents can do is prepare themselves for it with extra lolly bags and another box of party pies.

IT WAS LOVELY TO CATCH UP...

Nelly: Should I write thank you notes for three-year-old birthday parties?

(JV: This question refers to the host writing thank you notes to their guests for coming and for gifts.)

MELISSA: I like it. It's very common now. A little thank you note back in the post. Thank you for your gift, a little drawing or something. If it gets the kids involved and stops them just thinking about themselves for one second, that's got to be good.

LISA: I agree, it's good manners. It's a way of teaching them. I made the seven-year-old do it. We did something on the computer—just one line and a 'thank you for your present'. He thinks it's a real drag, but when you consider the time it's taken for someone to choose something and to come along, I think it's only right.

> **JV** This is the opposite of the adult convention where the guest would write and thank the host. Here the host is the thanking the guest. It's generally accepted that the five-year-old guest need not reply thanking the host for her thank you note.

IT'S THE COST THAT COUNTS

> *Krissy: My son has just started school and is being invited to lots of birthday parties. I send him along with a couple of Dr Seuss books or a Hairy Maclary and I notice that a lot of them turn up with Lego Star Wars and the bigger board games. I wondered if I should start to up the level a little? Usually when I go past one of those liquidation stores I buy up a whole lot of them very cheaply, but I'm starting to think I may be a bit out of step. You don't seem to be able to send them along with a colouring book and some pencils any more, do you?*

JANE: I have seven kids, so I face this problem quite frequently. This is all about materialism and we, as parents, have to take control and not let the kids run everything. My limit is ten dollars for primary, twenty dollars for high school. I'm the parent, I decide these things. I won't let them go to parties at fast food places because I don't approve of them. When we have a party at our place it's only for three or four children. How can a nine-year-old kid be a host for twenty? That's just present harvesting and greed. If my children go out with a present worth ten dollars and they feel a bit embarrassed, well, it's good for them. That's just part of being strong, of learning what it means to have a value system and learning to stand up for what you believe in.

HELEN: When my son was six, we had a party and he opened all the presents and when he was finished he said, 'Where's the next present?'. Put me right off the whole idea of kids' birthday parties. Next year we took him camping and then each year after that we just did something special. The next time he had a birthday party was his twenty-first and that was no big hoo-ha either.

JV I don't think any kid under about eight pays any attention to what present comes with what kid. Buy whatever you think is appropriate and don't worry too much about it. Any kid over eight who does notice is old enough to be told to be quiet about it and this offers an excellent chance to talk about presents and being greedy and all of the other rampant materialistic behaviour of your average child.

WE NEED SOME NEW TRADITIONS

Vanessa: How do you start a breakaway Christmas? We go every year to my mother's sister's house and it made sense thirty years ago, but it just doesn't now. It's all got a bit moribund, they won't do seafood and we just have chicken every year. No one really makes much of an effort, I want to do a new one for our kids and the new grandkids and just with my mum and dad, but how do I get started?

KATY: We broke away last year, and I'm happy that we did. Last year the family just couldn't make up their minds. Is it going to be Christmas Eve or Christmas? They shifted the date, we pretended they never told us. Just didn't front up.

JV: Any repercussions?

KATY: No one really cared, it had lost its excitement. They'd get the tablecloth out but they wouldn't iron it, know what I mean? Go off and get started, do something new.

BILL: Start by doing alternate years. Tell them you've got to do his parents, the in-laws, this year, and you'll be back at the family's one next year. It breaks it up and gives you an opportunity to start suggesting change. I know what she means, but isn't Christmas something we do even though no one really likes it?

JOANNE: We broke away the moment my husband and I got married. We didn't want to get locked in. We went to the zoo. It was open on Christmas Day and it was great, just us, the atheists and the tourists. Get in early, make the point.

JV: Did it cause a big ruckus?

JOANNE: Oh yeah, I suggested one year we use paper plates and it was World War Three. I suggested another time Dad might like to come and help dry the plates and he thought that was shocking. Accused me all of sorts of things. 'No, Dad', I said, 'I'm just wondering if you could pick up a tea towel'.

CAROLE: She should take a mature adult reasoned approach and run away. Our children are having children and then there's their in-laws, and really we'd had enough of it so we ran away to Jervis Bay. It was great!

JV: Oh, I see, you're the original parents and you ran away from your own children.

CAROLE: Yes! And, of course, next year all the kids came down, but it was better because we'd made the break. I come from a long line of runners away and I can heartily recommend it.

JV I wonder if Christmas is a festival that in each family has a peak and then many subsequent years are wasted in attempting to reproduce it. There's a time in every family—when the children are young, the parents proud and the grandparents still mobile—that the whole thing comes together and much joyeux noel is had. It can ossify and perhaps every family needs to think about freshening things up. Invite some friends, have a picnic, go out one year. Traditions and ritual are all very well, but they can get as stale as a mince pie in the New Year and that's when everyone starts wanting to run away.

WHAT DO YOU GET THE
EIGHTY-YEAR-OLD WITH EVERYTHING?

Susan: I'm currently organising an eightieth birthday party for my father-in-law and I've got the issue of whether 'no presents' should be written on the invite or not. The mother-in-law says write 'no presents' but I'm worried it might be a little offensive. People make their own minds up, don't they? And maybe they really want to bring a present, but he doesn't really need anything and we don't want people feeling like they have to buy a present.

VIRGINIA: I recently had a big birthday party and on the bottom of the invitation I just put 'your presence is your gift'. And some people did, of course, bring presents, but a lot of them didn't. They sort of got the message.

KATE: My mate's grandad had a party and on the invitation—he's renowned for telling the same joke over and over again—they said (he was about seventy), 'What do you get the man that has everything? A new joke!' So we all brought along a different joke and that was his present. But it made it good, because what do you buy him? He's got seventy years' worth of knick-knacks and I thought it was hilarious that finally we could get to give him some new material.

JV: Do you think there's any reason why Susan can't just write, 'No presents please'?

KATE: Absolutely not. If it's close family, family understands and they would have had, what, at least between sixty and forty years of buying you presents every year, so they would understand if they're good mates and family.

MICHELLE: You could say 'No presents, thank you, but your presence' or 'No presents needed, but your presence wanted'.

ROBERT I think in these busy times a lot of people would be relieved to see 'No presents' clearly written on the bottom of an invitation. Don't muck around with little phrases, it's too coy and makes people feel like they should still get a bit of a present. Just say 'No presents'. What on earth do you get eighty-year-old men anyway?

JV I also think if people indicate no presents on the invitation that it's slightly annoying to the host and to other guests if you turn up with a present. The host has to protest, 'Oh, you weren't meant to', and then they say, 'Oh, but we wanted to', and everyone else stands around feeling like they should have brought a little something as well. Do what the host asks you to do!

CHAPTER FOURTEEN

DEATH

A Brief History of Death

Death used to be quite common. Everyone died of TB. Women died in child-birth. Most children died. There was bubonic plague caught from the rats which scampered out of the straw as you lay yourself down after some pottage and some ruttage. The only treatment for everything was mustard seed in a hot flannel laid upon the brow. If that failed, the local dentist would be called and he would saw off your leg. Leeches were applied to the bloodied stump so as not to get too much blood on the sheets. The main job of a doctor was to stand at the bedside with a worried look and say, 'If he makes it through the night, I'll be surprised'.

All jobs were dangerous. Miners used to take small boys down pit. When they died, they knew it was too hazardous for the canaries. Miners used to bring up the contents of the mine in their lungs. It took a brilliant medical mind to make the connection. 'Miners fill their lungs with coal dust. Miners die at twenty-seven. Doctors don't fill their lungs with coal dust. Doctors live to be run over by horses at fifty-eight. Therefore, miners should be more careful when crossing the road.'

Not everyone was a miner of course. Some people worked at mill. Mill was a place where large spinning jennys could take your head off if you turned to gossip with your workmate. It was a place where you put workers in at one end, and after processing them, got bolts of cotton out the other. These were sent to Manchester Departments in Emporiums throughout the Empire (see my comments about Floorwalkers on page 263).

It was rare for anyone to come home from a shift at mill. Luckily everyone was breeding furiously. If women didn't die in childbirth, they went on to have seventeen children as a matter of course. Only three would survive, but you only needed one to become a doctor and then you would be looked after in your old age. Old age set in at forty-one, and within twelve months you would die of gout.

So, death was a part of life and no one made a big fuss about it. Death was to be got over and grieving was unknown. If a wife or child died, one was admired if one was bearing up well, and considered 'marvellous' if one just got on with one's life and didn't burden others with any sense of loss. If you witnessed Death on a mass scale—perhaps from a trench in the Somme—the correct response was to come home and never mention it. You were considered 'marvellous' if you never slept again and went quietly insane.

Funerals were quite funereal. Horses with black plumes would pull a gun carriage carrying your coffin. Mirrors would be covered for seven years and after standing in the rain by the graveside, the family would return to their home and serve sandwiches, showing everyone how 'marvellous' they were being. In Ireland, the death of a loved one would be marked by the women wailing until the pub opened and then all would drink and tell hilarious stories about the deceased.

Then: death was a part of life. Now: death comes as a great shock as we all believe ourselves immortal.

COULD YOU GET A DUMMY?

Bev: *I was watching on television the service from Canberra to mark the national day of mourning for the 2002 Bali bombing and throughout the entire thing there was a baby crying. The Prime Minister was speaking, the Governor-General and so on, and I thought it ruined the whole thing and must have made it very difficult for anyone to really get into the solemnity of the occasion.*

LISA: If someone stayed there with a crying baby then they must have had a good reason to be there. That lady does sound a bit intolerant. Babies cry and it could have been that baby's mother who was killed in Bali.

JV: Oh, sure, but there are several hundred other people there who are also dealing with loss and grief and who also have a good reason to be there. Wouldn't it be making it hard for them to engage in the solemnity of the event?

PETER: It's a symbol of the continuity of **life:** it's one of the most moving things to have a baby cry at a funeral; it's fresh life. Brings you up with a jolt when you hear it—that life goes on. It doesn't interfere with your desire to reflect on that life.

GILES: At a funeral of a lady friend, her young son cried and talked throughout the whole thing. I worried about it a bit, and the son said, 'Mum would have loved it'. It's not a whining toddler running up and down and playing. Let's face it, that baby at the memorial service probably made more sense than the people speaking. Take the baby out—solemn service, speech, dignitaries; it's not a shopping centre.

Two people, one of them takes the baby out, the other go out and relieve them.

ALAN: I disagree. There were hundreds of people there and thousands watching on television. It's a national event, a solemn occasion. I think it makes it very difficult for everyone else to get into the mood of the event. If it was a couple with the baby, then one of them should have taken it out or they should have left the baby with someone else. This taking the baby everywhere can get a bit ridiculous.

I think this is a generational divide. Older Australians often felt that you didn't take children to anything like this: family funerals, solemn occasions, formal observances. But today we see hundreds of kids at ANZAC Day parades, we see parents taking tiny babies everywhere and I think we can see from people's responses that most see nothing wrong with this and want babies and children to be around.

THE LATE JULIUS CAESAR

Amanda: I seem to remember that when people died, they'd be referred to for a certain period of time as 'the late Someone-or-other'. Now this was, I presume, a mark of respect, or to indicate to people who may not have read the paper that someone had recently died. Has the expression gone and was there a standard period during which someone was referred to as 'the late'? I mean, it's not the late William Shakespeare, but it's the late Johnny Cash, isn't it? And when does he stop being the late Johnny Cash?

FRANCES: When my husband died, he was reported as being 'late of Bullabanka'. And he was never late for anything. I rang and had it changed as I knew he would hate to be referred to as late for anything, let alone Bullabanka.

JV: That is an old-fashioned turn of phrase, isn't it?

FRANCES: It's still used in the funeral notices: late of Melbourne, late of a particular nursing home.

JANINE: I use 'late' when I'm talking to complete strangers. If I say 'My husband', they think he's at home or something, and if I say 'my ex-husband', they automatically assume that I'm divorced. So quite often if I'm talking to somebody that never knew him I use 'My late husband said so-and-so' or 'My late husband did so-and-so'. So it comes in handy just to inform people so that they understand the situation.

I have no idea if there's a standard use of 'late' when referring to the deceased. It doesn't seem as common when talking about public figures: is Steve Irwin being referred to as 'the late Steve Irwin'? And if so, for how long will he remain 'the late'? It seems to be a usage we don't use any more. Janine's gracious use of it when talking about her husband seems particularly adept. It pre-empts embarrassment and misunderstanding on both sides.

THANK YOU FOR YOUR KIND THOUGHTS...

Pamela: My mother recently died and as well as people at the funeral and lots of flowers being sent, I was sent a lot of cards. Do I reply to them as well?

RUTH: Look, I don't think you say thank you to a card because what do you do next? Send a card, then have to say thank you for that card. You send cards to people who've turned up at the funeral and signed the book and you send cards to those who have sent flowers. But you don't have to send a card to someone who sent you a card.

SUE: I disagree with the last caller, I actually think it's really nice to acknowledge all forms of cards or communication to do with a bereavement. It's part of the closure procedure. Also, a lot of people are left wondering if you got their card. It is just a very nice thing to do, to write to someone saying, 'Dear So-and-so, it meant so much to me to receive your card about my mother...'. I just think it's really about acknowledgement, and it's quite interesting that in this time where we have mobile phones and emails and we have such a world of communication, there are so many people who just do not know how to handle the communications around a bereavement. They really don't know what to do, and I think it's better to do something in a positive form than not do anything at all. A lot of positives can come of it. It is absolutely amazing how people find out and they'll get in touch. When my father died we got cards and letters from people who grew up with him in his country town, we're talking about forty years ago, and it was wonderful to write back and say 'Look, it was just fantastic that you acknowledged Dad', and send that on.

MARION: Can I just add that there's no real time limit to this. When my husband died there were around three hundred cards and letters, and it probably took me nearly six months to answer them all. But I just did it when I felt like it and there was something nice about it. Sometimes it was sad, but usually it made me remember something about him, about a time in his life, and it was nice.

JV Sue and Marion put it so well. Of course you acknowledge it, and it's not like sending a thank you note after a dinner party. It doesn't really matter when you do it, as long as you do it.

A MINUTE'S SILENCE

Frank: On Sunday, the day of mourning for the Bali bombing, my wife stood up in her café and said that they would be observing the minute's silence at eleven o'clock. I was proud she did this, she's not a bold person by any means, and some people just ignored her and she says quite a few looked at her like it was a weird thing to do.

COLIN: I work at a tourist attraction, an historical village, and we observed the minute's silence there. We announced it with the town crier, I work in the tavern and no one had any problem with it.

SUE: I was on the bus and the bus driver stopped the bus and turned the motor off. It was really good, everyone observed, no one said anything. We all just sat there for a minute and it was great.

ROBERT: I was running a mobile espresso van at South Curl Curl. At the beach everyone stopped and a lone piper appeared in the dunes and started playing; it was a very moving experience. Here was a surfing group thinking of lost mates. I think it's very important and if you run a café or whatever you've got to set up the mechanism for it to take place. It's part of being in the community.

JV I think back to the first Armistice commemoration of 11 November, an early ANZAC Day or RSL clubs reciting the 'Ode to the Fallen' at sunset and I imagine that a minute's silence used to be easier to achieve: less background noise, no mobile phones. Now people feel odd if they shut up for a second, if the piped music stops, and they get nervous if they don't check the phone. A minute's silence today is really worth something and should be respected.

THE MOBILE PHONE AT THE FUNERAL

Matthew: I was at a funeral service in a crematorium and some bumptious pompous bloody clown answered his mobile phone. He kept talking and walked out during the ceremony. We'd all been told to turn our phones off, he didn't and then answered it. I believe a couple of people afterwards told him in no uncertain manner not to come to the wake.

MARY ANNE: Not come to the wake, not deal with that guy ever again, taking the call is totally reprehensible. I think it should be made clear to him that when he dies, he doesn't have any choice of music. Everyone's just going to bring their mobiles and play the worst kind of ring tones they can find—all throughout the service—especially those cheap sounding ones, the really bad ones, the worse the better, I think.

JOSEPH: I'm a minister of religion and I officiate at funerals. I always ask people to turn their mobile phones off before I start the service, and I wait for two minutes until they do it. You have to, because leaving the phones on, it's just endemic.

JV: It's standard now at theatres and other gatherings to ask for the phones to be turned off, isn't it?

JOSEPH: People just forget. They've rushed to the funeral, they're late, they couldn't find parking, they forget to turn it off and suddenly there's this ring in the middle of the service when you're about to say something deeply meaningful and beautiful about a person and it feels like God's trying to interrupt you. What a terrible thing for a minister of religion to say.

JV And the Lord spake and he spake often as he had an excellent plan that allowed him to spake up to three minutes for free and a hundred free SMS per month. And he spaketh thus, 'And if a phone ring once it be deemed a mistake and the elders will frown upon him yet not send him into the wilderness. And if a phone rings twice, then may his ears be rent from his body and his tongue cleaved unto his soft palate that he may never need phone again. And if he yet answer the phone and discourse, then let him wander forever banished into the wilderness, beyond call strength, beyond battery life, let him call beasts and birds and chatter with them as he will, for this be the law; Thou Shalt Not Miscommunicate'.

317

WASTE NOT, WANT NOT

Kylie: Since my grandfather's death a couple of years ago, my grandmother has continued using their old address labels on the backs of letters she sends out, and just scribbles his name out with a black marker. It seems quite insensitive to me, but knowing my grandmother, I'm sure she's just being practical and doesn't like to waste anything. I've considered getting her some new address labels made up but I'm sure she'd still use the old labels first. What can I do? Am I overreacting?

MARGARET: I'm of the thought that your grandmother is being practical, a waste-not-want-not kind of person, and she would use the labels even if she got some new ones. She'd continue to use the ones she has, I reckon. And it may be a good way for her dealing with the grief of losing a husband, just to get rid of the name when she writes a letter.

JV: What if it's something like, look, Grandma, Kylie knows that everyone's laughing a bit at her about this. And a lot of people in fact aren't all that impressed with her. They find it a little bit offensive. Should she be telling Grandma this?

MARGARET: Hopefully Grandma's a bit over that, the idea of popular opinion. She's mature enough to let other people's thoughts waft away.

JV: So by this stage, if that's what Grandma's doing, that's it, don't interfere.

MARGARET: That's what I reckon. Maybe she could encourage Grandma to write her a heap of letters and use the labels up really quickly.

SONIA: As you say, it's about not wanting to waste them. But I'd steal them, actually, and I'd put them in the bin the day before the garbage goes. Make sure they go. And then, when she's discovered that she hasn't got them, you help her to search the house from top to bottom, and then when it's gone on a bit you offer to get her some new ones.

NEV: I've done this. My wife died over five years ago, and I've done the same thing. I've sent something and noticed our two names were on it, so I just put a line through hers. But my wife used to do this when she was alive, if it was a letter just from her. She'd put a line through me.

JV Every question in this book is about a relationship: with a child, with a neighbour, with a schoolteacher, a friend, a colleague. I loved this question because it contained so much. The grandmother's behaviour was amusing, a little sad, but perhaps also bold. Death is nothing more than a texta through a name. The grand-daughter is troubled over this and has obviously spent some time thinking about it. Is Grandma being insensitive? Are others mocking her practicality? It's very touching as it also reveals a relationship between a grand-daughter and grand-mother that's rich and long but close to its inevitable end. All that in a stroke of a pen through a name on a sticker!

Picture Credits

The publishers thank the following sources for allowing images to be reproduced in *The Form Guide*: